GOING GREEN

GOING GREEN
Women and Grassroots Environmentalism

Neera Agnimitra

SHIPRA

Rs. 800; US$ 40

ISBN: 978-81-7541-738-0

First Published in India in 2014

Going Green: Women and Grassroots Environmentalism

Published by:
SHIPRA PUBLICATIONS
H.O.: LG 18-19, Pankaj Central Market, Patparganj,
I.P. Ext., Delhi-110092, Tel: 91-11-2223 5152, 2223 6152
Br.Off.: 4617/18, Ansari Road, Darya Ganj,
New Delhi-110002, Tel: 9650028065, 9810522367
E-mail: info@shiprapublications.com
www.shiprapublications.com

To
My Father
My biggest source of inspiration,
My mentor, my guide, my role model
My guardian angel.........
He not only gave me life
But taught me how
To live it......
Love for nature was the most precious gift that he gave me
And it remains.... My passion and mission in life.

Preface

The world is currently facing an unprecedented environmental crisis and the situation is fast approaching the brink of a potentially catastrophic global disaster. So extensive and far reaching are the problems emanating from the environmental degeneration and manipulation that the future well being of humanity, together with that of the many other life forms on the planet is in serious jeopardy. We are losing not just time but the margin of planetary safety, as the world is precariously balanced on the edge....poised to overstep the various thresholds of environmental risk. With the human population continuing to rise by 75 million or more per year and with the harried economic growth in all corners of the world continuing to place humungous burdens of deforestation, pollution, greenhouse gas emissions, species extinction, ocean acidification and other massive threats, there exists a 'real' and monumental challenge to the survival and well being of the entire human race.

At one level, individuals and communities, especially those who are the poorest, most marginalised and suffering the most discrimination are facing the direct consequences of local environmental depreciation, which often result from exploitative business practices and destructive development projects. At another level, people all over the world are beginning to be affected by regional and global environmental changes. These critical environmental problems are primarily the result of unsustainable lifestyles, overconsumption and unrealistic and short term oriented patterns of development. What is however the most unfortunate is, that these environmental problems, which are largely the creation of an overtly consumerist, urban and economically privileged minority are impacting the poor and marginalised first, and with the most drastic of consequences. This reality that the worst negative impact of the environmental problems falls disproportionately on the individuals, groups, communities and societies, who are the most vulnerable, poor and disempowered, both within nation states and across the globe, leads one to contend that the crisis is also grounded in serious issues of environmental and social injustice. Unless curbed through wide ranging, structural changes in favour of the dispossessed, and the curtailment of over consumption by the privileged, these global environmental trends shall cause a threat to the entire planetary ecosystem and its essential life-supporting systems.

To achieve environmentally sustainable development, societies will not only require drastic changes in the current world order, they would also need to reconfigure and integrate alternative ways of thinking and 'being'. Within the environmental movement there is a huge wealth of ideas, experience and visions of what an alternative, just, environmentally sustainable and people-oriented society would be...and could be. The lasting key to addressing the environmental crisis is to have a longer term perspective that rejuvenates the role that humans play in generating sustainable growthCa: and that which does not disproportionately disadvantage either the ecosystems or human cultures.

The critics and the stalwarts of India's environmental policy advocate the primacy of local solutions, often arguing that only strong local governance and indigenous practices can tackle the social justice concerns and environmental issues simultaneously. Conserving and managing resources sustainably at the local level is a 'critical' for achieving the global goal of sustainable development. It is the combined impact of the small-scale initiatives undertaken by individuals and communities that will ultimately determine the fate of the natural resources and ecosystems, particularly in the Third World. The importance of people's participation in sustainable development has recently become increasingly acknowledged, yet there is little understanding of the multiple dimensions that such participation involves. Historically, great attention has been paid to persuading local communities to participate in externally-initiated environmental projects, yet requisite focus on the indigenous and locally evolved practices, structures and systems of environmental conservation have largely remained sidelined.

This book elucidates and analyses the viability and utility of the traditional management systems and practices garnered by the hill communities to save and rejuvinate their environment, especially their forest resources. The author analyses the social dynamics of local level conservation, both in situations where support is supplied from external agents, such as the state or the voluntary sector, and where local communities formulate their own plans and activities to protect and regenerate their environment. The book is a natural corollary of a comprehensive study undertaken by the author in the remote and ecologically fragile mountain ecosystem of the Garhwal Himalayas. A study of its kind, the insights generated by the rich data that was harnessed in engaging with the hill communities traversing more than eighty villages in the Bhilangana block of Tehri Garhwal district of Uttarakhand, has immense potential to guide and direct environmental conservation and management in the hill ecosystem. The study has inherent value, also because the area covered by the study is significant, both in terms of its environmental influence on the region, and by way of a rich historical tradition of environmental action.

Environment and environmental concerns are now the focus of interdisciplinary study, having captured the attention of the natural, behavioral and social sciences, with a proliferation of theoretical and application based content in the new and emerging areas of inquiry and action. The book reflects and reiterates the interest and the response of social work in understanding and engaging with the social and human aspects of the environment and environmental problems. The multifarious dimensions of the deep and intricate consequentiality of environmental well being and human well being are emerging, and it is only natural that the profession of social work locates its position and stance in the contemporary canvas of engagement. The questions that we need to ask ourselves are... Where does social work stand in all this? Have we, the social work professionals accepted the challenge and the opportunity of negotiating with the environmental issues and in mediating their impact on human well being? This book is a step in this direction and construes a modest attempt to understand and analyse grassroots environmentalism in an ecologically munificent locale. Without doubt, it should be of interest and value to postgraduate students, academics and researchers of social work, environmental sciences, resource management and geography, as well as to professionals in the field, who find meaning and a connect with 'green' social work.

I wish to acknowledge the direction and insights provided by my mentor in my environmental traversing, Prof. K.K. Mukhopadhyay, who challenged me to choose this remotest and most challenging locale. But for him, I would not have attempted to cover the length and breadth of the treacherous terrain, or have discovered the virgin beauty of the region or have acquired the unbounded love of the beautiful people residing there. Prof. Sushma Batra extended unlimited love, support and encouragement to me and I sincerely feel that words cannot express the deep sense of gratitude and respect that I feel for her and her role in encouraging me to complete this work. I owe Prof. Sanjai Bhatt a heartfelt thanks, as he has been a valuable colleague and friend, who has been consistent in his persuasion to me to complete this work.

Most of all, I wish to thank my dearest friend Dr Manoj Jha, who has been my student, yet who is also my biggest teacher, mentor, critic and a role model of sorts. His constant tagging led me to emerge stronger, not only in making sure that this book saw the light of the day, but also in letting me rediscover the joy of reading and writing as prolifically as I am able to do now. Sharing space with him has made me richer many times over, for he has enabled me to go much beyond what I had originally envisioned for myself. His thoughts, ideas, perspectives and arguments never cease to amaze, and they continue to add value and meaning to all that I learn and teach.

My parents have always been my biggest source of inspiration and my greatest supporters. Their gentle support, unlimited love and blessings, unshaken confidence and pride in their daughter became the driving force in the completion of this work. This achievement is theirs and not mine. This work is a tribute to the memory of my dearest father, whose strong presence still guides me and inspires me endlessly. My partner in life Ashwani has been my greatest source of strength and support. His unconditional love and encouragement kept me going and helped me to emerge as a strong researcher and practitioner. My dear children Arjun and Varun, my brothers Ashu and Vikram, and my sisters-in-law Sonu and Shilpa have contributed to my academic journey in their own special ways and they remain my fulcrum in life.

Neera Agnimitra

Contents

List of Tables

List of Figures

1
Introduction

Environment and Environmental Discourse

In the times, in which we are placed, it is near impossible to obviate the overwhelming presence of the environment, environmental discourses and perspectives, and undermine the environmental issues that are beginning to permeate our life and living. The criticality of the environment in defining the contours of life on this planet is acquiring a new thrust and significance, and all that is 'environmental' is beginning to matter. The advent of the twenty first century has been marked by the unfolding of an ecological consciousness across the countries of the north, as also the south.

Although the concept of environment is not new, nor is it that environmental issues and concerns have emerged only now, but the nature and quantum of changes that are beginning to become discernible in the realm of the environmental domain show a distinct change, and this change is substantial, for it has begun to register in our individualized and collective consciousness. There is definitely a rethink on the environment and environmental imperatives, and issues which remained peripheral and rhetoric are evolving as 'mainstream'. References to the interface between environment and development, which occupied centre stage more within the academic discourses and symposia of national and international development organizations, are entering the realm of the 'real', on account of the impinging reality that a threat whose possibility was notional and was located in the distant future has crossed the temporal boundaries, and is staring in the face at this instant.

This enhanced emphasis on the deeper understanding of the environmental contours has been precipitated due to escalating environmental problems, both in the micro context of individual nations and within the macro context of the world, which undoubtedly presents itself as the largest ecosystem unifying the living and the non living constituents that together define the environment. The reality that environment as an entity disregards and obfuscates the presence of national borders, existential in the territorial, marine and air space, is enough to validate the drawing in of all nations and governments to collude and think through options to prevent and mitigate the worst impacts of an environmental crisis that is lurking round the corner. Environmental considerations or the lack of them within the context of a nation state may most certainly impact its micro environment, but the fact that they would play a role in altering the global well-being of the environs is now a given, and is therefore curtailing the autonomy of the individualized nations to undermine or invisibalize the same.

The environmental imperative was brought to centre stage with the publication of Rachel Carson's classic of 1962. Titled *Silent Spring,* the document stimulated the 'green discourse' which was the first formal reckoning of the impact that development creates on nature and it effectively inaugurated self conscious environmentalism in the West. Ten years later, the Club of Rome's *Limits to Growth* spurred a debate on the upper limits that an unbridled utilization of the environmental 'goods' poses for the growth story and the development potential of any nation.

The larger debate about the criticality of conserving the environment distinctly arose in the year 1972, when the United Nations Conference on the Human Environment was held at Stockholm. This heralded an undisputed acknowledgement of ecology and environment as an integral component in the cognizable frame of the developed, and even the developing nations. The Conference was attended by the then Prime Minister Mrs Indira Gandhi, and it was she who took the lead in initiating a new chapter on environment in the mainstream of the Indian development discourse. Consequently, environmentalism came to India in the seventies, but it was heavily tinged with western concerns and perspectives.

However under the new environmental stimuli, important legislations and policies in the environmental domain were drafted. It was beginning to emerge that environmental conservation was not a luxury afforded only by the rich and the powerful in the global axis, but an 'essential' that needed to be paid heed to by even the less powerful and less privileged in the global hierarchy. However, a downside of the Stockholm Conference was the statement of Mrs Indira Gandhi that 'Poverty is the worst polluter', as it led to a whole generation of Indians to believe that it was poverty and the poor who were the main culprits in the continuing decimation of the environment, and also that India being predominantly poor, did not have to contend with serious environmental regeneration till its poverty bar showed a downward trend. Development continued to mesmerize and the appropriation and misuse of resources by the rich and the powerful in the North and within the South, remained outside the dominant consciousness.

The World Commission on Environment and Development (WCED) popularly known as the Brundtland Commission was created in 1984, and it initiated studies which culminated in the publication of 'Our Common Future' (The Brundtland Report) in 1987. This was a landmark initiative, as it initiated the global recognition and understanding of 'Sustainable Development', as a common denominator of all development. The concept which was defined as 'Development that meets the needs of the present without compromising the ability of the future generations to meet their needs' was a powerful concept that needed to provide direction and dimensions to the developmental thrust, that seemed to be permeating the context of all of the world's nations. It called for policies which recognized the need for economic growth in a way that did not jeopardize the possibility of the future viability of the natural resource base and denigrate the position of the vulnerable sections of the world's peoples. This necessitated an attitude to economic development in which both, the quantitative and qualitative dimensions of growth were equally significant. It postulated that poverty, resource depletion and environmental stress arise from disparities in economic and political power, and that the goals of sustainable development would require different approaches to resource exploitation, investment patterns and decision making processes, as also newer thrust on environment friendly technological development and institutional change. An environmental thrust and perspective needed to be pursued by all the countries of the world, in their own individualized domain, as also in their more collectivized context The Report therefore set a broad agenda for change, but the mechanisms to remove the barriers that existed to achieving the goals of Sustainable Development were not addressed.

Both within the Indian context, as also on the international front, the decade of the 1980's witnessed the manifestation of events denoting an environmental resurgence, in that the civil society emerged as a viable and a committed force to counter balance the resource intensive and environmentally 'non' sensitive mandates of the state and posed fundamental questions on the GNP led and GDP primed development agenda drawn out by the nations of the world. They rallied to create some impact in the slowing down of the march of modernization and industrialization, and to stall some potentially catastrophic state driven 'development' projects. These non-state actors focused on diverse environmental issues, articulated and espoused an alternate development paradigm as opposed to the more conventional one. Consequently, a proliferation of environmental movements emerged around the globe, and the same transpired in India too, following the Chipko Andolan in the seventies.

While the processes of globalization, privatization and liberalization, which were unleashed under the aegis of the regime of structural reforms, had been predicted to create unprecedented opportunities for economic rejuvenation and poverty reduction, they simultaneously posed a serious threat to the environmental well being of the planet. Already, the implications have proved to be severe for the countries of the South, and they have not insulated the Northern bloc of countries also, from seething under the environmental repercussions that have arisen in the wake of the economic restructuring of the global economy and economic processes. The market and export driven growth ideology is geared towards a perpetually upward moving profile of the economic output and towards the integration of the national economies into a global economy. As a consequence, a competition of the already overstretched environmental resources has intensified, resulting in the severe decline in the ability of the ecosystem to regenerate and boomerang back into its normal dimensions.

As things stand, the spate of economic liberalization in India has translated into the Indian natural resources being readily made available to the outside markets and the Indian market being opened up to the foreign corporate sector. This has implied that the natural resources which form the basis of sustenance for an increasingly disproportionate section of the population have a greater propensity to move towards the sectors and sections which proclaim greater economic returns. The trend of sacrificing the natural habitats and resources for short term economic gains and of ignoring the reality of the struggle of the local rural communities and indigenous people has become the written and the unwritten norm for the pundits of the development story being written in contemporary times. The hitherto diligently protected and sustainably utilized nature's bounties found many claimants other than those who persevered to preserve them. In this manner, the trail of globalization has meant serious repercussions, not only for the environment, but also for employment and livelihoods and for human well-being, in general.

The recent times are also clearly marked by the incessant ravages of recurring environmental calamities, both natural and manmade. The frequency and the intensity of these events have increased to extremely disconcerting levels. Evidence of the all pervading global climatic changes and the implications that they behold for impacting livelihoods, life and living of people across the globe, and for the living beings in all the three realms of the ecosphere are all too real. Climate change will ultimately curtail the ability of the developing countries to reach their poverty reduction and sustainable development objectives.

All of these trends and developments are markers of the eroding man environment relationship that define the contemporary context. The intensification of the contradiction between the claims of environment and development within the neoliberal context of the world, and in India, cannot be ignored any longer, as they seem to be too pervasive and too overpowering for comfort. The increasing hardships faced by people in the context of a depleting and deteriorating natural resource base, and the newer challenges thrown up by the neoliberal model of development are forcing people to delve deeper into understanding the complexity of environmental issues, and on the existing and emerging threats that these pose for the human race. The significance of understanding the inextricable and two-way linkage between environment and development was always an imperative, but to do so with reference to the rapidly transforming economic and environmental frame becomes an urgent and inescapable priority. The need to develop, propagate and promote an alternate perspective on development, the idea of 'human well being' and 'social justice' woven into its frame is increasingly finding uncontested support.

Concepts of Participation and Development

The concept of participation is characterized by a sense of diversity, both in terms of its meaning and interpretation and its usage in the practice domain. Although it is not a new concept in terms of its presence in the development scenario, it continues to remain an ever dynamic concept, in more ways than one, as many different definitions, perspectives and interpretations continue to surface. Several authors have rightly argued that it is impossible to establish a universal definition of 'participation' and in that sense clarifying the term and the concept is problematic. Given its complex nature, the concept can be explored, but not contained in a single, comprehensive and formal definition. Understanding the plethora of definitions and perspectives is crucial as it opens up the possibility of a wider range of possible applications and more meaningful outcomes.

Often the term participation is modified with adjectives, resulting in terms such as *community participation, citizen participation, people's participation, public participation,* and *popular participation*. The existing definitions of participation reflect a wide range of perspectives. The way participation is defined also depends on the context in which it occurs. For some, it is a matter of principle; for others, practice; for still others, an end in itself (World Bank, 1995).

The Oxford English Dictionary defines participation as "to have a share in" or "to take part in," thereby emphasizing the rights of individuals and the choices that they make in order to participate. It implies, 'the process of taking part in something' or 'having a "part", which in turn signifies 'some level of collaboration and of shared ownership or responsibility'. In its simplest of avatars, it is also considered as 'a voluntary contribution by the people to one or another of the public programmes supposed to contribute to national development' (Economic Commission for Latin America, 1973).

Participation can also be perceived as a method to co-opt dissent, a mechanism for ensuring the receptivity, sensitivity, and even accountability of social services to the consumers. Armitage (1988) defined citizen participation as a process by which citizens' act in response to public concerns, voice their opinions about decisions that affect them, and take responsibility for changes to their community. In the context of rural development, Lisk, 1981) characterized participation as 'people's involvement in the decision-making process, in implementing programmes, their sharing in the benefits of the development programme and their involvement in efforts to evaluate such programmes'. It connotes 'the process by which the rural poor are able to organise themselves, and through their own organisation are able to identify their own needs, share in the design, implementation and evaluation of the participating action' (FAO, 1982).

Participation has also been interpreted as 'the distribution of power which enables groups to determine which needs, and whose needs will be met through the distribution of resources' (Curtis, 1978). Brager, Specht, and Torczyner (1987) described 'participation as a means to educate citizens and to increase their competence'. It is considered to be a vehicle for influencing decisions that affect the lives of citizens and an avenue for transferring political power. It is inclusive of 'the organized efforts to increase control over resources and regulative institutions in given situations on the part of groups and movements of those hitherto excluded from such control' (Pearse and Stiefel, 1979). Citizen participation may also be a response to the traditional sense of powerlessness felt by people, when it comes to influencing government decisions and that people often feel that access to services are beyond their control because the decisions are made outside their community by unknown bureaucrats and technocrats. Westergaard (1986) defined participation as 'collective efforts to increase and exercise control over resources and institutions on the part of groups and movements of those hitherto excluded from control'. This definition points toward a mechanism for ensuring community participation. The World Bank's Learning Group on Participatory Development (1995) defined participation as 'a process through which stakeholders' influence and share control over development initiatives, and the decisions and resources which affect them'. Participation is also understood as an essential element in human development in that when people participate, they 'are closely involved in the economic, social, cultural and political processes that affect their lives. It means people have constant access to decision making and power'. (*Human Development Report*, UNDP, 1993).

A descriptive definition of participation programs would imply the involvement of a significant number of persons in situations or actions that enhance their well-being, for example, their income, security, or self-esteem (Chowdhury, 1996). Chowdhury states that the ideal conditions contributing towards meaningful participation can be discussed from three aspects:

1. What kind of participation is under consideration?
2. Who participates in it?
3. How does participation occur?

Evens (1974) also points out the importance of the following issues in order to assess the extent of community participation:

1. Who participates?
2. What do people participate in?
3. Why do people participate? There are:
   (a) Cultural explanations (values, norms, and roles.)
   (b) Cognitive explanations (verbal skills and knowledge about the organizations)
   (c) Structural explanations (alternatives, resources available, and the nature of benefit sought)
4. Implications (how the benefit contributes to the ends or principles they value).

Oakley and Marsden (1987) defined participation as 'the process by which individuals, families, or communities assume responsibility for their own welfare and develop a capacity to contribute to their own and the community's development'. In the context of development, participation refers to 'an active process whereby beneficiaries influence the direction and execution of development projects rather than merely receive a share of project benefits' (Paul, in Bamberger, 1986).

The five objectives to which community participation might contribute are:

1. Sharing project costs, in that participants are asked to contribute money or labour (and occasionally goods) during the project's implementation or operational stages.
2. Increasing project efficiency, through beneficiary consultation during project planning or beneficiary involvement in the management of project implementation or operation.
3. Increasing project effectiveness, via greater beneficiary involvement to help ensure that the project achieves its objectives and, that benefit goes to the intended groups.
4. Building beneficiary capacity, either through ensuring that participants are actively involved in project planning and implementation or through formal or informal training and consciousness-raising activities.
5. Increasing empowerment, which has been defined as, seeking to increase the control of the underprivileged sectors of society over the resources and decisions affecting their lives and their participation in the benefits produced by the society in which they live (1986, 4-5).

At the level of project/programme level participation, Bamberger (1986) points out that the objectives and organization of project-level activities are different from those of programs at the national or regional levels and the three distinct kinds of local participation included the following:

1. Beneficiary involvement in the planning and implementation of externally initiated projects or community participation.
2. External help to strengthen or create local organizations, but without reference to a particular project, or local organizational development.
3. Spontaneous activities of local organizations that have not resulted from outside assistance or indigenous local participation.

The first two are externally promoted participatory approaches used by governments, donors, or NGOs, while the third is the kind of social organization that has evolved independently of (or despite) outside interventions (Bamberger, 1986). At a community level, there is a separation of community participation into two distinct approaches: (1) the community development movement and (2) community involvement through conscientization (Freire, 1985). The basis of conscientization, according to De Kadt, started from "the existence of socioeconomic inequalities, the generation of these by the economic system, and their underpinning by the state" (De Kadt, in Abbott, 1995).

The word development is fraught with ideological, political, and historical connotations that can greatly change its meaning depending on the perspective being discussed. The following three definitions of development are most helpful and suitable in relation to this endeavour: Development is a process by which the members of a society increase their personal and institutional capacities to mobilise and manage resources to produce sustainable and justly distributed improvements in their quality of life consistent with their own aspirations. (Korten, 1990). This definition emphasizes the process of development and its primary focus on personal and institutional capacity. It also touches on justice, equity, quality of life, and participation. The second definition is from Robinson, Hoare, and Levy's (1993) work. Robinson adds the dimension of empowerment to Korten's idea of development, wherein he says that '...(Empowerment) is a social action process that promotes participation of people, organisations, and communities towards the goals of increased individual and community control, political efficacy, improved quality of life, and social justice' (Robinson, 1993, 199).

Finally, Zachariah and Sooryamoorthy (1994) emphasize that development must promote economic growth, but the encouragement of economic growth must take account of and be restrained by three other equally important objectives:

1. Protection of the environment and consideration of the ecological impact of industrialisation and commercialisation.
2. Fair and equitable distribution as well as redistribution of goods and services to enable poorer people to get a fairer share of society's wealth and to participate fully in the economy.
3. Creation of opportunities for everyone to increasingly participate in the political, artistic and other activities of society. (1994: 22-23).

Zachariah and Sooryamoorthy's criteria for development recognize the environmental and ecological dimensions of development as an imperative to all community development initiatives. Within this perspective, the environment is considered to be an integral part of development, since any impact on a person's environment also influences the state of well-being or welfare of the person and the community the person belongs to. Environment and development are thus linked so intricately that separate approaches to either environmental or developmental problems are piecemeal at best (Bartelmus, 1986).

Community/Peoples' Participation

A review of perspectives on community development reflects that the said approach emphasises self-help, the democratic process, and leadership in community revitalization (Barker, 1991). Most community development work involves the participation of the communities, who are often perceived simply as 'beneficiaries' involved (Smith, 1998). Given that there is so much that is written and discussed about the subject, community participation emerges as an important component of community development and reflects a grassroots or bottom-up approach to problem solving.

In social work, community participation refers to '...the active voluntary engagement of individuals and groups to change problematic conditions and to influence policies and programs that affect the quality of their lives or the lives of others' (Gamble and Weil, 1995). One of the major aims of community development is to encourage participation of the community as a whole. Indeed, community development has been defined as a social process resulting from citizen participation (Rahman, 1990). Through citizen participation, a broad cross-section of the community is encouraged to identify and articulate their own goals, design their own methods of change, and pool their resources in the problem-solving process (Harrison, 1995).

It is widely recognized that participation in government schemes/ programmes is most often confined to using the service offered or providing inputs to support the project (Smith, 1998). This is contrasted with stronger forms of participation, involving control over decisions, priorities, plans, and implementation; or the spontaneous induced or assisted formation of groups to achieve collective goals (Arnstein, 1969; Cohen and Uphoff, 1980; WHO, 1991; Rahman, 1993). Community participation, as it is practiced, is only expected to pertain to mobilization of the community as a beneficiary of the deemed programme, or at most its involvement in the implementation of externally driven initiatives of the government or the non-governmental agencies. 'Real' and higher forms of participation in planning and decision making, and effectively transferring the ownership of the initiatives to the community are the 'essential' missing ingredients.

Effective community participation may lead to social and personal empowerment, economic development, and socio-political transformation (Kaufman and Alfonso, 1997). Yet there are obstacles: the power of central bureaucracies, and their disinclination to devolve power; the lack of local skills and organizational experience; social divisions and conflicts within the communities; and the impact of national and transnational structures (Kaufman and Alfonso, 1997). The need for community participation in development is nonetheless accepted, recognized and considered as the core element in professional literature.

Approaches to Community Participation

Scanning through literature, there is a multiplicity of approaches that have been delineated for community participation. Some of the most important approaches to participation, and which have a bearing or implications for the study at hand are presented below:

United Nations Research Institute on Social Development (UNRISD) Approach

The most important and original aspect of UNRISD is the focus on peoples' power and organization of the disadvantaged groups, hitherto bypassed in development. The significant factor in this approach is not that it focussed on the poorest of the poor, but that it crystallises questions of power and organization, and also views the allies and adversaries of the hitherto excluded to be included in the purview of the analysis (Chowdhury, 1996).

Framework on Participation: Norman Upoff: In 1976, USAID requested the interdisciplinary Rural Development Committee at Cornell University to come up with some practical concepts and measures of community participation in development (Uphoff, 1997). The committee worked on the concept and practice of participation and its framework. In fact, they gave a new thrust to the older Community Development (CD) approaches (Chowdhury, 1996). The four kinds of participation they identified were: decision-making, implementation, benefit sharing, and evaluation. Even if these kinds of participation are distinct, there are usually connections and linkages among them; for example, participation in decision making is likely to contribute to participation in benefit sharing. The more there is of any one kind of participation, the more participation there is in total (Uphoff, 1997). Uphoff also emphasized that who participates (and how they participate) is as important to consider as to whether there is participation, and of what kind. Just saying, 'there was participation' does not tell us very much. We want to know who participated, why they participated, and how they participated (Uphoff, 1997). The framework of participation provided by Upoff and his team added the requisite detailing and the analytical perspective to the understanding of participation.

Self-Reliance and Self-Help Approach: During the development decade of the 1960s, self-reliance and self-help projects became the order of the day. Chowdhury notes that the main components of this developmental process included participation in taking initiatives to identify unmet needs, and self-reliance, that is, breaking away from the dependencies that suppress the creativity of the poor. According to him it was more a psychological process, than being an economic or a physical one (Chowdhury, 1996, 13). It is evident that participation as it relates to development is a process that includes a set of activities and takes place through different stages. A literature review suggests that participation in development projects needs to be understood based on the following elements, which form an integral part of the process:

Identification of Appropriate Stakeholders: The involvement of stakeholders in the development projects is widely recognized as a fundamental element of the process. Timely, well-planned, and well implemented public involvement programs have contributed to the successful design, implementation, operation, and management of proposals (UNEP, 1996). For instance, the range of stakeholders involved in a local project shall typically include:

1. The people (individuals, and groups) in the local community
2. The proponent and other project beneficiaries (and even those who have a stake in resisting the project or initiative)
3. Government agencies
4. Nongovernmental Organizations (NGOs)
5. Others, such as donors, the private sectors, academics, and so forth.

Needs Identification and Goal Determination: Participation of the people in development activities implies enhanced capacity to perceive their own needs. Through participation, local people identify their needs as well as the relevant goals of a programme. By participating in decision making and implementation activities, local people help the project officials to identify (1) real/felt needs, (2) strategies to meet those needs, and (3) the necessary resources required to implement the various strategies (Yadama, 1995). For example, community participation would be discouraged if environmental issues are given priority in agendas without addressing issues such as poverty, homelessness, health, and other basic necessities perceived to be more important by the coastal communities.

Information Dissemination: This is a one-way flow of information from the proponent of the development project to the people. The proponent should provide sufficient relevant information about the project such as the benefits of the project to the beneficiaries, the costs of implementation, the potential for financing and implementation, and possible risk factors. The proponent must allow sufficient time for individuals to read and discuss the information provided, and listen to the views held by individuals as well as to issues and problems. Lack of transparency often fosters mistrust and misunderstanding between project authorities and local communities (UNEP, 1996).

Consultation: Consultation involves inviting people's views on the proposed actions and engaging them in a dialogue. It is a two-way flow of information between the proponent and the people. Consultation provides opportunities for the people to express their views on the project proposal initiated by the project proponent. Rigorous planning and implementation of projects should be undertaken only after considerable discussion and consultation have been undertaken. Consultation includes awareness building, education, information sharing, and negotiation, with the goal being a better decision making process through organizations consulting the general public (Becker, 1997). This process allows those who are usually bypassed by the planners and programme managers to articulate their concerns, interpretations and opinions in the present and the future initiatives.

Depending on the project, various methods are used during consultation such as public hearings, public meetings, general public information meetings, informal small group meetings, public displays, field trips, site visits, letter requests for comments, material for mass media, and response to public inquiries. The knowledge of local people should be recognized and they should be enrolled as experts in designing development projects. Participants should be encouraged to articulate their ideas and the design of the project should be based on such ideas.

Genuine Interests: Participation depends on people's legitimate interests in the project or development activities. Therefore, participation needs to be considered as an active process, meaning that the person or group in question takes initiatives and asserts an independent role (Chowdhury, 1996).

Public Involvement in Decision-Making: The project should encourage a maximum number of people to participate in the development projects. Such involvement should give the participants full inclusion in designing, organizing, and implementing activities, and for that to materialise, workshops to create/facilitate deliberations, build functional consensus, encourage ownership, and support action may be a good, viable option. The process should include all people and all the groups constituting the community. Public involvement is a process for involving the public in the decision making of an organization (Becker, 1997, 155). Participation actually brings the public into the decision-making process.

White (1989) stressed community involvement in management of marine protected areas. According to the author, public involvement can take place at several stages in the establishment and management of marine protected areas. These stages are: (1) the recognition of a need; (2) discussions with interested parties and integration with the community; (3) baseline studies and monitoring; (4) education; (5) core group building and formalization of reserves; and (6) enforcement.

Accountability: The requirement of accountability applies to all parties involved in the project, such as project management, external organizers, and traditional leaders, as well as any emergent leadership from the ranks of the poor and the disadvantaged. The authors also note that the agencies involved in project management and implementation are procedurally and periodically answerable to the people in the project area, as well as the citizens of the country in general. All people should be aware of their roles in the project and the planning of activities of the project. Accountability of concerned community members must be ensured, particularly after the decision is taken.

Repeated Interaction: Often there is an interaction at the beginning of the project, but no dialogue or any other form of interaction occurs during or after the project. This ultimately creates a big gap between the proponents of the development projects and the communities.

Consequently, the local people abandon a project based on such an idea. Therefore, it is suggested that there should be an ongoing communication throughout the project period, and even post project participation of people in the evaluation of the intervention and the identification of 'lessons learnt'.

Ownership and Control: Participation plays a major role in people's management of their own affairs. Ownership and control of resources have a profound impact on participation in development projects (Mathbor, 1990). Ferrer (1988) emphasized four areas to be worked towards in a participatory coastal resource management programme: greater economic and social equality, better access to services for all, greater participation in decision making, and deeper involvement in the organizing process resulting from the empowerment of people.

Sharing Benefits: It is evident that without sharing the benefits of the project, participation is a frustrating process for the poorer people. Zachariah and Sooryamoorthy (1994) note that there should be a fair and equitable distribution of benefits, as well as redistribution of goods and services, to enable the poorer people to get a fairer share of society's wealth and to participate fully in the development process. The Centre on Integrated Rural Development for Asia and the Pacific (CIRDAP, 1984), a regional rural development organization in South Asia, has highlighted that participation entails three distinct processes: first, the involvement of the people in decision making; second, eliciting of their contribution to development programs; and third, their participation in *sharing the benefits* from the development process.

Partnerships: Partnership in the development process allows stakeholders to work, talk, and solve problems with individuals who are often perceived as the experts, and thereby attributed a higher position in the hierarchy of the relationship. Instead of projecting the relationship to be primed on such unequal terms, evolution and facilitation of a spirit and structure of 'partnerships' needs to be ushered. An expression used by the Latin American activists to describe their relationship with the people (communities, groups) with whom they are working is *accompanamiento*, or "accompanying the process" (Wilson and Whitmore, 1997). Wilson and Whitmore identified a set of principles for collaboration in a variety of settings and situations. These include non intrusive collaboration; mutual trust and respect; a common analysis of what the problem is; a commitment to solidarity; equality in the relationship; an explicit focus on process; and the importance of language.

Determinants of Participation: Molley Joseph

An alternative approach to study participation has been offered by Molley Joseph (Joseph, 1997, 62). She highlights the frame of determinants of participation and these are as follows:

1. In-built organisational and institutional arrangements;
2. Nature of leadership, local or organisational;
3. Socio-economic characteristics of the participants, including the social values, gender bias, literacy level, income, class and other such parameters;
4. Nature of the programme, in terms of the type of benefits entailed, cost, requirements and other specifics;
5. Orientation and Ideology of the organisation and its personnel;
6. Anti-participation ideology in the society;
7. Programmes for participation, encompassing education, training and extension.

Some current ideas affecting definitions of participation include the integration of the concept of social capital, as provided by Robert Putnam. Robert Putnam (1993; 2000) introduced the idea of 'social capital' and elucidated it as the 'connections among individuals-social networks and norms of reciprocity and trustworthiness that arise from them' (Putnam, 2000, 19) and associated civic virtue and civic involvement to the building up of social capital. Putnam (2000) further attributed the decline of social networks and social connectedness with a reduction of 'social capital', which in turn undermined public and civic engagement (voting, political trust and grassroots political activism, as also membership and activity in all sorts of civic organizations). Because social capital relates to the nature and depth of existing social relationships and networks, it is often argued that high levels of social capital augur sustained and meaningful participation, and also that more effective participation contributes to enhanced social capital. The value of community bonding and inter connectedness through 'high' social capital; therefore becomes a pre requisite to community participation in a programme of governance or development.

In the present context, voluntary and development organizations often rely on the use of campaigning (including demonstrations, confrontations and other forms of direct action) concurrently with negotiations and the more formal consultation exercises, which are recognized by governments as the more legitimate avenues for influencing policy making/legislation formulation. When participation is perceived as involvement in decision making, it has to negotiate the context of policy and legislation building. Within this context, the option of the more benign form of 'consultation' has been usually the traditionally favoured option. However, increasingly participation practitioners are tending to consider consultation as a weaker form of participation, which undermines commitment to genuine power sharing and the 'right' to have a say' in the process of decision making, considering the prevailing centralizing thrust of governments and other decision making agencies. Community voices and peoples' preferences are often excluded from the analyses of such participation and campaigning as a method allows for an incorporation of the same. The possibility for campaigns to be community-led, also emanates from the possibility of evolving participatory community projects, which then help build the capacity and interest of those involved, so that they may be more willing and more competent to participate in the larger policy initiatives.

The Idea of Participatory Development

Participatory development has assumed significance, as an increasing number of organisations are finding that they can get significantly better results using participatory methods rather than traditional policy development and project management approaches. Sometimes participation happens just because it is required, but more often these days, government and development organisations are finding that participatory models fit very well with the idea of modern government 'enabling' as much as directly 'delivering' services, where consumers, citizens and communities all have a role to play in creating effective public services, together with public/governmental agencies.

According to Involve (2005), an organization focused on the practical issues of making public participation work, the four main objectives of participatory development in current public policy circles are delineated below:

1. Governance, in terms of strengthening democratic legitimacy, accountability, and facilitating active citizenship.
2. Social cohesion and social justice, by way of building relationships, ownership and social capital, equity, and empowerment.
3. Improved quality of services, interpreted as more efficient and better services, especially public services, that meet real needs and reflect community values; and
4. Capacity building and learning, for individuals and organisations, to provide a basis for future growth and development and, especially, to help build stronger communities.

Good participation also requires that the following principles are followed:

1. Makes a difference: The purpose of participation is to achieve change in relation to the purpose identified; it may also make a difference to all those involved in terms of learning, confidence and sense of active citizenship. This requires active commitment to change by all parties.
2. Voluntary: People may be encouraged to be involved, and even paid for involvement, but effective participation requires them to choose to be involved. Participation cannot be compulsory.
3. Transparency, honesty and clarity about the purpose, the limits of what can and cannot be changed, who can be involved and how, and what happens as a result.
4. Adequate resources, to manage the process well and to deliver on the results.
5. Appropriate participants, representative and/or inclusive, depending on the purpose of the exercise, with traditionally excluded groups given special support and encouragement when their involvement is appropriate.
6. Accessibility, so that no participant is excluded because of lack of physical access to meeting places, timing, appropriate support (e.g. child care), etc.
7. Accountability: Participatory processes need to be accountable to all those involved (including the organization that may be running/commissioning the exercise, and to the wider 'community'). This requires good record-keeping and reporting of both processes and outcomes.
8. Power: Participatory processes should have sufficient power to achieve the agreed objectives. This may require a change in the existing power sharing arrangements.
9. Learning and development: Participatory processes should seek to support a climate of mutual learning and development among all those involved.

People's participation in development is imperative for the following reasons:

1. Development is for the people and the involvement of people in the process of development is therefore indispensable. Participation ultimately aims at self-help and self-reliance among people.
2. Involvement of the people in schemes of development is expected to result in the local people having a better insight about their needs and preferences and a comprehensive understanding of the conditions as also the potentialities of development of their locale. Moreover, it helps in the preparation and execution of effective development action plans through a self-assessment of people's own 'felt' needs and constraints.
3. Participation of people in their own development generates 'trust', which in turn facilitates the process of implementation and a more equitable benefit sharing. Furthermore, it enables a more effective use of local resources and local initiative. It also minimizes the cost of implementation of the developmental programme by reducing the cost of supervision, and steps up the speed of implementation by mobilization of popular support and cooperation between groups having diversified objectives and interests.
4. Development often leads to confrontation and conflicts. Consensus based participation of people in the process of development can greatly reduce the scope of confrontations and violence by promoting the spirit of sharing and holding responsibilities together. However, this does not necessarily undermine the participation of people in negotiation, bargaining, confrontation and direct action to seek their rightful share in the process and the benefits of development.
5. Participation helps to raise the level of awareness of people about their rights and responsibilities, which in turn facilitates social change.
6. It develops people's own potentialities to plan, implement and evaluate, and thus provides them with an opportunity for advancement on the basis of self help and mutual cooperation. It strengthens people's self-initiative and weans them away from the traditionally ingrained dependency syndrome.
7. People's participation makes the process of development sustainable, as it harnesses indigenous energies and is grounded in people's own efforts. Dependency on outsider support is minimized; people perceive the programmes as their own; and assume responsibility for their continuation and diversification.

Conversely, the developmental context also has an important bearing on the quantum and quality of people's participation. Many a times there are constraints to people's participation which may require a transformation in the developmental context. This may necessitate change in structures, forms and functions of a society. It may mean overcoming illiteracy, ill health and poverty. Apart from physical and economic transformation, it may entail changes brought about by education, training, motivation, occupational mobility and exposure to modernity. It means promoting such development which will enable people to deal with their situation, become aware of the forces and impediments that restrict them, and take charge of their own lives. It implies a holistic and coordinated approach to development which empowers communities to initiate their full and active participation in the process of development. Such development must lead to their self-reliance, self-initiative and self-esteem.

Concept of Sustainability

The concept of sustainability was made popular by the United Nations' World Commission on Environment and Development (WCED), which coined the term 'Sustainable Development'. 'Sustainable Development', as defined by the WCED Report, titled "Our Common Future" is 'a process that meets the needs of the present without compromising the ability of the future generations to meet their own needs'. It requires the 'promotion of values that encourage consumption standards that are within bounds of the ecologically possible and to which all can reasonably aspire'(WCED, 1987).

With this interpretation, the notion of sustainability assumed a wider temporal context, having broadened its range from a few years to many generations in time scale. Further, a review of the many different definitions and interpretations of the concept of Sustainable Development reveals that Sustainable Development requires: (1) the maintenance of the environmental and human resource base that is essential for long term economic growth; (2) a focus on environmental management; and (3) a broader view of both economics and ecology than most practitioners in either discipline are prepared to admit, together with a political commitment to ensure that development is sustainable. Thus, while conventional economics and ecology offer competing, and not complimentary approaches to development, sustainability as a desirable attribute of development imparts a judicious compromise between the two extremes.

Most importantly, if we look at the definition of 'Sustainable Development', the focus is on the means by which 'development' is made to meet the needs of the present without compromising the ability of future generations to meet their needs (WCED, 1987). Since the needs of future generations are indefinable, and the future potential for generation of (natural) wealth and inputs is equally unknown and undetermined, the concept quite naturally implies that the total biological assets by and large remain unchanged, in the long-term. A sustainable use of resources thus, not only involves conserving biological diversity, fauna and flora, but also maintaining ecological functions such as soil quality, hydrological cycles, climate and weather, river flow and water quality. It also implies maintaining the supply of natural products-food, wood, game, fish, fodder, fruits, nuts, resins, dyes, construction materials, fuel wood, and all categories of minor forest products, all of which are integral to the sustenance of the critical livelihoods of the local people. Needless to say, the proportion of populations of the developing countries, who show a direct dependence on the natural resource base remains pegged at very high levels, and in that vein, sustainability of the environment justifiably and implicitly links itself to the availability of the nature and natural resources for this critical mass of people.

It is important to distinguish between the WCED definition of sustainability, with its emphasis on human needs and sustaining livelihoods, and those definitions which were subsequently adopted by many development institutions, and wherein the more technical definitions of sustainability entailed the ability of ecosystems to maintain a continued production of goods or services through the provision of a continued supply of inputs or the so called factors of production, or the maintenance of biodiversity (see, for example, Pearce, *et al.*, 1989; World Bank, 1991). Many such definitions strip the concept of 'sustainability' of the social and political issues implicit in the notion.

As the WCED study acknowledges, achieving sustainability implies a radical transformation in present-day economies. It requires a fundamental change in the way natural resources are owned, controlled and mobilized. To be sustainable, development must meet the needs of local people, for if it does not, people will be obliged by necessity to take from the environment more than that which is planned or desirable and coerce them into committing 'environmental crimes'. Sustainability is fundamentally linked to concepts of social justice and equity, both within generations and between generations, as well as both within nations and between nations (UNEP, 1989; WCED, 1987). Achieving sustainability thus implies major political changes, and the way resources and opportunities are distributed and redistributed over the sub national, national and global canvas.

As the WCED notes, the pursuit of sustainable development requires a political system that secures effective participation in decision-making, and this is best secured by decentralizing the management of natural resources. Sustaining the natural resources upon which local communities depend and giving these communities an effective say over the use of these resources is the only viable way of ensuring sustainability. Mandatorily, this will also require promoting citizen's initiatives, empowering peoples' organizations, and strengthening local democracy. Such a notion of popular 'participation' in development is very close to that adopted by the United Nations Research Institute for Social Development, which defined Popular Participation 'as the organized efforts to increase control over resources and regulative institutions in given social situations, on the part of groups and movements of those hitherto excluded from such control' (UNRISD/79/C.14, cited in Turton, 1987: 3).

The WCED develops this concept even further in its discussion of indigenous and tribal peoples, of whom it notes that in terms of absolute numbers these isolated, vulnerable groups may be small, but the fact of their marginalization is a symptom of a style of development that tends to neglect both human and environmental considerations. In such a context, a more careful and sensitive consideration of their interests is a 'touchstone' of a sustainable development policy. The traditional rights of these constituencies should be recognized and they should be given a decisive voice in formulating policies about resource development in their areas (WCED, 1987: 116, 12, emphasis added).

The same principles are echoed by the International Union for the Conservation of Nature and Natural Resources (IUCN) which, in its 'Guidelines for the Management of Tropical Forests' notes that, 'the people who live in and around tropical forests should control their management' (IUCN, 1989). In the same vein, the Tropical Forestry Action Plan states that one of its basic principles is to promote the 'active organized and self-governed involvement of local groups and communities in forestry activities, with a particular focus on the most vulnerable and on women and on commonly shared resources' (FAO, 1989).

The concept of 'Sustainable Development' provides a framework for the integration of environment and development on the one hand, and people's participation and their development on the other. The emergence of this concept is a result of the realization that sound environment not only leads to development which can be sustained over a long period of time, but also has the potential of sustaining the well being of the people who depend on it, directly and indirectly, in myriad ways. It also acknowledges the uncontested right of the people themselves to protect, manage, and regenerate the natural resources. By means of this right, people's participation in environmental protection and preservation becomes the chosen means to augur in sustainable development. Viewed within such a frame, while on the one hand, sustainable development works to assure that the growing economies get firmly attached to their ecological roots and these roots are protected and nurtured, so that they may support development over the long run, on the other hand, it also provides support to the importance of people's participation to ensure the sustainability of all developmental efforts, including environmental conservation.

The aforementioned discussion has clearly indicated the transition in the manner in which the concept of development has evolved. From being determined and characterized by economics alone, it shifted its stance to amalgamate the nodal concepts of peoples' participation and sustainability. No wonder then that the essence and the value of 'Participatory Development' and 'Sustainable Development' have an unequivocal presence in the academic and practice contexts and continue to be the buzz words of all development agenda and discourse.

People's Participation in Environmental Conservation and Management

The concept of sustainability emphasizes certain basic principles when applied to rural communities: that basic needs must be met; that resources should be subject to local control; that local communities must have a decisive voice in planning; they should represent themselves through their own institutions; and innovative political organization must exist at the community level. These principles have been notionally accepted by development planners and conservationists at all levels. Yet, they continue to be systematically over looked and deliberately undermined by the international and national policies and development programmes, leading to increasing poverty, social conflict and rapid decimation of the land, forests, water and air.

Traditional knowledge and systems of land use have proved far more environmentally appropriate, resilient and complex than initially supposed by outsiders. Management of resources for the market and market economics is very different from the way the local and indigenous people interact with the natural resources and engage in land use and resources use in terms of long term sustainability. They have been known to live in their resource rich environs with common ownership on resources and utilize them based on certain social norms, rules, customs and traditions. Indigenous Knowledge System or the traditional wisdom of the people denotes the cumulative human experience in the distinct natural and social compound, adapted to local culture and environment, and is a vital base for various kinds of information about the conservation and protection of environmental resources, including seed preservation, appropriateness of tree species and their propagation, indigenous technology, and management systems based on local political system. This vast reservoir of locally tested and contextually relevant and inter generationally preserved knowledge constitutes a rich source of according protection to the environment.

Therefore, the current global trends to dislocate and alienate the people from their habitat and their natural resources constitutes a monumental threat to the environment and to development of all hues, economic, social, and human, to begin with.

Forest and indigenous peoples have successfully opposed many socially and environmentally destructive development schemes proposed for their forests and lands. The pressure for the limited resources by an ever increasing population and the internal dynamic for development have created a plethora of social and environmental problems, and much of their impact has to be borne by the forest communities and other natural resource dependent communities like fisher folk, pastoralists and others. Livelihood requirements being central to the life and living of these communities, they 'create' an integral 'stake' in ensuring the sustenance and well being of their natural resource base. Their dependency on nature is built upon a symbiotic 'give and take', leading to the preservation of the local ecosystems, even without the fanciful application of the more celebrated environmental programmatic component of the government, donor agencies and developmental lobby. Thus stems the need and the relevance of keeping people as central in any effort for the rehabilitation and conservation of the natural resource base. While the local people are quite naturally the worst victims of environmental degradation and ecological disasters, they are also the first beneficiaries of a sound and healthy environment. In every sense of the word, and owing to the fact of their survival being inherently linked to the health of the ecosystem, it naturally follows that people be meaningfully involved in any efforts to protect and promote the environment.

People's participation in programmes/schemes of ecological conservation is also expected to yield better results because the local people have an intimate understanding of their environment. They possess an inherent 'traditional wisdom', attained by their long standing and inseparable links with their natural habitat. This traditional wisdom, if harnessed, can yield more effective strategies of action and better solutions/results. Secondly, the local people have a vested interest in securing the sustenance of their resource base, and therefore, they should ideally act as the legitimate guardians of their resources, and play an active role in managing them. People's participation is also important in recognition of the right of the local communities to decide how they should manage and use their resource-base, as against centralized management without any concern for the devolution of environmental rights and obligations. It emphasizes the notion of empowerment of local communities to manage their own resources. Thirdly, participation in programmes of environmental action helps the people to raise their level of consciousness about their own environment and their rights and responsibilities towards it. Both are complementary in that expecting people to protect the environment without recognizing their rights in the environmental resources is not justified. Fourthly, peoples' participation based on action may not always be in alignment with the state policies and programmes. Conversely, government policies and programmes may not be integrated with the interests/

wishes of the people. A tradition of popular involvement brings about popular consciousness and watch over governmental action. Moreover, it empowers local groups and communities to mobilize their own action programmes and environmental movements, based on their own contexts.

Additionally, certain other factors add to the importance and relevance of people's participation in traditional hill societies, like the Garhwali society. These are: (a) Scientific environmental management may require land use changes. But these changes may not be readily accepted by people, as quick incomes and produce are required for the subsistence of people and land use changes may cause interruptions in income or cause returns to flow in a longer time frame; (b) Scientific land use may also involve rational forest/grazing land closures, which are also not acceptable to all local people, especially when alternatives to traditional resources are not easily available or affordable in mountain areas, such as fuel for domestic needs or fodder for livestock (especially for traditional grazing communities); and (c) Such changes may be looked upon, initially by the rural poor as attempts aimed at depriving them of access to these resources, of which they had full and free use earlier. Thus, the problems are deeply related to the implications of such changes for the affected communities. Experiments have shown that such scientific environmental management is capable of being achieved if community involvement and community acceptance are entailed from the very conception of a project to its implementation. All of the above goes to support the need and urgency for people's participation in environmental conservation and management. There is development when people and their communities act as subjects and are not acted upon as objects; assert their autonomy, self-reliance and self-confidence, when they set out and carry out projects.

A people-centered approach, a people-oriented strategy and a people-participatory ethos of planning as well as implementation yields better results in terms of achievement of environmental goals/objectives as opposed to pure government initiatives. Essentially, the real people and real work are in the 'micro' of the contexts and we really need to redress the past preponderant imbalance of the macro-institutional world, by putting the micro world in the centre of the picture. A review of community-based initiatives in South and South-East Asia shows that in some countries, positive initiatives have been taken by local and national governments to promote a community-based approach.

This speaks eloquent about the need to analyze environmental issues, legislations, policies and programmes within a holistic framework that integrates the ecological context with the economic, social and political processes. The critical issues confronting environmental sustenance such as the nature and role of the principal actors responsible for environmental protection and promotion; the manner in which ecological changes interact with livelihood options/strategies, gender roles in the context of the environment; the presence and contribution of social institutions (both, traditional and emerging; individual and collective responses to environmental crisis; and conservation initiatives by the state, the donors, the NGOs and the local communities need deeper reflection and a more conjoined framework for practice. An analysis of the pervasiveness of conflicts engendered by competition over natural resources and the emergence of environmental movements also needs to be woven in. It is only such an analysis that is likely to reveal the vital elements of an alternative approach to sustainable development linking livelihood security, environmental protection and community empowerment.

Women and Environment

This book has been based on a study which was aimed at drawing on the discourse of peoples' participation, with a special emphasis on women's participation in the protection and promotion of the environment. While women comprise one half of the population, it automatically follows that women's participation is crucial to the success of any developmental programme. Undeniably, women's participation assumes a fundamental significance in the realm of environmental conservation programmes, due to the fact that in all societies, including India, women play a distinct and a predominant role in almost all activities related to nature and natural resources.

Women have an essential role to play in the development of sustainable and ecologically sound consumption and production patterns and approaches to natural resource management, as was recognized at the United Nations Conference on Environment and Development (UNCED, 1992) and the International Conference on Population and Development and reflected throughout Agenda 21. Awareness of resource depletion, the degradation of natural systems and the dangers of polluting substances has significantly increased in the past decade. The environmental plundering is destroying fragile ecosystems and displacing communities, especially women, from productive activities and are an increasing threat to a safe and healthy environment. Needless to say that poverty and environmental degradation are closely interrelated. While poverty results in certain kinds of environmental stress, the major cause of the continued deterioration of the global environment is the unsustainable pattern of consumption and production, particularly in the developed countries of the Northern bloc, which leads to aggravating poverty and imbalances within and among the countries of the Southern bloc.

The deterioration of natural resources displaces and dispossesses communities, especially women, from income-generating activities, while greatly adding to unremunerated work. In both urban and rural areas, environmental degradation results in negative effects on the health, well-being and quality of life of the population at large, especially girls and women of all ages. Their 'gendered' roles require them to negotiate with nature in the most integral of ways and to form inherent and intimate linkages with their surrounding resource base. Through their management and use of natural resources, women provide sustenance to their families and communities. As consumers and producers, caretakers of their families and educators, women play an important role in promoting sustainable development through their concern for the quality and sustainability of life for present and future generations.

The culturally accepted and culturally determined division of labour within the family leaves the collection of biomass and water to women. Biomass plays a crucial role in meeting the daily survival needs of the vast majority of rural households in the country: food, fuel, fodder, fertilizer for agricultural fields, building materials and medicines (herbs) are all different forms of biomass, and it is the women who have traditionally provided for these core needs of the household. Water is another crucial element in human survival and again, it is the women who face the extremely arduous task of carrying water, sometimes across long distances and treacherous terrain. Women have also traditionally contributed to agricultural operations like sowing, weeding and harvesting, and also looking after the domestic animals. Women in many communities provide the main labour force for subsistence production; hence, their role is crucial to the provision of food and nutrition, the enhancement of the subsistence and informal sectors and the preservation of the environment.

Women have often played leadership roles or taken the lead in promoting an environmental ethic, reducing resource use, and reusing and recycling resources to minimize waste and excessive consumption. Women can also play have a potential role in influencing sustainable consumption decisions. In addition, women's contributions to environmental management, including through grass-roots campaigns to protect the environment, have often taken place at the local level, where decentralized action on environmental issues is most needed and decisiveIn certain regions, women are generally the most stable members of the community, as men often pursue work in distant locations, leaving women to safeguard the natural environment and ensure adequate and sustainable resource allocation within the household and the community.

Fulfilling all these roles has given women a special understanding of, and special 'connect' with nature and natural resources, which is inherently different from that of men. Women, especially indigenous women, have particular knowledge of ecological linkages and fragile ecosystem management. Their "ecological knowledge" has been age old and remains a traditional storehouse of generational experience. Their engagement with their role has made them appreciative of the benevolence of Mother Nature and a deep regard for the sustenance of all that she has endowed on them. The woman's role and image, as that of a nurturer has been a theme of much academic work, and is attributed to offer her a special ability to nurture life, in all its forms, including all that is 'living' within nature. It is perhaps due to this ability that, from times immemorial women have striven to maintain a delicate balance between 'taking from' nature and 'giving back' by nurturing nature.

It is an unfortunate saga that this traditional and mutually fulfilling relationship between women and nature has been disrupted by the processes of urbanization, industrialization and the advance of the cash economy. These have inadvertently led to the destruction of the critical biomass through the onslaught of deforestation and de-vegetation. It has also meant another significant transformation of the biomass, in the sense that its use has been reformulated. It has blatantly been moving away from rural and household needs and has been shifting closer to urban, commercial and industrial needs. While this is having a major impact on the lives of all those who live within the non-monetized, biomass-based subsistence economy, probably no other group is more affected by this phenomenon than the poor village women. Since it is they who interact with the environment for survival, it is their drudgery that has increased manifold. As ecological conditions have worsened, their long march in search of fuel, fodder and water has become longer, more tiresome and more burdensome.

Gender differentials already place women at a disadvantage with double work burdens, unequal distribution of resources, and lack of access to education, health, cash and productive assets, like land, all of which stem from their inferior status in the household and the society. Given this all pervading imbalance, the reality of an ever continuing environmental decimation exacerbates women's already acute problems in multiple ways, which are very different from those experienced by men. For example, a declining natural resource base implies reduced food availability, which translates into less food for women and girls. The disproportionately increasing workload and longer hours devoted to the collection of fuel, fodder and water implies more drudgery for women and less time for themselves. Already surveys show that women have less access to health care, stemming out of the social and cultural factors like women's traditional shyness in reporting illness and general neglect of female health in a patriarchal society. But the extraordinary work burden on women means that often they do not have enough time to seek health care, even if they want to. Environmental risks in the home and workplace may have a disproportionate impact on women's health because of women's different susceptibilities to the toxic effects of various chemicals. These risks to women's health are particularly high in urban areas, as well as in low-income areas where there is a high concentration of polluting industrial facilities.

Despite the significant role that women play, they largely remain absent at all levels of policy formulation and decision-making in the domain of natural resource and environmental management, conservation, protection and rehabilitation, and their experience and skills in advocacy for and monitoring of proper natural resource management too often remain marginalized in policy-making and decision-making bodies, as well as in educational institutions and environment-related agencies at the managerial level. Women are rarely trained as professional natural resource managers with policy making capacities, such as land-use planners, agriculturalists, foresters, marine scientists and environmental lawyers. Even in cases where women are trained as professional natural resource managers, they are often underrepresented in formal institutions with policy-making capacities at the national, regional and international levels. Often women are not equal participants in the management of financial and corporate institutions whose decision-making most significantly affects environmental quality.

Even within the context of grassroots participation, despite their traditional role with regard to their engagement with the natural resources, and the knowledge base that they possess, they have been almost completely marginalized from processes that seek to formulate strategies for the use and management of these resources. More significantly, in the process of this marginalization, women have further lost status and power, by losing access to resources and decision making with regard to the same. In contrast, men have not only gained control over resources and access to technology but, given their orientation and motivations, have continued to derive primary benefits from all development initiatives. In cases where men of certain socio-economic groups have been deprived of access to natural resources, or have been impacted by an ever decimating resource base, they have found options such as migration, and have moved to distant locales, and have simply transferred the collective responsibility of managing home and hearth to the women, leaving them in a worse position.

In such a situation, the need to mainstream women in environmental conservation and management programmes becomes imperative on several counts. First and foremost, their intensive involvement and links with the environment have given them a special understanding of the environment, which will certainly lead to greater success in environmental conservation. Field experience has shown that lack of will on the part of the government to involve women in governmental programmes has often resulted in the ineffectiveness or complete failure of these programmes. An apt illustration is that of the Social Forestry projects launched by the government with aid from international organisations like the World Bank. Almost no effort was made to involve women and virtually all the schemes ended up as schemes for farming trees as cash crops, thus defeating the very objective of social forestry. On the other hand, when women were integrated into such processes, usually through NGO initiatives, the success rate of programmes was high. Thirdly, involving women in environmental programmes shall not only achieve the environmental objectives, but also address certain crucial direct needs of women like generation of income and drudgery reduction. It would ameliorate the impact of environmental degradation on them, which in turn will reduce their workload.

The last justification, though significant within the context, is several times more relevant in view of the fact that any reduction in the drudgery and workload of women, would imply the availability of some free time for the women, which could be then utilized by them in more productive or self-development oriented activities, or those avenues that could potentially pull them out of their limited spheres of existence. These would therefore constitute for them the much needed means for the acquisition of power and status by the women, because organizing and attending meetings, increasing awareness and articulation, achieving literacy and of course, financial independence would contribute directly or indirectly to women's empowerment and family well-being.

Particular attention and recognition needs to be given to the role and special situation of women living in rural areas and those working in the agricultural/forestry sectors, where access to training, land, natural and productive resources, credit, development programmes and cooperative structures can help them increase their participation in sustainable development. The strategic actions needed for sound environmental management require a holistic, multidisciplinary and inter sectoral approach.

Women's participation and leadership are essential to every aspect of that approach. The recent United Nations global conferences on development, as well as regional preparatory conferences for the Fourth World Conference on Women, have all acknowledged that sustainable development policies that do not involve women and men alike will not succeed in the long run. They have called for the effective participation of women in the generation of knowledge and environmental education in decision-making and management at all levels. Women's experiences and contributions to an ecologically sound environment must therefore be central to the agenda for the twenty-first century. Sustainable development will be an elusive goal unless women's contribution to environmental management is recognized and supported.

The aforementioned arguments amply justify the need for promoting women's participation in programmes of environmental conservation. This participation can be strengthened and promoted only when the exact state of their present participation is understood. It would be relevant to know the forms in which women participate and the factors which hinder or promote women's participation. This is precisely what the study aims to do, and in doing so it strives to promote the cause of popular participation, and especially women's participation in environmental protection and promotion.

2
Methodological Parameters of Engagement with the Field

The analysis of peoples' participation in environmental action initiatives, with a distinctive focus on women's participation in their interface with the environment and environmental action has been attempted, based on an empirical study and an intensive engagement with the locale provided by the Bhilangana Block of Tehri Garhwal District of Uttarakhand State, and its people, who formed the subjects of the action component of the discourse.

It must be shared that the chosen locale is extremely pertinent to the said theme on account of its strategic location within the Garhwal Himalayas, and the significant environmental influence that this region exerts on a large part of the Indian subcontinent. Moreover, the selected block has a rich history of peoples' struggles and movements, especially those in the realm of environmental issues and concerns, with the celebrated Chipko Movement being a part of this historical frame. The contemporary arena within the locale is also replete with initiatives in the domain of environmental action, thus paving way for its selection as the 'field' for basing this work.

The methodological parameters pertaining to the study have been encapsulated in this chapter, as they provide the methodological grounding and justification for the empirical work that was undertaken, and which forms the basis of the discourse forwarded by the study.

Objectives

The primary objective of the study was to understand the nature, forms, extent, scope, methods and problems of people's participation in the environmental protection and promotion programmes based on the study of a block, and to focus on women's participation, in particular. The specific objectives were:

1. Understanding the state of the environment and the problems of environmental degradation and depletion in the Tehri-Garhwal region in general and Bhilangana block in particular.
2. Gaining a familiarity with the setting, that is, Bhilangana and its people, with particular emphasis on the participants in environmental action.

3. Acquiring an understanding of the programmes of the government and people's groups and organizations being implemented for the protection and promotion of the environment.
4. Understanding the nature, forms, extent, scope and methods of participation, with a particular focus on women's participation, and identifying and describing the factors promoting or hindering participation.
5. Examining the perception of people about their participation and also assessing the impact of participation on the participants, their families, and on the state of their environment.
6. Developing a perspective on environmental action, based on an analysis of the past efforts as well as the contemporary (post-Chipko) programmes of environmental protection and promotion.

In addition to the above objectives, the study also aimed at providing some perspectives and insights for the promotion of people's participation in environmental action programmes, based on the observations of participation in the block covered by the study.

Research Design

'Descriptive' Research Design was used for the purpose of the study, as the focus of the study was on describing and analyzing the different aspects of people's participation, with specific focus on women's participation in the protection and promotion of the environment in an ecologically sensitive locale.

Operational Definitions

Operational definitions of three concepts engaged with, within the context of the study are as follows:

People's Participation: 'People's participation' for the purpose of the study, refers to the individual or collective involvement of the following six categories of people, as planners, implementers, evaluators or programme recipients, in programmes for the protection and promotion of the environment, conducted either by governmental or non-governmental organizations, including people's groups.

The six categories of people are:

- Members of Village Councils (including members of Panchayats);
- Members of Mahila Mangal Dals;
- Members of Nav Yuvak Mangal Dals;
- Functionaries of Voluntary Organisations;
- Members of Van Panchayats; and,
- Local Activists.

Environment: 'Environment', herein, refers to the land (soil and forests), water, wildlife (fauna), plants and trees (flora) components, and is inclusive of human-beings and their interaction with the other components. The air component has been excluded, as within the region under study, problems pertaining to air pollution were not significant, and thus, action with regard to the protection and promotion of this environmental component was deemed insignificant.

Protection and Promotion of the Environment: This consists of two terms 'protection' and 'promotion', in context of the environment. Both are independent, yet inherently inter-related. In fact, environmental 'promotion' begins with the 'protection' of the quality and quantity of the existing environmental components/resources. Both 'protection' and 'promotion' are two components of sound environment management, aiming at the conservation of species and biological processes, as also the simultaneous conservation of the biotic resources of the environment. However, the difference between the two terms is reflected by the following operational definitions:

'Protection' of the environment is that part of environmental management which is undertaken to maintain or safeguard the quality and quantity of environmental components/resources and/or to prevent a deterioration or degradation in the same, so as to ensure the survival of the maximum diversity of species and the maintenance of the biosphere functions. Thus, prevention of tree felling/deforestation and overgrazing, soil and water conservation, protection of wildlife, preservation of indigenous varieties of trees, plants, including medicinal herbs, etc. comprise environmental protection.

'Promotion' of the environment is that part of environmental management which focuses on the improvement, enhancement or regeneration of the quality and quantity of the environmental components/resources, so as to allow replenishment to keep pace with depletion. Thus, activities like forestation, water harvesting, use of non-conventional energy sources, promotion of biomass alternatives, etc. constitute environmental promotion.

Relevance of the Study

There is a paucity of comprehensive studies on people's participation in environmental action related to the area under study. In this regard, the study is not only relevant, it is an imperative, considering the contemporary context which is characterized by a series of prevailing and emerging environmental crises and threats. To be precise, it has a twofold relevance, theoretical and practical.

Theoretical Significance

(a) Bridging the Existing Gaps and Addition to the Body of Knowledge: As far as the theoretical significance is concerned, the first and the foremost contribution of the study is that it has added to the body of knowledge by exploring and analyzing different aspects of people's participation. As has been mentioned earlier, there has been a dearth of empirical studies on the theme of people's participation in environmental action programmes. There is no comprehensive study covering different categories of participants, and focusing on differential aspects of people's participation, at the level of a block in this particular geographical locale. The present study has attempted to provide an empirical basis for the description and analysis of different aspects of participation, of a variety of participants, in both government and non-governmental environmental programmes, at the level of a block.

Additionally, by providing a special focus on women's participation, the study has contributed to the understanding of the gender perspective in environmental management. As has already been highlighted in the introductory chapter, women share a special relationship with the environment in the hill-based economy of Uttaranchal. But not much has been known about the exact status of women's involvement in the environmental conservation and management initiatives in the region as such and more so in governmental programmes. This has depicted a serious gap in the existing body of knowledge on women's participation. Hence by studying people's participation, and particularly women's participation, the study has most certainly attempted to bridge this critical gap. It has combined empirical and theoretical concerns and has added to the knowledge base of the subject.

(b) Providing a Database: The study also attempted to provide a database about the state of environment of the region. No comprehensive effort has been made in the recent context to study the same, either in a micro or macro perspective. Although the study area has been a specific block, but it shares the problems and issues with the wider regional context. Therefore, by exploring the ecology and the ecological problems of the study area, this micro-level study has shed light on the ecological status of the macro area, that is, the entire Central Himalayan Region. Any attempt to ameliorate the environmental problems of the region has to also be based on a realistic understanding of the contemporarily determined status of the environment. The study is significant due to its potential of having generated valuable information on the environmental components, namely, land, soil, forests, water, flora and fauna of the region, and problems pertaining to each of them.

The study also aimed at providing a database about environmental action. It is important to note that the region that has been covered by the study has been the home ground of the famous Chipko Movement, which has been heralded as the most successful people's movement and which had set new landmarks in the realm of people's action.

While in the Chipko period, that is, in the late seventies and early eighties, the region had attracted immense attention of researchers, scholars and academicians, no attempt was made in the subsequent period to examine whether or not the tradition of popular participation, generated during the

Chipko period, continued to thrive or not. This study could be viewed as an effort to update information on the nature and level of environmental action in the post-Chipko period. It has attempted to examine the status of people's response to the more contemporary environmental challenges, with special emphasis on the strategies/methodologies of participation, and thereby has tried to develop a perspective on environmental action, based on an analysis of the past efforts, as well as the more contemporary initiatives.

(c) Developing Notions and Theories: The study is also pertinent in that it has clarified ideas and developed notions on different aspects of people's participation, especially nature, forms, duration and methodologies of participation, as also the factors promoting or hindering the participation of people in general, and women in particular. By attempting to formulate ideas and notions the study has aimed to contribute towards concept formulation and theorization.

(d) Generating Indigenous Resource Material: The study has assumed special significance in view of the emerging recognition of the relevance of ecology and environment within the developmental thrust of the developing countries. Like other disciplines, social work is also striving towards an increasing association with environmental issues and concerns. Since it is a new field of study and intervention, not much is available by way of relevant resource material to enable social work educators, students and practitioners to develop a better understanding of this field. This study has attempted to fill this gap, by not only focusing on the environmental situation at a micro level, but also bringing to the fore action/initiatives being taken to protect and promote the environment. By doing so, it has generated indigenous resource material on different aspects of people's participation, especially the methodologies of participation and strategies of action. It has sought to provide valuable case material for discussion, both at the level of social work educators and scholars, as well as the environmentalists. The study can also form the basis for more detailed studies on similar themes.

Implications for Practice

As far as the practical value of the study is concerned, the study can contribute in multiple ways. These include:

- **(a) Providing Data Base for Environmental Action:** The study has generated information on the state of the environment in a specific area of the particularly eco-sensitive Garhwal Himalayas. This information can form the basis of environmental action programmes for both the government and voluntary sectors. It has the potential for facilitating new project formulation by different agencies.
- **(b) Strengthening Existing Programmes:** The study has immense utility for the existing organizations, both governmental, (including the local

self-governments or panchayats) and voluntary, working in Uttaranchal, as also people's own self-help groups. It can enable them to critically examine and evaluate their own programmes, approaches and strategies.

(c) **Promoting People's Participation, Particularly Women's Participation:** As the study has shed light on the scope and avenues for people's participation, it can help to illustrate how people's energies can be meaningfully harnessed to resolve common issues concerning them. It can enable agencies to refine/upgrade their operational strategies to secure effective people's participation in their own action programmes. In view of the fact that the study has provided a special focus to women's participation, the results of the study have special relevance for organizations working with women. It can help them to draw appropriate strategies to secure women's participation, based on a better understanding of the factors promoting and/or hindering their effective participation.

(d) **Forming the Basis for Policy Formulation and Implementation:** It will not be an over estimation to say that an empirical and comprehensive study like the present one shall not only have a relevance in the micro context, but shall also have special significance in the regional context. Uttaranchal, as a relatively new state, relies primarily on its rich natural resource base to generate and sustain its socio-economic development. The need to adopt a cautious approach with regard to its ecology and environment, as also mobilize people's energies to protect and promote the environment will form the mainstay of its developmental strategy. Thus, this study has important implications for policy formulation and implementation at the level of the block, district and the state as a whole.

To summarize the discussion, it can be said in no uncertain terms that the present study has been meaningfully able to contribute, not only to the corpus of knowledge on the subject, but also presents immense scope for use by the people and agencies involved in securing people's participation in environmental action programmes, both in the region and elsewhere.

Dimensions of Coverage

The study was confined to the Bhilangana block of Tehri Garhwal district of the state of Uttarakhand.

The district of Tehri Garhwal was selected due to certain important reasons:

Firstly, it is the source of the two major river systems of the country, viz. the Ganga and the Yamuna, and thus has a strategic importance vis-à-vis its environmental influence on a large part of the country. Secondly, indiscriminate commercial exploitation of the natural resources of the region has already led to severe environmental damage. Consequently, the people have been facing many natural hazards like earthquakes, floods, droughts and landslides, on a recurring basis. This coupled with the fact that Tehri district is the poorest district of the state renders the economy and people very vulnerable. Moreover, being located in an environmentally sensitive zone, the entire development of the district, as also the state has to be based first and foremost on environmental conservation. In view of this, there is an immense need and scope for sound environment management practices and programmes in this area. This also contributed towards the researcher's choice of area for the study. Thirdly, Tehri district has a rich history of environmental action. The period up to 1947 (when it was governed by rulers) was replete with instances of popular conflicts, resistances and movements, the basis of which was the 'Haq-Haqooq' or the traditional and inherent rights of the local people to their environment and natural resources. Even after independence, there have been a number of popular movements, based on environmental issues. The Chipko Movement and the Tehri Dam Agitation launched by the local people are prime examples of such indigenous initiatives. Both these movements had a stronghold in this district and had elicited widespread popular support and participation from people. This rich history of popular collective action, especially revolving around environmental concerns, made Tehri a rich locale to study people's participation in environmental action.

Lastly, a multitude of groups, (both formal and informal) and organizations are working in this area and are concentrating on environmental conservation. These presented ample scope for the researcher to study the theme of people's participation in environmental programmes.

Bhilangana, as a block of Tehri Garhwal district shares all the advantages mentioned above. Some more points of consideration determined the choice of this particular block. These were:

1. Rich history of people's movements: Bhilangana block, in particular has had a rich history of people's movements. Apart from environment linked action, the women of this block have led a successful war for the prohibition of alcohol consumption both at the level of the block, as well as in the region as a whole. Moreover, this block has been the home ground of Shri S.L. Bahuguna and had been a very active area for the Chipko movement and the Tehri Dam Agitation. Thus, it was expected that people would show a high level of awareness and participation in environmental initiatives.

2. Presence of a number of active voluntary organizations: There are a few very active voluntary organisations working in the block, like Parvatiya Nav Jeevan Mandal in Silyara village (which was run by Shri Sunder Lal

Bahuguna, and his wife Shrimati Vimla Bahuguna) and Lok Jeevan Vikas Bharti in Budha Kedar. These agencies were found to be doing exemplary work in the area of environmental action and have been able to mobilize people, especially women in their programmes. Personal interest of some of the organizations in a study of this nature for the furtherance of their work was also a reason which prompted the researcher to choose this block.

3. Existence of a number of women's groups: There exist multiple very active Mahila Mangal Dals in the block, some of which have been doing exemplary work in preserving their environment, in participating in action against the Tehri Dam and in the Anti-Liquor Movement. The presence of these Dals also motivated the researcher to choose this particular block as it could provide her with a meaningful avenue to study women's participation.

Sampling Frame

The study covered a total of 320 respondents, specifically belonging to the six categories of 'people', comprising of those persons who were perceived to be the participants in environmental action programmes, either at their own level, or in liaison with governmental and people's groups and organizations. These categories were:

1. Members of Village Councils (including members of panchayats) residing in the block.
2. Members of Mahila Mangal Dals (women's groups) of the block.
3. Members of Nav Yuvak Mangal Dals (youth groups) of the block.
4. Functionaries of Voluntary Organizations working in the block.
5. Members of the Van Panchayats functioning in the block, and
6. Local Activists of the block.

Multistage Stratified Random Sampling Technique of the probability type was used to select the respondents from the six categories of people. It involved two stages, both of which have been described below:

Stage I: Selection of Sample Villages

The block consisted of a total of 268 villages divided into seven revenue zones or 'pattis'. The first stage comprised of selecting villages at random to give an equal representation to all the Pattis. This was achieved by selecting thirty five per cent villages from each patti. (Some minor adjustments had to be made later due to practical considerations). Thus, the total universe comprised of 268 villages, while the final sample consisted of 75 villages, comprising 40 Gram Sabhas/Gram Panchayats.

The patti-wise distribution of the selected villages is provided by the following diagram:

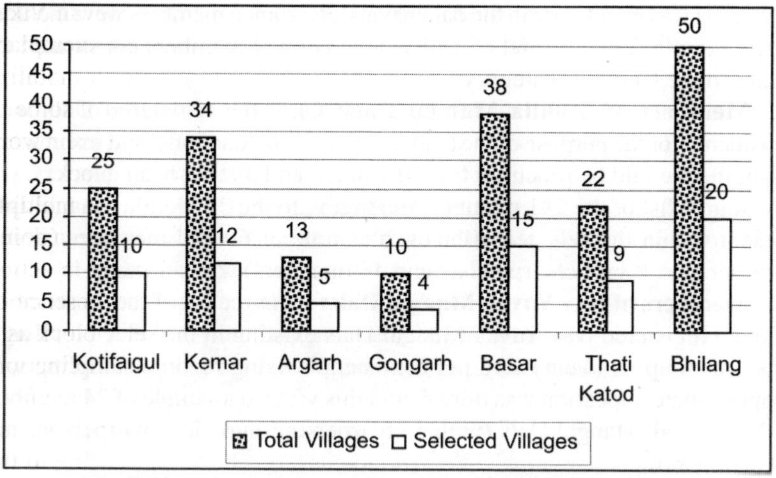

Fig. 2.1: Patti-wise Distribution of Total and Sample Villages

Stage II: Selection of Sample Respondents from the Selected Villages: In the second stage, differential sampling techniques were employed to select the respondents from the six categories of people. The category wise sampling design is presented below:

Members of Village Councils (including Panchayat Members): In Bhilangana, a number of village councils, either individually or in collaboration with neighbouring councils have traditionally been managing or protecting their common property resources, especially forests. These councils are not necessarily co-terminus with the Gram Sabhas (constituted under the Panchayati Raj Act), and are usually single village settlements. They have even constituted committees known by varied names like Van Suraksha Samitis, Van Samitis, and Jungle Samitis, primarily for the purpose of forest protection and promotion, besides taking up other environmental causes.

Moreover, gram panchayat members residing in the selected villages were also included separately in this category, as they were both members of the village councils and elected representatives of the local self-government. Thus, they were found to be participating, both in the programmes of the village council and other village groups, and in government programmes, Thus, this category comprised of two sub-categories. Out of a total of 360 members of all the village forest/environment committees existing in the selected villages, a twenty five per cent sample selected randomly yielded a sample of 90 members from this sub-category. Out of the 362 members of gram panchayats belonging to the selected villages, a twenty five per cent sample, selected randomly yielded a sample of 90 members (comprising 30 chairpersons, 30 vice-chairpersons and 30 panchayat members). Since one-third representation of women was mandatory in the panchayats, 30 women members were included in the sample. Thus, a total of 180 village council members constituted the final sample from this category.

Members of Mahila Mangal Dals: Only the registered Dals were considered for the purpose of the study, as they were functional and information about them could be procured from the block and district head quarters. Out of a source list of the 241 members belonging to the 22 Mahila Mangal Dals present within the selected villages, a sample of 60 Dal members (with 6 chairpersons, 6 vice chairpersons and 48 members) was selected.

Members of Nav Yuvak Mangal Dals: A source list of the 96 members of the 9 registered Nav Yuvak Mangal Dals existing in the selected villages was drawn up. A twenty five per cent sample using random sampling with proportionate allocation was drawn, and this yielded a sample of 24 members of Nav Yuvak Mangal Dals (with 5 chairpersons and vice-chairpersons and 19 members).

Functionaries of Voluntary Organisations: Seven active voluntary organizations, which were genuinely involved in environmental action programmes, along with other developmental work were functional in the block. Information about these organizations was initially procured from the block and district headquarters, as also the Block Pramukh. Later all these organizations were visited. The universe for this category comprised of the 82 functionaries/staff working for these seven organizations. This included 7 chief workers and 75 other workers. A twenty five per cent sample yielded a sample size of 20. While all seven chief workers were selected, the rest of the 13 functionaries were selected randomly from the list of 75 workers

Local Activists: This category comprised of those activists from the sample villages who were known to have associated or were associating themselves with environmental initiatives at the level of a village or a group of villages, or even the block. Information about their identity was procured from various sources like block officials, voluntary organizations and Panchayat members. The local activists were working without being a part of any registered organization and mainly through informal village groups. Many such local activists belonging to activist groups like Rakshasutra Andolan, Meera Van Bachao Andolan, Balganga Shiksha Prasar Samiti, as also the erstwhile Chipko activists were found to be working in the block. Since the researcher was unsure of the exact number of such activists, (and therefore, about the size of the universe), a pre-determined sample size could not be set, and 20 local activists were selected using purposive sampling technique.

Members of Van Panchayats: At the time of data collection, a few Van Panchayats had been constituted in the block. A source list of the 32 members belonging to the eight Van Panchayats in the selected villages, and comprising of 8 chairpersons, 8 vice-chairpersons and 16 members was prepared. Due to the smallness of the universe, a fifty per cent sample was drawn using random sampling with proportionate allocation to provide representation to all three sub-categories. This yielded a sample of 16 Van Panchayat members (with 4 chairpersons, 4 vice-chairpersons and 8 members).

A schematic representation of the sample design used for the study is provided in Figure 1 in order to present a comprehensive picture of sampling undertaken by the researcher to select a representative sample of the different groups participating in the environmental programmes of the block:

Data Collection

Primary Sources: The six categories of respondents covered by the study formed the primary sources of data. Additionally, officials at the block and district levels were also used as sources of first-hand information about the district and block situation (including information about the state of the environment, environmental problems, environmental programmes etc.) especially wherever data was unavailable.

Secondary Sources: The secondary sources were used for processing available literature to gain information about the study area, the state of its environment, environmental problems as well as different programmes of environmental protection and promotion being undertaken by different agencies and groups in the past and in the contemporary context. This information was procured from published and unpublished reports, records of government departments, and voluntary organizations involved in environmental action programmes. Apart from the block headquarters at Ghansali and district headquarters at New Tehri, reports and records at the 'Ministry of Environment and Forests', at New Delhi, state departments at Lucknow, and thereafter Dehradun were also utilized for this purpose. Additionally, literature in the form of reports, records including census reports, and other materials available at the block and district headquarters was also processed in order to derive an understanding of the block in terms of its land and population parameters.

The following methods and tools were used to achieve the stipulated objectives:

Interview

1. An **Interview Schedule** was used to collect data from the respondents. The schedule was very comprehensive and sought information relating to the background of the respondents; their organizational/group affiliations; their awareness with regard to the environment, environmental problems and programmes; as also detailed information pertaining to the various aspects of their participation in governmental and non-governmental programmes of

environmental protection and promotion. The schedule was in Hindi and was pre-coded at relevant places (Refer to Appendix I).

2. A self-made **Scale** for the measurement of the levels of participation of respondents in different forms of participation (viz. in planning, implementation and benefit-sharing) was used (Refer to Appendix II). Separate indicators were first identified for determining the level of participation in the three forms. For planners the indicators were four in number and included: (i) Regularity in attending meetings; (ii) Raising relevant issues in meetings; (iii) Participation in discussion; and (iv) Role played in arriving at decisions.

For implementers the indicators were five in number and included:

(i) Regularity in meetings; (ii) Expression of views on implementation of the programmes; (iii) Extending new ideas and strategies; (iv) Carrying out assigned tasks satisfactorily; and (v) Participation in orientation/training. For beneficiaries there were four indicators, which were: (i) Role in selection as beneficiaries; (ii) Role in choosing nature of benefits; (iii) Redressing grievances; and (iv) Confrontation, in case grievances were not met.

Each indicator was assigned three responses: 'Active, 'Average' and 'Passive' (with scores 3, 2 and 1 respectively.) describing different levels of participation pertaining to each indicator. Summated scores were then worked out for each respondent by adding up the individual scores obtained by the respondent on the specific indicators. The respondents were ranked as 'Active', 'Average' or 'Passive' as planners, implementers and beneficiaries based on their summated scores.

(3) An **Interview Guide** was used to collect data from relevant officials at the block and district levels. Data pertained to the state of the environment of the area as also the different governmental environmental programmes functioning at the district and block levels, together with information on the scope of peoples' participation in the same.

Focus Group Discussion

Focus groups were used for collecting qualitative information from the different categories of respondents. Purposive sampling of the non probability type was used to select those groups whose members were willing and had good communication between them. The role of the moderator entailed engagement of all the participants in discussion to promote a lively exchange of views, for modulating conflict (by proactive intervention) and to ensure that the interview guidelines were followed. The issues for discussion were: (i) State of the Environment; (ii) Government and Non-Governmental Environmental Programmes. (iii) Women's Participation, (iv) Future Course of Action for Environmental Conservation; (v) Position of Women in the Region; and (vi) Traditional/Indigenous Environmental Conservation Systems/Practices and Scope of People's Participation.

Focused Group Guidelines were used to guide FGDs into desirable deliberations and data sharing.

Non-Participant Observation

The researcher attended meetings of Van Panchayats, Block Development Council (BDC), Mahila Mangal and Nav Yuvak Mangal Dals, Forest Officials, Panchayats, as also Van Sammelans and Van Shivirs (organized by women and voluntary organizations), and used non-participant observation to procure information on relevant portions of her study. She also attended the special programmes organized on the occasion of World Environment Day (over three consecutive years) and Van Mahotsava, as also the programmes of social action conducted by a few voluntary organizations, as a non-participant observer. Non-participant observation was used to understand the background of respondents, their life and living conditions, community dynamics and functioning of their groups/organizations. It also enabled the researcher to examine the role and performance of respondents in meetings and action programmes, and to understand the nature and extent of their participation. It was also used to observe first hand, the environmental problems faced by the area, as also the impact of the different environmental action programmes. Observation data was used not only to supplement information, but also to verify the information collected through primary methods.

An **Observation Guide** was pre-determined to capture all the themes to be covered using this method.

3
The Landscape
Ecology and People

This chapter describes and analyses the ecology of the area, that is Bhilangana block, both in terms of the land and the people. This description and analysis assumes importance from the point of view of developing a deeper insight into the issue of people's participation, which is closely related to the nature and constraints of the land and area. Moreover, people's participation, and especially women's participation is also impacted by the particular socio-economic and cultural situations prevailing at that time and in that particular place.

This chapter is divided into two parts. Part I deals with the setting, i.e. Bhilangana block in terms of its location, topography, climate, administrative set up and development infrastructure. Part II focusses on the people of the area, and describes and analyses their background features. It also highlights the status of the women of the area. An insight into the position of women is important, as it has implications for women's participation, which constitutes an important objective of the study under consideration.

The Area

The block of Bhilangana is one of the nine community development blocks of the district of Tehri Garhwal. Prior to 1997, Uttarakhand comprised of eight hill districts, divided into two administrative divisions of Garhwal and Kumaun. While the Garhwal division comprised of the five districts of Uttarkashi, Chamoli, Dehradun, Pauri Garhwal and Tehri Garhwal, Kumaun division had three districts viz. Pithoragarh, Almora and Nainital. In September 1997, a reorganisation of districts led to the creation of three new districts. viz. Bageshwar, Champawat and Rudraprayag, which were carved out of the eight parent districts of Uttarakhand.

In November 2000, the Uttarakhand region of Uttar Pradesh, which had a distinct geographical, cultural, social, historical and administrative identity became a separate state of the Indian republic and came to be known as Uttarakhand. On acquiring the status of a separate state, Uttarakhand got two new districts in the process of the states' reorganisation, viz. Haridwar and Udham Singh Nagar. These were added due to their geographical and physiological proximity to the area included in the new state. Consequently, Uttarakhand state comprises of thirteen districts, again divided into two major administrative zones, viz. Kumaun zone (with districts Nainital, Udham Singh Nagar, Almora, Pithoragarh, Champawat and Bageshwar) and Garhwal zone (with districts Pauri Garhwal, Tehri Garhwal, Uttarkashi, Chamoli, Dehradun, Rudraprayag and Haridwar).

Location and Expanse

Bhilangana block is located in the north-eastern part of Tehri Garhwal district which in turn is located in the central Garhwal region. From Delhi, about 12 hours of journey, by bus and train, would lead one to Ghansali, the headquarters of the block. The nearest railway station is at Rishikesh, which is at a distance of 114 kms from Ghansali. While driving through the mountainous region beyond Rishikesh, one is struck by the beauty of the landscape. The typical image of the area as painted in a booklet by SBMA titled "Home in the Himalayas" reads, "*a small stream, rushing along the bottom of a steep rocky valley. On the banks of the stream and in the terraced hills above, there are small fields in which are grown potatoes, rice, barley and spinach, and sometimes apples, apricots and peaches. On the higher slopes there are forests of pine, and deodar, oak and rhododendron. In the mountains laced with boulder-stewn rivers and villages one finds chequered a few lonesome dwellings*". The above account provides the most apt description of Bhilangana.

Bhilangana block is located within the latitudes 3°3'10" and 30°52'45" N and longitudes 79°2'45" and 79°8'15"E. It has been named after river Bhilangana, which also forms its eastern boundary. Uttarkashi district and Pratap Nagar blocks of Tehri district lie to the west of the block. The snow-clad mountains of Chamoli lie in the north and Jakhnidhar block of Tehri district constitutes its southern boundaries. Most of the block area either lies in the snow-belts of the Himalayas or is comprised of rugged mountains with deep and precipitous glues in between the ridges.

Dimensions and Constituents

The total geographical area of the block, as per 2001 figures was 1096 sq. kms., which made it the biggest block (area-wise) in the district of Tehri Garhwal. The block headquarters at Ghansali is at a distance of 68 kms from the district headquarters, located at the New Tehri township.

For revenue purposes, the block has been divided into seven zones or 'pattis'. These are Thati Katod, Gonegarh, Argarh, Kemar, Kotifaigul, Bhilang and Basar. As per the 2001 census Bhilangana block comprised of 268 villages, out of which 10 villages were depopulated. The 258 populated villages have a population ranging from less than 10 to 2000.

Subsequent to a reorganisation of the block and districts (in the year 1997), the total reported area of the block increased from 130765 hectares, to 144066 hectares, as villages from an adjoining block were added to Bhilangana block. The number of villages in Bhilangana also increased from 192 to 268. Out of the 268 villages, 258 were populated and 10 of them were depopulated. Again, a majority of the villages are small settlements with respect to population size, with about 203 villages having a population less than 500 and only 14 of them having a population of more than 1000. In the area, it is a common feature for a person to have two settlements, one located at a higher altitude comprising a cold site for summer season, and another one at a lower altitude or comparative hot location for the winter season (twin village concept). Seasonal migration therefore occurs.

Historical Background

The district of Tehri Garhwal, in which Bhilangana is located, was the erstwhile Tehri Garhwal state, ruled by the Raja of Tehri in the pre-independence era. To trace a brief history of the region, one has to go back to the period 1000-1790 AD, which can be described as the medieval period in the history of Garhwal region. In the early years of this period, the entire Garhwal was ruled by a number of petty princes, who at a later date assumed the form of a loose federation or 'Baoni' of 52 states or principalities. The Pala dynasty was one of the most prominent dynasties which ruled a large part of what is now Tehri, Uttarkashi, Chamoli and Pauri districts. Raja Son Pal was the first of the Rajas of Garhwal about whom there were precise records and his headquarters were in the Bhilangana valley. King Ajaypal (1493-1547 AD) was credited with the unification and consolidation of the various principalities or "Garhis" of the region into one kingdom, which came to be known as Garhwal. Balbhadra Sah (1581-1591 AD) was the first king who adopted the title of "Sah" which is still borne by the descendents of the erstwhile state of Tehri. Man Sah who inherited the throne of Garhwal Kingdom in 1591 AD was a very rich and powerful king. During his rule the king of Kumaun invaded Garhwal on seven occasions only to be driven back each time, suffering a considerable loss. The conflict with Kumaun continued for more than two hundred years and was primarily in the form of raids and counter raids into each others territories. Pradip Sah was one of the most important rulers of Garhwal. He came to the throne in 1717 AD and was able to make temporary peace with the kings of Kumaun.

The Gorkhas of Nepal started attacking and plundering the border parganas of Garhwal from 1791 AD onwards and they finally invaded Garhwal in 1803 A D. The region remained under the regime of the Gorkhas for about

11 years. During their rule, there was exploitation of the people. The government was ruthless and officers were corrupt. It was quite evident that the Gorkha rule in Garhwal was very harmful, both for the people and the land. At last in 1815 AD, with the help of the East India Company, Sundershan Sah got back his state from the Gorkhas, but a major portion across the river Alakhnanda was given to the British government. As per agreement, the portion of this ancient kingdom on the west of river Alakhnanda was returned to Maharaj Sundershan Sah. He established the capital of his kingdom at a place on the left bank of the Bhagirathi river, which was known as Tehri and the whole kingdom was known as Tehri Garhwal state. The portion of Garhwal under the jurisdiction of the British came to be known as Garhwal district or British Garhwal.

Narendra Sah shifted his capital from Tehri to Narendranagar in 1920. In 1949, the state was merged in the Indian union and become a separate district of Uttar Pradesh. In the year 2000, after the creation of the new state of Uttaranchal comprising of the hill districts of Uttar Pradesh, Tehri Garhwal became a district of Uttaranchal state.

The district of Tehri Garhwal is still a backward district, not only in the Garhwal region, but in the entire Uttaranchal state. This is because of the rulers who had long ruled the region and exploited the people. It was only after independence that the people of this district achieved their civic rights for which they had been suffering under the rule of the Rajas.

Topographical Traverse

The area has special geographical characteristics. The elevation varies from 885 meters to above 5000 meters above sea level. The minimum height of the area is at Ghansali and the maximum height is at Bhartikantha, which is the origin of river Bhilangana. The area is characterized by rugged mountains, containing a tangled series of ridges with innumerable spurs, separated by low valleys of the rivers, namely Bhilangana and Balganga. The general direction of the ridges is North East to South West.

From the physiological point of view, the land can be divided into four main parts or altitudinal zones (a) the valleys which lie below the altitude of 1200 meters above sea level, (b) the middle heights, which vary between 1200 meters and 2400 meters, (c) the upper heights, which lie between 2400 meters and 3600 meters and, (d) the area in the highest altitude zone, with altitude above 3600 meters. The habitational area of the block lies between the heights of 800 meters to 2800 meters above sea level. Out of the total 268 villages in the block, approximately three-fourths are in the valleys or the middle altitude zone.

Most part of the block lies in the mountainous region. The valleys have been created by the rivers and mountain streams. Deposits brought down by the rivers and streams covered the valley bottom, and have made them fertile, as compared to the other regions. The lower and middle regions of the area consist of pebbles, soft earth and rocks. Here one can see dense forest with a luxuriant undergrowth of bushes, weeds and herbs. Brown forest soil is found in these hills because of relatively extensive forest cover. The soil found in the valleys is generally alluvial in nature, being either loam or sandy loam. The upper region lies in the snow belt of the Himalayas and comprises of dry hills which are covered with snow and wild grass.

The slopes in the lower tract and along river terraces are moderate; however they are very steep in the upper reaches. Bhilangana, along with the blocks of Jaunpur and Pratapnagar falls in the high altitude zone of the district.

Climate

There are climatic variations and complexities due to the complicated relief, altitude, slope and the presence of a large tract of forests in the region. The climate of the area is diversified and ranges from tropical hot in the valley region to severe cold in the high altitude region. Thus, geographical heterogeneity leads to climatic variations.

The low lying valleys (below 800 m of elevation) have hot and humid tropical climate. Between 800 m to 1200 m elevation, the climate is sub-tropical. It is temperate between 1200-2000 m elevation and cool temperate between 2000-2400 m elevations. Cold temperate climate is found between the altitude range of 2400-3000 m and above 3000 m elevation, very cold alpine climate prevails. The temperature varies between 8° C and 38° C in the region.

Broadly speaking, there are three main seasons:

(a) Winter season (mid October to mid February), which is locally known as "Huind".
(b) Summer season (mid February to mid June), which is known as "Rudi".
(c) Monsoon season (mid June to mid October), which is locally known as "Chaumasha" or "Badkal".

The area receives maximum rainfall, that is, almost 80 per cent during this season, depending on favourable and unfavourable conditions. Not only temperature, but rainfall also varies from place to place, depending on the physiographic location of the place. Places located at high altitude, facing the south receive high rainfall, whereas valleys or sheltered places have scanty rainfall. In general, the rainfall varies from about 60 cms to 250 cms. The maximum downpour takes place during July and August. Almost half of the total rainfall occurs during these two months. Fog is common in the ridges during monsoons and in the valleys during winter.

In spite of this heavy rainfall, the area suffers from scarcity of water for irrigation and drinking purposes mainly due to: (a) uneven distribution of rainfall during the year, (b) high run-off, (c) inadequate storage, and (d) low moisture absorbing capacity of the soil.

The irregularities in the amount and nature of rainfall and temperature variations in the recent years, in the area, as also in the entire Himalayan belt, are mainly due to the environmental degradation taking place there. A small section on "Climatic changes" in the wake of environmental degradation has been included in the next chapter.

Transport and Communications

For the development of a region, the availability of a well-developed transport system is essential, but owing to the harsh and mountainous terrain, there is no railway line to the block or even to the parent district Tehri. Railway connection is only available up to Rishikesh or Dehradun, but beyond these, road transport is the only alternative. Since Bhilangana represents an area of relatively higher elevation, it is characterized by a poor network of roads. As a result it has been devoid of much development. The block headquarters at Ghansali is connected by bus service with the district headquarters at New Tehri, as also other important towns like Tehri, Narendranagar etc. The total length of 'pucca' or motor able roads in the block was still limited i.e., 258 kms. It was 170.84 kms per lakh population and 166.97 kms per 1000 sq kms, as per 2008-09 data. Most of the villages are still connected to each other by mule paths or bridge paths or 'kuccha' paths. As per 2000-2001 data less than half the total number of villages are connected by all weather roads.

There are only 119 bus stations/bus stops in the block. In other words, 119 villages had a bus station/stop. For as many as 49 villages, the distance from the bus stand varies between 10 kms to 30 kms. Only 21 villages have a bus stand/stop, at a distance of less than 3 kms. A large part of the block remains inaccessible, particularly during the rainy and winter seasons. As far as the availability of a communications network is concerned, 52 villages have post offices within the village itself and for 92 villages the post office is located between 1 km and 3 kms. There is no telegraph office in the block. The block had 53 villages with PCOs. For 196 villages, a PCO was more than 5 kms away. Inspite of recent efforts to enhance the reachability and communications network, difficulties related to accessibility and communication persisted, restricting the developmental activity in the area.

Administrative Set Up

The block is under a Block Development Officer, based at the block headquarters. The overall administrative machinery overseeing all the community development blocks within the district is located at New Tehri, the district headquarters. The DM, Police Commissioner and the office of the Chief Development Officer are at New Tehri. All developmental work in the district is undertaken by the office of the Chief Development Officer (CDO). The District Rural Development Organization is located at Narendranagar.

For the purpose of the revenue administration, the district is divided into five tehsils and one of them is Ghansali. The tehsil is further divided into "Patwari regions" and "Supervisors Kanungo regions". The judicial work is under the jurisdiction of the Chief Judicial Magistrate, New Tehri. Construction work for the block is supervised by the office of the Chief Engineer under whom there is an Asst. Engineer at Ghansali.

The work of the Forest Department is looked after by the Divisional Forest Officers (DFOs). The offices of the DFOs, Tehri Forest Division and Tehri Dam Forest Division are located at New Tehri. The DFOs are assisted by Sub divisional Forest Officers, Range Officers, Deputy Rangers, Foresters and Forest Guards.

The block has 11 Nyaya Panchayats. These are Budhakedar, Kathod, Jakh Nailchami, Dalla, Khirbel, Kothiara, Devanj and Thati Bhilang. These are panchayat courts which adjudicate disputes between villagers without the aid of elaborate or complicated legal machinery. As per the 2000-2001 data, there are 178 gram sabhas and gram panchayats in the block, covering all the populated villages, with the number of villages comprising a single panchayat depending on the population of the constituent villages.

The People of Bhilangana

Demographic Characteristics

1. Population size and population density: As per the 2001census, the total population of Bhilangana block is 1,07,118, which is about one sixth of the population of Tehri district (the population of Tehri district being 6,04,747). The following table (Table 3.1) presents the demographic profile of Bhilangana block. Additionally, figures for the district of Tehri Garhwal are provided to facilitate a comparative picture.

As is indicated by the table, Bhilangana block with a population size of 1,07,118 and a population density of 97.47 is the most sparsely populated block of Tehri Garhwal district, as all other blocks demonstrate a much higher population density. The difficult terrain, inaccessibility and remoteness of the area and inhospitable conditions exiting in the block have led to it being sparsely populated.

While the density of population for Tehri district increased from 90 to 113 in the period 1971-81, it further increased to 131in 1991 and to 154.44 in 2001. Correspondingly, the density of population in Bhilangana block had increased from 34 in 1971to 41 in 1981. It further increased to 49 in 1991 and

Table 3.1: Demographic Composition of Bhilangana Block and Tehri District (as per 2001 Census)

Sl. No	*Region*	*Population Size*			*Population Density*
		Total	*Male*	*Female*	
1.	Bhilangana Block	1,07,118	49,247	57,871	49
2.	Tehri Garhwal district	60,47,47	29,51,68	3,09,579	131

Source: Annual District Plan, year 2000-01, Tehri Garhwal District, p. 3

to 97.94 in 2001. The number of families residing in the block, as per the 2001 census, is 20,456.

2. Sex Ratio: Table 3.1 also depicts the sex-wise distribution of population of the block. As per the 2001 census, out of the total population of 1,07,118, the males are 49,247 and 57,841 persons are females. In other words, 54 per cent of the block population is female and the rest i.e. 46 per cent comprises of males. The sex ratio for the block is 117.5 and is biased in favour of the females. The main reason behind this imbalance in sex ratio is the heavy out migration of the male population from this remote mountainous and under developed block, devoid of any opportunities for productive employment, to valleys and urban areas in search of employment and livelihood. The sex ratio of Tehri district as a whole is also skewed in favour of females (that is 1049) but is less than that for Bhilangana.

3. Population Belonging to Scheduled Castes and Scheduled Tribes: As per the 2001 census, the total Scheduled Caste population of the block is 19,172, out of which 9,417 are males and 9,755 are females. The Scheduled Caste population is approximately 17.9 per cent of the block population. The important Scheduled Castes of the block are: Chamars, Bedas, Anjees, Lohars, Sunars, Rurias, Chunaras, Kolis and Kumbhars. The Scheduled Tribe population of the block is almost non-existent i.e. only 17 persons belong to this category.

4. Age Structure: Separate information pertaining to the age distribution of the block population did not exist, but if trends at the district and regional level are examined, a pyramidical age structure of population is observed. Table 3.2 provides information pertaining to population in various age groups, for Tehri district.

Thus, a significant proportion of the population of the district is less than 14 years of age. This category comprises almost 37 per cent of the population and represents the broad base of the population pyramid. Almost 27 per cent of the population falls in the age-group of 15-29 years. Only a small proportion of people (7.91%) were 60 years and above in age. This category represented the top of the population pyramid. So, 45 per cent of the district population comprises of the dependent population assuming that the age group 15 to 59 years works to support the rest.

Table 3.2: Percentage of Population in Various Age Groups, Tehri Garhwal District (2001census)

S. No.	Region	Age Groups					Total
		Below Years	15-29 Years	30-44 Years	45-59 Years	Above 60 Years	
1.	Tehri Garhwal district	37.00	26.74	16.62	10.79	7.91	100

Source: Statistical Diary, District Tehri Garhwal, 2012, p. 16.

5. Level of Urbanization: The level of urbanization indicates the trend displayed by the population to settle in urban settlements, and is a reflection of an increase in the proportion of the urban population to the total population over a period of time. The stage of socio-economic development of any society is often viewed by the degree of urbanization attained by that particular society in the specified space and time. For the block, this trend is totally missing. The entire block population is rural, that is, resides in rural settlements only. Tehri District is also primarily rural based, with 90.10 per cent population residing in rural areas. Viewed in the traditional context, both the district and the block should therefore be considered backward in terms of socio economic development.

6. Religion and Caste Distribution: Almost the entire population of the block is Hindu. There are a few Muslim families, but exact numbers pertaining to the block are not available, (either at the block or district headquarters). As per 2001 census, 98.68 per cent of the district population is Hindu.

The block is inhabited by people belonging to diverse ethnic backgrounds. They could be divided into three main castes viz. the Rajputs, and the Brahmins, who constitute the higher castes, and the Kols, Koltas and Doms, who are the lower castes. Approximately 60 per cent of the block population comprises of Rajputs, 20 per cent of them are Brahmins, 16.6 per cent are Scheduled Castes and the rest i.e. 3.4 per cent comprise OBCs and Muslims.

The work pattern or the distribution of occupations is reflective of the social system. In the area, the dependence of the majority of the high caste population is primarily on agriculture, with a secondary dependence on animal husbandry, while the low status artisan caste lives by the caste specialties such as basket-weaving, tailoring and so on. Thus, the distinction between a high and a low caste is basically an economic one.

7. Family Size and Structure: The number of families in the block is 1,07,118 and the average size of the family is 6 members (as per 2001 census). Most families are joint families, consisting of the man, his wife, grown up sons, daughters-in-law, unmarried children and grandchildren. Although family size could be larger, it does not get reflected due to the fact that males have migrated to other areas in search of jobs. Compared to the plains, the average household size of the hill villages is high mainly due to out migration of the males and the resultant dependence on the larger family to look after the women, elderly and the children. In addition, low fertility agriculture and a declining pastoral economy make it essential for households to adopt labour intensive strategies to sustain themselves. This also helps to keep the joint family together.

8. Literacy Levels: Out of the total block population, 54,743 persons are literate, as per 2001 census figures. In other words, 61.82 per cent of the total block population is literate. This includes 33,031 males and 21,712 females. Thus, there was a vast difference between the male literacy rate of 83.19 per cent and the female literacy rate of 44.46 per cent. The low female literacy rate has adverse ramifications for the socio-economic status of women in the block. Thus, low literacy continues to be one of the main problems of the block, and is one of the main contributory conditions leading to the poor socio-economic status of women of the locale.

9. Educational Background: Detailed information pertaining to the educational background of the block population is not available. Information pertaining to the educational background is available at the district level only. As per data pertaining to 2001 census, almost 44 per cent of the district population is illiterate; about 15 per cent of the population is literate but without any education at all; 14 per cent of population has completed primary schooling and about 10.8 per cent people has completed middle-school education level. Only about 11.7 per cent of the district population has attained higher secondary education level. Only a miniscule proportion i.e. 3.8 per cent of the population is graduate or possesses a higher educational qualification. As far as the block situation is concerned, the situation should be no different from the district. A number of factors including the lack of appropriate educational infrastructure (both in terms of quality and quantity), the distance factor, complex terrain intercepted by hills, valleys, rivers, and forests, weather hazards and the like, coupled with poor economic conditions and lack of means of transport facilities prevented students from availing schooling. Women and girl children bear the burden of grueling household chores, as well as agriculture, and thus, remain the deprived lot with little or no opportunities for schooling or intellectual engagement.

Economic Life of People

1. Occupational Distribution: The occupational structure for the workers of the block is presented in Table 3.3. As per the 2001 census, there are a total of 34,307 main workers in the block. As far as the primary sector is concerned, a total of 27,280 (or 80%) main workers are engaged in agriculture and associated occupations. There is a predominantly high dependence of the block population on agriculture for their sustenance and livelihood and more importantly, women play a dominant role in agricultural activities.

Table 3.3: Occupational Structure of Bhilangana (2001 census)

S. No.	*Occupation*	*Main Workers*
1.	Cultivators	27,167
2.	Agricultural Labour	113
3.	Family based Manufacture	210
4.	Other Occupations	6,817
5.	Total Main Workers	34,307
6.	Marginal Workers	12,984
	Total	47,291

The available data is indicative of the almost total lack of employment opportunities in manufacturing and other secondary sector occupations at the block and even at the district level. It fact, this is the main reason for the very high male out migration from the block and the district. Arable land being limited, and a virtual non-existence of secondary sector occupations, has compelled the male population to migrate to the valleys and plains for suitable employment opportunities.

As far as agriculture is concerned, it is characterised by the predominance of marginal and small farms, fragmented and small land holdings, lack of irrigation and dependence on rainfall for irrigation, and prevalence of traditional methods of cropping and livestock management, with low productivity. The per capita land is far below the standard requirement, and the net cultivated area is extremely limited. Although the block has an abundant water supply and natural sources of water, including the two main rivers, and a number of nalas, gads and gadheras, yet the topography of land sets limitations for their use in irrigation. Thus, only 32.6 per cent of the cultivated area is irrigated. Irrigation is mainly by canals, guls, hauzes and hydrums.

Agricultural holdings are very small. Almost 60 per cent of the holdings are less than 0.5 hectare, while 81 per cent are less than 1 hectare or are marginal sized holdings. Another 12.7 per cent are small sized holdings (i.e. between 1 to 2 hectares). The main crops grown in the block are wheat, paddy, pulses, sawa, jau (barley), mustard, maize, soyabean, and potatoes.

The block does not have any industrial units. Only a few cottage industries exist, comprising of spinning and weaving of wool, basket making, carpentry, oil crushing, fruit preservation and stone craft. The main reasons for the industrial backwardness of the area are: (a) Long distance from railway head, (b) Lack of transport facilities, as also adequate infrastructure like power, communication network etc., (c) Migration of skilled persons to the plains, (d) Smallness of the local market, (e) Inadequate availability of raw material, (f) Strict control over extraction of forest wealth, and (g) Ban on mining of limestone and dolomite.

Women in Bhilangana

The position and status of women in Bhilangana block has been explained in terms of their sex ratio, caste, age, family position, ownership of property, education-literacy rates and educational standards, occupation, income, organizational affiliation, role in the decision making process in the family, and, participation in the socio-economic, political life of the village.

1. Sex Ratio: As per the 2001 census, out of a total population of 1,07,118 in Bhilangana, 57,871 persons are females, that is, 54 per cent of the population. The sex ratio for the block is 117.5 and is biased in favour of the females. The main reason behind this imbalance in sex ratio is the heavy out migration of the male population from the hills to the plains in search of employment and livelihood. This has both positive and negative ramifications. The positive impact is that it leads to an active participation of women in production activities, leading to a special position that they enjoy in the agro-pastoral economy of the area. The negative impact pertains to the added responsibilities that women have to bear in the absence of the male members of the family. In fact, many households in a village have defacto female heads.

Traditionally, the functional value of women is very high, as she shares abundant responsibilities and performs a wide spectrum of duties, both indoors and outdoors. They form a reserve force of labour and contribute to various spheres of productive and non-productive activities. Their contribution to production is significant, albeit often hidden as "non-remunerative" shadow work. However, due to her crucial role in production, the birth of a girl in Garhwali families in general, is not considered a curse, unlike the other regions of northern India. In fact, a system of bride price (dam marriage) was earlier practiced among low income households, which indicated that a girl was not a liability to her parents.

The health of the women however continues to be a neglected aspect of the households. Health is ignored, until it becomes absolutely necessary. Women's access to health is found to be mediated by men, especially, the use of family planning. There is a tendency towards prolonged motherhood, ranging from 16-40 years, in the expectation of more male progeny, lack of awareness and lack of access to family planning facilities, making women more prone to delivery-related deaths, increased morbidity and an overall poor health status. The general nutritional standard of women is otherwise poor. Though men and women should have an equal access to nutrition, men and children are traditionally given the best food. Pregnant and lactating mothers are not given any special nutritional diet. Due to lack of adequate nutrition, rest and medical care, women often suffer from anaemia, diarrohoea and cough. In some areas, women still give birth in cowsheds and are allowed minimal rest

2. Caste Grouping: Among the Hindu families, which constitute an overwhelming majority in the block, dominant Hindu customs prevail. Brahmins and Rajputs constitute about 80 per cent of the population and the Scheduled Castes (artisan groups locally known as Harijans) account for about 16.6 per cent of the population. The birth-ascribed, purity-pollution oriented caste system has given birth to discriminatory social values, and women are the worst sufferers of this system (especially women of low caste groupings), who find their access to various resources such as education and health further curtailed.

3. Literacy: Female literacy rate was 44.46 per cent, whereas overall literacy rate for the block was 61.82 per cent and that for the males was 83.19 per cent. This reflects a very low literacy rate among women in comparison to men. Literacy rate among women varies according to their age group and caste. There is higher literacy among the younger generation i.e. those between 18-35 years of age, while a majority of the women above 45 years of age are illiterate. Women belonging to the scheduled caste groups show very low literacy levels (as revealed by grassroots workers of Mahila Samakhya, as recorded data was not available).

Access to education for girls is mediated by men, because of limitations on mobility. Mobility is primarily limited to the home and field for girls, and access to the outside world requires male permission. This has reinforced men's control of and dominance over knowledge and information. There has however been a change in the last few years with the coming of a few NGOs focusing on education, as also the spread of the communication media and implementation of development programmes. This has created an element of attitudinal change among men and awareness about sending girls to school. People tend to send their daughters to school, though they drop out from school at a much earlier age than boys.

While the Government emphasizes the enrollment of girls between the ages of 6-11 years, but certain local constraints continue to be ignored even by the governmental programmes. These include the presence of more male teachers, making parents hesitate in sending their daughters to schools. The number of girl's schools is almost negligible. Moreover, the distance from school discourages the attendance of girl children. The region also faces the problem of migration, forcing girls to work. These problems are not attended to in the setting up of the educational infrastructure within the hilly terrain.

4. Work Pattern and Gender Based Division of Labour: Work patterns continue to be based on a distinct division of labour, with women undertaking responsibilities for farm and household activities, whereas men are mostly engaged in marketing and activities involving skilled modes of work.

As was mentioned earlier, a main reason for the dominant role played by women in the hill-based subsistence economy of the region is on account of the large scale out migration of menfolk for want of jobs to the plains. This has contributed to the development of the 'remittance economy', also popularly known as the 'money order economy', wherein men leave their villages for long periods to earn household income, which provides support to the household economy. This has resulted into an added workload for women.

Data for the sex-wise distribution of the occupational status was not made available in the statistical booklets for the district post 2000, but older data pertaining to the 1991 census showed that out of the total persons engaged in production in Garhwal, 46 per cent were women. Occupational pattern for the block showed that out of a total of 26,047 main workers, as many as 13,685 or 52.5 per cent were female workers. Female cultivators comprised 58.6 per cent of the total cultivators (i.e. 13,581 out of a total of 23,247 cultivators). This showed that not only were more women than men engaged as the main workers, they showed a greater involvement in agricultural operations. The peculiar geo-climatic conditions of the hills do not allow the women to remain aloof from production activities. The role of women in agricultural operations continues to be very significant and their contribution works out to more than three-fourths of the labour required for agricultural operations. Women participate in almost all the agricultural operations including land preparation, manuring, sowing, transplanting, weeding, hoeing, applying fertilizers, protecting and taking care of crops, harvesting, threshing, and carrying the produce from fields to home, storage of food grains and so on. At times, even ploughing, which is considered to be the only agricultural operation to be solely undertaken by men, is also done by women. While men use draught power, women's work is manual and to that extent unskilled. Agricultural operations have become even more burdensome with the introduction of cash crops, as women are forced to spend more time in the fields. Young girls generally assisted their mothers in agricultural operations, while young boys only help in watering the fields. During harvest season, while boys attend schools, girls are found working in the fields. This highlight the adherence to gender based division of labour, right from childhood.

Apart from agriculture, livestock and animal husbandry are important secondary activities. Livestock and agriculture go together, yielding no separate income. Cattle and animals are mostly looked after by women and girls. It is important to note that the percentage of women engaged in agriculture, and related activities like animal husbandry, plantation, and afforestation in the area was about 59 per cent, whereas the corresponding figure for Tehri district was 57 per cent (1991 census).

It is also noteworthy that although the overall involvement of people in secondary and tertiary sector occupations continues to be low, women are conspicuous by their total absence from such occupations. In Bhilangana block, 2678 males were involved in forestry, fishing, mining/quarrying, manufacturing and processing, construction, trade and commerce, transportation, storage and communications and other services. In contrast only 103 females were involved in the same activities, that is, only 3.7 per cent of persons engaged in non-agricultural occupations in Bhilangana comprised women. Additionally more women than men were marginal workers (i.e. 2,607 women, as compared to only 278 men).

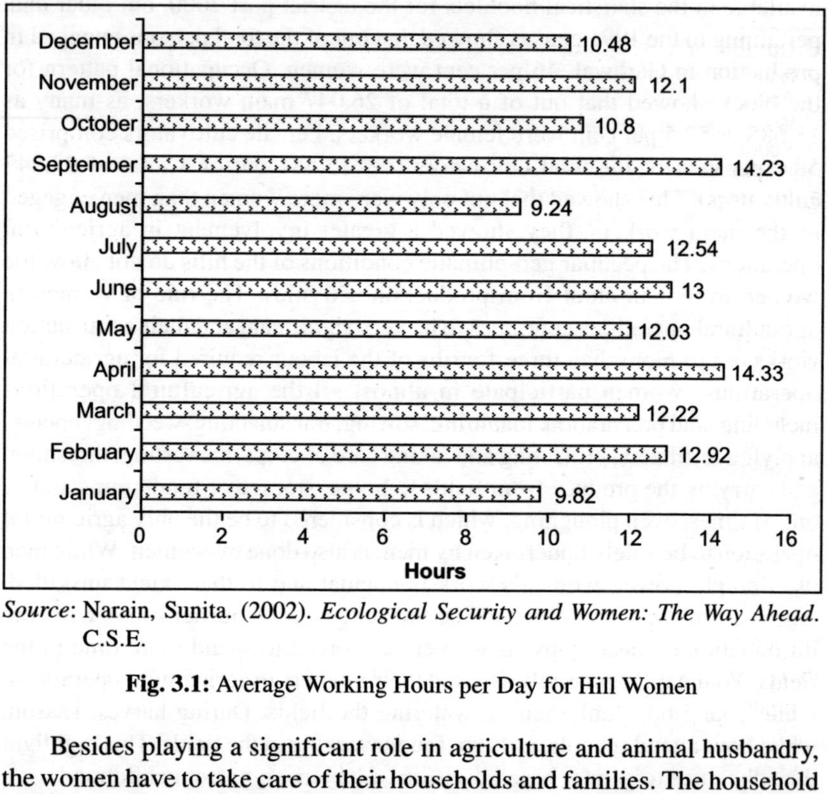

Source: Narain, Sunita. (2002). *Ecological Security and Women: The Way Ahead.* C.S.E.

Fig. 3.1: Average Working Hours per Day for Hill Women

Besides playing a significant role in agriculture and animal husbandry, the women have to take care of their households and families. The household activities centre around rearing of children, looking after the aged, cleaning utensils, washing clothes, cooking, milking cattle, arranging fodder for cattle, bringing water, collection of fuel, knitting, spinning, stitching etc. The diagram (Figure 3.1) depicts the average working hours of a Garhwali village woman and is reflective of the extreme hardships of her routine.

In villages where potable water, fodder or fuel is not available in closer vicinity, the women have to cover long distances to fetch the same. In such cases, their day which begins even before dawn was obviously, more busy and tiring. Thus, womenfolk of the block work for almost 16 to 18 hours daily, most of which goes unaccounted, and even unnoticed and naturally unappreciated. The following Table 3.4 depicts the outcome of a survey based study conducted in a district of Garhwal, and which clearly brings out the drudgery of the women of the area:

Table 3.4: Disposal of Daily Time and Percentage Distribution of Work of Hill Women

Activities performed by womenfolk	*Per women per day hrs of work*	*% age distribution of work disposal*
A. Outdoor activities		
Agriculture	4.11	24.92
Animal husbandry	0.73	4.43
Water fetching	1.42	8.61
Fodder collection	1.96	11.88
Fuel wood collection	2.03	12.31
B. Indoor activities		
Cooking	1.32	8.00
Washing clothes	0.88	5.33
House cleaning	0.74	4.48
Grinding and husking	1.21	7.34
Care of children/aged	0.65	3.93
C. Leisurely and Recreational Activities		
Craft and business	0.10	0.60
Reading and writing	0.18	1.09
Entertainment	0.05	0.30
Social work	0.55	3.33
Religious activities	0.57	3.45
Total	16.49	100.00

Source: Pande, P.N. (1996). *Drudgery of the Hill Women*. New Delhi: Indus Publishing Company, p. 86.

The table shows that a hill woman tends to devote an average of 16.49 hours a day performing different activities. The percentage ratio of work disposal, according to outdoor, indoor, and recreational activities was recorded at 62.17 per cent, 21.11 per cent and 8.72 per cent respectively. This highlights the amount of physical labour that women of the area have to perform. The outdoor activities continue to be highly time consuming and about 10.25 hours out of a daily routine of 16.49 hours is usually absorbed towards their performance. Apart from agriculture and animal husbandry, the amount of time devoted for fuel and fodder collection and water fetching add to the drudgery of women and absorb about 5.41 hours in a day or 32.80 per cent of the total time. Moreover, there are seasonal variations in the hours of daily work performed by women in different seasons.

5. Ownership of Assets: As in most parts of the country, the parental property is inherited by the sons, except in case there are only daughters. Even if the husband wants to sell off the property, the wife has little, if any say, though it is mainly she who manages the property in the real sense of the word. An unmarried daughter can exercise rights over the property till her marriage. All property (generally productive) is owned jointly by male members of the patrilineal, patrilocal extended family and is shared equally. Women show no ownership of land, house and other capital goods. This is reinforced by the gender unequal tenurial legislation and/or customs. A woman's access to land is mediated by men, and her lack of control makes it difficult for her to apply for loans and credit. Women thus continue to manage agricultural activities and family, not only with little male assistance, but without any titles of the land that they are cultivating. Access to farm equipment and other tools in a household depends on the basis of their use by sex, and therefore, on the basis of skilled and unskilled labour, e.g. simple tools like sickles, pick axes etc. are used by women for manual work. Handling ploughs and small tractors requires skill and are therefore used and controlled by men. Surprisingly, most women do not give much thought to the owning of these assets for themselves, but the younger women did voice their feeling that owning assets, especially the house and land would make women's position more secure, as also prevent ill treatment of women.

6. Economic Position: Although data pertaining to the income levels of people of the district or the block were not available, it is however quite obvious that generally the economic condition of women tends to be miserable and they usually lead a hand to mouth existence. The mode of agricultural production is backward; land holdings are small, fragmented and far flung. Farm production is mainly for family consumption. Over the years, the vulnerability of agriculture has intensified due to rapid ecological degradation. Agricultural activities are backbreaking and increasingly non remunerative.

Among the upper castes in the village, due to NGO intervention and formation of women's groups (Mahila Mandals), some women have gradually gained access to local employment opportunities. However the types and nature of jobs are determined by the male members. Because of division of labour in the household, it is a problem for women to find outside employment. Since very few avenues for employment, access and control exist for women, their economic position is low. Cumulatively, all these have resulted in the pauperization of the hill people, especially women.

7. Social Status: The dominant role played by women in production should not lead us to believe that women have achieved social equality with men, and no atrocities are perpetrated against them. Inspite of their high and fundamental contribution in the economy of the hills, women are by and large considered to be unpaid domestic servants. It is true that, to a certain extent they enjoy more freedom in matters like marriage and divorce, but by and large, they too face the same inequality and injustice within the family and society as their counter parts elsewhere.

Poor access to health, education, information, knowledge and productive assets, as also lack of exposure to the outside world beyond the closed rims of the mountains keeps the women tradition-bound. Still wedded to tradition, the socio-cultural environment offers little scope for personality development. Technology and development have largely bypassed them, and a vast majority of them continue to persist in the rut of illiteracy, ignorance and drudgery. In a vast majority of cases, marriage of girls takes place by 16 years and in case of illiterate girls, it is even earlier. High human fertility, scarcity-ridden family life, and drudgery keeps women in a state of tension and anxiety. Men are by and large unconcerned and unsympathetic towards the high work incidence and drudgery associated with women's work. A sort of defeatism, acute fatalism and pessimism dominates the psyche of women facing the worries of a migrant husband, scarcity ridden conditions, in terms of water, fuel, fodder and remunerative employment, and the problems of children. This frame of pessimistic psyche is often seen to be transmitted to the younger generation specially the girls, who see their mothers in constant tension and worry.

Thus, the woman's position in the household and society is still subservient to that of men, due to lack of independent economic status, economic freedom, decision making power and work discretion. This is reinforced by cultural norms and traditions which give preference to boys and accord a secondary role to womenfolk, both in family and society.

8. Women's Role in Decision Making: Women's involvement in decision-making within the household is rather complex. In the management of the farm, storage and distribution of agricultural products primarily meant for internal consumption, women have a crucial role to play and have equal authority with men. However, any decisions on sale, purchase, and/or transfer of productive assets, such as house or land, are made by men. Women can only make suggestions, the entire decision making authority rests with the men. This is because women have no rights to immovable property. In matrimonial alliances, women's suggestions are considered, though the final say is in men's hands. Decisions concerning monetary transactions of dowry and so on are also made by men. Women are implementers of the decisions taken by men. Most women-headed households which need to purchase agricultural inputs, have to rely on male support from the community, reinforcing men's control of and dominance over knowledge and information. The introduction of cash crops has further marginalised women's role in agriculture. Emphasis on outside inputs, such as HYV seeds, fertilizers, agricultural technologies and implements are inaccessible to women, and therefore they cannot take appropriate decisions. This also undermines their traditional knowledge about farming, which has been passed down from generation to generation.

At the community level, women deal with wider social issues and thus have greater decision making capabilities than men. This is apparent from various social movements introduced in the region like the Anti-Liquor Movement, Chipko Movement and Anti-Tehri Dam Movement. Yet, in the society as a whole, women's effective participation in decision-making is less than that of men due to traditional and conventional views. Factors that have an impact on women's decision making are: (a) new technologies and cash crops in agriculture; (b) male out migration; (c) lack of access to information; and (d) illiteracy and lack of exposure.

9. Organisational Affiliation and Participation in Socio-Economic and Political Life of the Village: In the region, men continue to dominate formal gatherings like the Gram Sabha and Panchayats. However, with the reservation of one third seats for women, women have come to occupy the posts of members and chairpersons. Illiteracy, lack of time and lack of confidence had prevented women from becoming active participants in formal organisations in the initial phases of their assumption of these posts. However, with time, women are coming forward and putting in a more active participation in the political life of the area. Similarly, initially Van Panchayats were also male-dominated, but government support and NGO intervention is helping to empower women to become a part of these groups. Special 'Women Sarpanch Van Panchayats' have been constituted to enable women to participate in forest protection.

Although women have not been active participants in formal settings, they have been associating themselves with informal groups and organisations. The Mahila Mangal Dals are one such type of informal groups. These are collectives of women, formed to address local village problems. These have played a significant role in providing informal forums to mobilize women to organise themselves and participate in community life. Women have also played a traditional role in protecting and managing their common property resources through the constitution of committees/samitis like Mahila Van Suraksha Samitis, Van Samitis etc.

As mentioned earlier women have been dealing with wider community issues and problems, with which they can identify, and to which they can relate. In such instances their presence is easily mobilized with effective leadership at the grass roots level. Although not much has been known about women's participation in the national movement or in the Anti-Feudal Peasant uprisings in the Tehri Riyasat during the period of local dhandaks (uprisings), it was in the 1970s that they started participating in agitations on a large scale. The Anti-Liquor Movement, the Chipko Andolan and the Anti-Tehri Dam Movement are all illustrations of active women's participation. These are issues which continue to be close to women's hearts.

10. Perception of Self: A women's perception of herself has been seen to differ over generations. However in general, women hardly find the time to reflect on their status and position in the family and society, and are found to be more resigned to fate. During focussed group discussions, it was found that women, by and large accepted their inferior, subordinate status in society. They felt that their lack of independent economic status and economic freedom curtailed their discretion and decision making power. Their poor access to education, information and knowledge marginalized them and put them in a poor bargaining position, both within the household and the society.

While most women acknowledged their inferior and subordinate status, the older women tended to support and justify the existing male domination and their subservient role as a part of their social and cultural tradition. Younger women tended to voice their dissatisfaction with their low status. However, they acknowledged that they also felt resigned to their fates due to their persistently high work burden which offered them no respite to do something about the present state of things.

By and large women considered their male counterparts as more competent. Although women of the region had been active in movements like Anti-Alcohol Movement, Chipko Andolan and the Tehri Dam Agitation, as also in contemporary collective action to protect their community resource base, their image of their own self and their organizational abilities was lower than those of men. They acknowledged their poor outlook, low perception of themselves, and lack of confidence, arising out of their low socio economic and educational status and denial of decision making authority.

11. Ascribed and Achieved Status: It is clear from the above that the status of women ascribed by society and societal norms has tended to be low in comparison to men. But changes in the status of women are more in her achieved context. While her already active role and dominant position in the economy provide her with a head start in comparison to her counter parts in the plains, her exposure and opportunities to participate in community life have been enhanced through the interplay of several factors. One such notable factor is the reservation provided to women in Panchayats. While in the initial phase, many women remained Panchayat members in absentia, the situation in the contemporary period is quite different. With support from the local NGO groups and the personal efforts of an enthused woman Block Pramukh, most women have entered the public domain and are participating in panchayats. As mentioned earlier, they are active in working as informal groups to conserve and manage their natural resources, but have not made much head way in sharing authority with men in formal groups and organizations. Here again, the government has introduced compulsory membership for women in Van Panchayats and all other village user groups to encourage their participation in community affairs and to formalize women's ongoing involvement with the protection of the community resource base.

4
State of the Environment and Environmental Action

This chapter attempts to explain and analyze the state of environment of the locale in an effort to provide a deeper understanding of the environmental context, particularly the important environmental issues and problems confronting the same. Following this, it describes the various governmental and nongovernmental initiatives, being undertaken in order to deal with the delineated issues and problems.

The chapter has been divided into two parts. While the first part focuses on the state of the environment, the subsequent part highlights the policies, legislation, and programmes pertaining to the environment of the area.

The State of the Environment

Attempts to describe and analyze the state of the environment of the chosen area have been undertaken with the ultimate objective of developing an appreciation of the issue of protection and promotion of the environment by the people, especially women. Both Bhilangana block and Tehri Garhwal district have been covered together, as well as separately, when necessary. This has been necessitated in order that: (i) a comprehensive picture of the state of environment of the region as a whole, as also the specific situation of the block and the district emerges; (ii) in recognition of the fact that most of the problems and potentialities pertaining to the block are shared and manifested by the district as a whole; and (iii) in view of the constraint with regard to the segregation of the environment of a micro-area from the larger environmental context.

The state of the environment of the area has been discussed in relation to (i) Land and land use, (ii) Water; and (iii) Wild life, the three environmental components of relevance in the frame.

Land and Land Use

The total land area under Tehri Garhwal district is 53642 sq kms (as per 2001 data). The highly complex and rugged mountainous nature of the terrain plays a very important part in determining the land use pattern in this hill region. Land use dynamics is of focal concern for this natural resource rich region, as changes in land use directly influence its fragile ecosystem. Table 4.1 depicts the land use pattern of the district and the block in the year 2006-07.

Table 4.1: Land Use Pattern for Tehri Garhwal District and Bhilangana Block (2006-07)

(in hectares)

S. No.	*Category of Land Use*	*Land Area*	*Percentage (%)*
1.	Total Land Area	4,85,517 (1,28,736)	100.00 (100.00)
2.	Forest Land	3,21,564 (1,12,255)	66.23 (87.74)
3.	Net cultivated area	53,480 (5,737)	11.00 (4.46)
4.	Area under uses other than Cultivation	7,586 (750)	1.56 (0.58)
5.	Usar and not suitable for Cultivation	5,595 (743)	1.15 (0.58)
6.	Current Fallow	7,089 (779)	1.46 (0.61)
7.	Other Fallow	8,674 (779)	1.79 (0.61)
8.	Cultivable Wasteland	78,852 (8711)	16.24 (6.77)
9.	Permanent Pastures and other grazing land	480 (23)	0.50 (0.10)
10.	Area under trees, gardens, and bushes	2,198 (73)	0.45 (0.06)

Source: Statistical Diary, District Tehri Garhwal, Uttaranchal, 2008.
Note: Figures in parentheses indicate figures for Bhilangana block.

As far as the district was concerned, as per the 2006-07 data, the largest tract of land was under 'forests' that is 66.23 per cent of the total land area. This was followed by the categories 'cultivable wasteland', comprising 16.24 per cent of the total area and 'agricultural land', which was about 11 per cent.

A brief description of land use pattern of the district is given below:

A. 'Forests' constitute the most important and valuable land use category in this region. Information relating to land use pattern over the last few decades revealed that after an initial increase between 1975-76 and 1981-82 (by about 10%), the proportion of land under forests had remained unchanged (i.e. about 70% of the land area) up to the end of the century. This was obviously due to the importance accorded to forests by the National Forest Policy and the legislative provisions restricting diversion of forest land to non-forest uses. However, as per the latest data provided by the district through its Statistical Booklets, the forest cover for the district has declined to 66 per cent.

It is noteworthy that the data pertaining to the forest cover, as presented through different sources indicated a difference. While the Statistical Booklet (2006) of the District Tehri projected a 'recorded' forest cover pf 66.23 per cent, data gathered through satellite imageries captured by the State of Forest Report (2007), by the Forest Survey of India gave the actual forest cover of the district as 58.95per cent. Details are as follows:

Table 4.2: Forest Cover of District Tehri Garhwal (2007)

1.	Total Geographical Area of the District (sq kms)	3462
2.	Actual Total Forest Cover Assessment (sq kms)	2147
3.	Percentage of Forest Cover to Geographical Area	58.95

Source: State of Forest Report (2007), Forest Survey of India (Ministry of Environment and Forests), Dehradun.

It is very important to note that the actual forest cover of Tehri district (being 59%) was much less than the desirable 66 per cent stipulated by the National Forest Policy, 1988 for hill districts. This bespeaks the declining forest cover and is also indicative of the façade of the ideal cover projected by state governmental sources. In reality, the truth, as evidenced by the satellite imageries shows a much less than optimal scenario, as far as forests of this important hill district is concerned.

B. 'Cultivable Wasteland' comprises 16.24 per cent of the total reported land area. It is worthwhile to mention that this category of land was maximal in Tehri district when compared with other districts of the state. This category of land is not concurrently used for cultivation, either due to problems of accessibility or due to the unproductive nature of land or migration of users to other places. Moreover, information relating to land use pattern under this category during the last three decades reveals that this category of land increased from being only 1.62 per cent of the total land area in 1975-76 to 13.5 per cent in 1998-99, to 16.24 per cent in 2006-07. This has accrued primarily on account of the declining productivity of land and its consequent non-use in agriculture, as also the abandonment of inaccessible and steep land by the purported users.

C. The third important land use category, namely 'Agricultural Land' comprises 11 per cent of the total land area of the district. The reasons for the limited availability of cultivable land are: (i) government policies for this hill region emphasized foremost the expansion of 'forest' land use and so they conversely restricted 'agricultural' land use in the region; (ii) diversion of forest land to non-forest uses has been severely curtailed by legislation [Forest Conservation Act, 1980] and (iii) topographical constraints of a hilly terrain limiting the availability of land for cultivation.

Information pertaining to change in land use indicates that there is a progressive decline in the land under cultivation from 16 per cent in 1975-76 to about 11 per cent in 1998-99, and the same remains applicable even in 2006-07. This has been mainly due to the pressure of increasing population and the consequent demand for housing and other infrastructural facilities and, decline in productivity/quality of land making it unfit for cultivation.

D. The 'Usar land and land not suitable for cultivation' was about 2.3 per cent of the total land area. This comprised of rocky land, scrub land, steep and slopy land, area under landslides, streams and rivulets, and other unproductive land categories. Although relatively insignificant in terms of absolute area, this category was slowly increasing if trends for the last three decades are observed. The main reason for this has been the declining forest density. Since forests are no longer under full tree canopy (as will be elaborated upon in the subsequent section), the community lands (comprising of the soyam and the panchayati forests, grazing land, land other miscellaneous tree crops, and others) are getting successively eroded and severely denuded. These lands have been the victims of what is popularly known as the 'tragedy of the commons' and are slowly getting converted into unproductive land.

E. The categories of land under productive uses like 'Pasture land/Grazing land' as also 'Land under trees, gardens and bushes' was very small (i.e. only 0.50% and 0.004% respectively). Trends over the last few decades has revealed a declining trend, mainly on account of the prevalence of increasing encroachment of community lands, especially on the common 'gauchar' (grazing) lands, by local vested interests and for extending cultivation or habitation by the individuals, groups and the community. Moreover, the productivity of these lands in terms of forage, grass, fodder, food production and fuel wood has also been declining.

Comparing the land use pattern of the district and the block, it is interesting to note that there are some differences at the micro level. A brief description of the same, based on 2006-07 data is presented below:

1. Bhilangana block had much greater forest coverage than the district forest cover. As much as 1,12,955 hectares or 4.46 per cent of the land area of the block was under forests, as compared to 66.2 per cent at the district level. This could be attributed to: (i) the rural nature of the block, as in blocks with higher urbanization levels, as also the district, there continues to be a greater demand for habitational land and supportive services for the growing population, which in turn leads to a lower and declining forest cover; and (ii) the remoteness of the block and the inaccessibility of large tracts of its forests (due to their location at high altitudes), leading to the preservation of a larger forest cover.

2. The block showed a low coverage in terms of agricultural land. Only 4.46 per cent of its total land area has been under cultivation as compared to 11 per cent for the district. This has mainly been due to: (i) a high forest cover in the block; and; (ii) its topographical constraints and inaccessibility leading to limited availability of land for agricultural purposes.

As far as the other categories of land use are concerned, the block and district showed similar trends. These were with regard to:

(i) 'Cultivable wasteland', which comprised 6.77 per cent of the total land area of the block, has shown gradual increase overtime, on the lines of the parent district;
(ii) 'Usar land and land not suitable for cultivation', although relatively insignificant in terms of absolute area, has also shown an increase overtime, like the trends within the district. (The reasons for these trends have already been discussed in context of the district.)

In context of the land use pattern, it is important to highlight that: (i) the land under forests has declined over time, i.e. from about 70 per cent in 1998-99 to 66 per cent in 2006-07, for the district, but has remained constant for the block, i.e. about 87 per cent, (ii) While the land under productive uses has been showing a gradual decline over time, the unproductive and under-productive land use categories, for the district and the block have been showing a gradual increase. If the current trends are not remedied, they can have a very adverse impact on the economy of the region.

'Forests' and 'Soil' constitute the two important environmental components of land. Each of these have been described and analyzed in detail in the following sub sections.

1. Forests

As mentioned earlier, forests constitute the largest and the most important land use category, from the point of view of the environment of the region. Hence a discussion on the forest component gets precedence over other environmental components. This discussion on forests focuses on: (a) Types of forests; (b) Changes in the forests; and (c) Problems pertaining to the different types of forests.

A. Types of Forests

Forests have been classified on the basis of two criteria and these are: (i) Nature of vegetation, and (ii) Ownership and management of forests. Both these classifications have been discussed in some detail in the following section:

(i) Forest Zones (as per nature of vegetation): Forests of the area have been divided into four broad zones, depending on the nature of vegetation. Different topographical conditions and climatic characteristics determined the different forest zones. These forest zones are depicted below:

Table 4.3: Nature of forests according to type of vegetation

S. No.	*Forest Zone*	*Altitude (m)*	*Main trees*
1.	Sub-Tropical Forests	Below 1200	Sal, Kanju, Haldu, Khair, Sissu, Bamboo, Semal, Haldar, Tun, Kharik, Guriyal, Bimal, etc.
2.	Temperate Forests	1200-1800	Chir Pine, Akhrot, Deodar, Banjh, Khilonk, Darly, Dinken, Kharik, Chambharik, etc.
3.	Sub-Alpine Forests*	1800-3000	Banjh, Maru, Kharsu, Burans, Deodar, Spruce, Birch, Silver Pine, Kail, Rai, Moranda, Ustha, Pangar, Padam, Bhooj, Kachula, etc.
4.	Alpine Forests	3000-4500	Birch, Silver Fir, Xerophytic bushes and pastures (Bugyals).**

Note:

* Moist coniferous with a mixture of broad leaved trees have been the dominant vegetation of the lower sub-alpine forest zone. Higher sub-alpine zone consists of conifers.

** Bugyals are the extensive grasslands of the greater Himalayas which are used as summer meadows for the Himalayan sheep.

Apart from the large number of plants, continue to fulfill the demands of the people, wildlife and livestock, some very rare and highly valuable drug yielding plants are also found in the region. These include Choru, Kharsani, Thuner, Chairata, Summaya, Vajradanti, Gabrya, Haldu, Kutki, Keu, Dolu, among others.

It is important to note that the quality of the forests in the diverse forest zones is not the same. Changes have occurred due to extensive human intervention. At lower elevations, the forests are regularly degraded due to over exploitation for commercial purposes. Prominent timber species like sal are the worst impacted in this process. Moreover, the forests in the lower altitude zones are more accessible to people, owing to the fact that the main human settlements lie in these zones, and are therefore under heavy pressure for meeting the biomass needs of people. Consequently, these forests are qualitatively poorer and degraded.

The middle zones comprising mostly of pine and oak trees (1300-2300 m) are relatively better off in terms of quality, as forests are better protected and offer greater scope for regeneration. The ban on commercial felling in the Uttar Pradesh Himalayas above 1000 meters in the wake of the Chipko Movement has been instrumental in contributing to this relative protection.

While pine is regularly exploited for turpentine and timber, oak forests are mainly reserved forests under the State Forest Department.

The Upper zone forests (2300-3650 meters) are dense and qualitatively superior due to very less inhabitation and very limited access due to difficult terrain and topography. Above this region, only pasture land, barren land and snow covered peaks can seek to exist.

(ii) Categories of Forests (as per ownership and management): There are three different categories of forests in the region, as per ownership and management. These are:

(a) Reserve Forests, which are under the ownership and management of the Forest Department. They constitute more than two-thirds of the total forested area, that is, 278116 sq kms. or 68.5 per cent of the total forests (as per 2001 figures). They are managed in accordance with the objectives of the Union Government instituted through the Provincial Government.

(b) Civil and Soyam Forests, which are under the Revenue Department. In Tehri district, the nomenclature for this category of forests is 'soyam' forests. These forests cover 845. 10 sq. kms and comprise 20.8 per cent of the total forests of the district. Being under the management of the Revenue Department, the Provincial Government enjoys a greater stake in deciding the uses of these forests.

(c) Panchayati Forests/Van Panchayat Forests, which are under the jurisdiction of the locally elected panchayats. About 10.7 per cent of the forest area constitutes the Panchayati forests. The village community enjoys a greater stake in the protection and management of these forests.

It is interesting to note that the Panchayati forests were constituted rather late in the Tehri district. The 'State of Forest Report 1995' did not report this category of forests in Tehri and it was only in the year 1997-98, that the state-driven Van Panchayat formation was initiated in Tehri Garhwal under the Uttar Pradesh Village Forest Joint Management Rules, 1997. The Revenue Department demarcated 432.64 sq kms of soyam forest lands which were under its jurisdiction as village forests to be managed by the officially constituted Van Panchayats. Although a detailed analysis of the functioning of the Van Panchayats is attempted later, it is important to point out that as these bodies had been constituted late, and for quite some time in the context, they were not fully functional in real terms. Since their constitution and till the time of the study, less time had elapsed for the Van Panchayats to show an active involvement and contribution to the protection and management of the panchayati forests in Tehri.

It is to be noted here that the fourth official category of forests, viz, protected areas, private municipal, cantonment and unclassified forests do not exist in Tehri.

The role of the government and people in the development and management of the forests is different for different categories of forests. The same is depicted through Table 4.4.

Table 4.4: Role of People and Government in the Management of Different Categories of Forests

S. No.	*Categories of forests*	*Role of Government and People in the Development and Management of Forests*
1.	Reserved Forests	Under the exclusive jurisdiction of the Forest Department of the State Government. People/ community had no role in the development and management of forests. The extraction of the non-timber forest produce was done by the Forest Department through the local people. Villagers had timber rights (haq-haqooq) but the quantities of these had not been revised since the forest settlements of 1910-17, and were completely inadequate. Timber was extracted through the Forest Corporation of the State Government.
2.	Soyam Forests	Under the jurisdiction and administrative control of the Revenue Department. They were managed by the government in collaboration with the people (Gram Sabhas), which were elected bodies. Forest Department rendered technical guidance. People enjoyed unlimited rights and concessions. Lack of protection and mismanagement had almost depleted and destroyed these forests and they needed remedial measures to rehabilitate them.
3.	Panchayat Forests	Traditionally, the Panchayat forests were managed and protected by the Van Panchayats, which were elected forest councils, under the provisions of Forest Panchayat Rules 1976, framed under section 28 of the Indian Forest Act, 1927. The administrative control was vested in the district administration and the Forest Department rendered technical guidance. But recently, in the year 1997-98 with the promotion of the Village Forest Joint Management (VFJM) with autonomous Van Panchayats being funded by a World Bank Forestry Project, the decision making autonomy of the Van Panchayats participating in the VJMP was now subject to the supervision, direction, control and concurrence of the Divisional Forest Officer (D. F. O). A functionary of the Forest Department was made the joint account holder and the Member Secretary of Van Panchayats3. Thus, under the VJMP the forests were placed under the joint management of the Van Panchayat and nominated officers of the Forest Department.

B. Change in Forests

Although the coverage of forests, in terms of area has remained virtually unchanged, other changes have taken place in the forests. These changes mainly pertained to (i) changes in the ownership pattern of forests, and (ii) changes in the nature, pattern, and density of forests.

(i) Changes in ownership pattern of forests: As far as changes in the ownership pattern of forests are concerned, these have mainly been in the context of the soyam forests. These forests have been developed to meet to needs and demands of the people for biomass. It was expected that people's participation would be secured in the protection and management of this genre of forests. However, this did not happen. Neither have these forests been able to cater to the fodder and fuel requirements of the people on a sustained basis, nor has people's participation in their protection and management been secured. It is the government agencies which have remained dominant in the planning and organization of conservation and management for this category of forests.

To devolve control of forests to the community, the third category of Panchayati forests and the institution of Van panchayats were initiated in the region on the lines of the Van Panchayat system in the Kumaun division and Pauri Garhwal district.This was achieved by bifurcating the existing soyam forests into Panchayati forests. As mentioned earlier, only 432.64 sq. kms. of Soyam forest lands had been handed over to Van Panchayats in the district in the initial phase of their formation.

(ii) Changes in the nature, pattern and density of forests: The changes that have taken place in the forests, with regard to their nature, pattern and density are specific to the two different categories of the Reserve forests and the Soyam forests. These have been discussed in detail in the following section:

***(a) Changes in Reserve forests*:** Over the years, the Reserve forests of the region have undergone many changes, largely due to human interference. Two main changes which were discernible related to:

Changes in the nature of forests: During the last many years, although the magnitude of forest cover has by and large remained unchanged, the forests of the region have shown a change in terms of their nature and pattern. Although no recent recorded data pertaining to these changes is available, it is a fact that the original forest vegetation of mixed forests has gradually been replaced by monocultures of commercially viable trees, largely owing to the silvicultural practices followed by the state, in both the pre and the post independent times. As a result, the chir pine area has increased, but the oak and other deciduous forests have declined. This is due to the preference of the Forest Department for fast growing, commercially viable species like chir pine, as opposed to the more environment friendly and people friendly, broad-leaved varieties of trees like oak or fruit trees. This change in the nature of vegetation has not only been detrimental to the life and living of the local communities, but also harmful to the cause of the environment, as species like pine are known to expose forests to fire, diminish soil fertility by reducing moisture content, and prevent the development of any undergrowth. On the other hand, oak is instrumental in developing a thick mass of undergrowth (bushes, grasses and creepers), and in naturally harvesting rainwater to generate natural springs and other sources of water.

Thus, it is easy to see that the nature of forest vegetation of the region has been registering a change towards an expansion of mono cultures and a decline in forests under mixed tree cover.

Changes in forest cover density: It is not only the extent of forest cover, but also the density of this forest cover, which gives us a true picture of the state of the forests. This component sheds light on the quality of the forest resource. Although specific data on the earlier situation was not available, discussion with the local people revealed that the erstwhile thick forests in the vicinity of their villages have degraded and have transformed into open forests. Elders of the community reminisced about the times when the reserve forests adjoining their villages used to be so thick that it used to be dark inside, even during daytime, whereas presently there were large, gaping spaces in them. An analysis of the forest area based on satellite imageries done by the Forest Survey of India in the year 1999 was already showing the poor forest cover density even then:

Table 4.5: Analysis of Forest Area of Tehri Garhwal District based on Satellite Imageries by the Forest Survey of India, 2007

Geographical Area	*Actual Forest Cover Assessment (sq kms)*				*Percentage of Forest Cover to Geographical Area*
	Very Dense Forest	*Moderately Dense Forest*	*Open Forest*	*Total Forest*	
3462	298	1232	617	2147	58.95

Source: The State of Forest Report 2007, Forest Survey of India, Dehradun.

The data indicates that in the year 2007, out of a total forest cover of 2147 sq kms in Tehri District, only 298 sq kms consisted of 'very dense forests' that is 13.87 per cent of the total forest cover. Another 1232 sq kms of forest area was 'moderately dense', that is 57.38 per cent of forest cover. The rest of forest cover of 617 sq kms or 28.74 per cent of the forest cover comprised of 'open forests'. On the whole, about 71 per cent of forests could be deemed as good quality forests, while 29 per cent of the forests were tending to have a low crown density (between 10% and 40%), and were therefore forests of 'doubtful' quality. Another 85 sq kms of 'scrub' area was also reported by the Forest Survey Report.

(b) Changes in Soyam Forests: The erstwhile open forests which were earlier known as class III forests are now referred to as 'Soyam Forests'. Soyam forests were envisaged to be 'protected' forests, belonging to the Revenue Department and formally shown within the revenue boundaries of villages or gram sabhas. Thus, they come closer to the definition of the village commons, as they are loosely regarded as belonging to the people. The demarcation between reserve forests and the villages had left narrow strips of land for the free use of villages as a kind of a buffer zone between the reserves and the village settlements. They are an artificial introduction into the native land management system which was destroyed at the time of expropriation of village forests and notification of reserves by the native state of Tehri, following the practice followed by the British government in British Garhwal. In actual fact, these strips of land were carved out of a mix of forest fallow, uncultivated waste or 'benap' and winter grazing grounds, and was qualitatively inferior even at the time of their creation.

Transformation into open access common property resources: Over the passage of time, these non-cultivated lands transformed into 'open access' common property resources. With the reserved forests being out of limits for the local population, the soyam forests have come under increasing pressure of rising human and livestock population, and are victim to reckless exploitation by the local people and vested interests. The influential or otherwise well placed farmers benefit by the extension of cultivation into these areas.

Gradually, most of the common lands have been appropriated in this fashion and instances of conflicts have also become frequent. The policy of extension of cultivation has been undertaken at the cost of the valuable resources in soyam lands, many of which were earlier covered by dense oak forests.

Having continued to be treated as common access lands, the soyam forests have suffered, what is now widely known as the "tragedy of the commons". In the words of Madhava Gadgil, "the commons have now become property that is everybody's to exploit and nobody's to guard."

C. Problems Faced by Forests

Multiple problems are being faced by the forests of the region. While some problems like increasing decimation due to population pressure, and overgrazing are common to all categories of forests viz. Reserved forests, Soyam forests and Panchayat forests, there are certain specific problems faced by specific categories. Some of the important problems faced by the forests of the region are presented in Table 4.6.

A brief description of the aforementioned problems faced by the three categories of forests is presented below:

Table 4.6: Problems Faced by Different Categories of Forests

Categories of Forests	*Problems faced*
Reserved Forests	(a) Biotic stress due to increasing fuel wood and timber demands of population. (b) Recurring incidence of forest fires. (c) Commercial exploitation of forests (d) Overgrazing by livestock (e) Transfer of forest land to other uses. (f) Inadequacy of protection infrastructure
Soyam Forests	(a) Unlimited access with no specific responsibilities for protection and promotion (b) Increasing biotic stress. (c) Increasing encroachment by vested interests (d) Ambivalence in policies governing these forests. (e) Administrative problems related to control. (f) Increasing accessibility leading to uncontrolled exploitation. (g) Lack of successful regeneration initiatives
Panchayat Forests	(a) Increasing degradation due to biotic stress. (b) Ineffective and weak Van Panchayats, leading to lack of adequate protection and regeneration.

1. Problems Faced by Reserved Forests

(a) Biotic stress due to fuel wood and timber demands: In the absence of alternatives, the fuel needs of the population are met by firewood from the forests. For the region, the demand for fuel imposed by the population, especially living in the municipal areas is quite significant. Data provided by the Forest Department suggest that between the period 1991-92 and 1995-96, an annual average of 10,224 cu. mts round stacks of firewood per year were produced in the district. It is also important to note that the worst victim of this cause had been the rich oak forests, as oak has both a high calorific value and it also yields high quality charcoal. Large scale departmental extraction of fuel wood has therefore led to widespread decimation of oak forests of the region.

Apart from the heavy departmental extractions, intensive lopping particularly near the villages has led to the degradation of the reserve forests, particularly the kokat and oak forests, and even chir forests. Grass cutting is widely practiced, and on the steeper slopes it does considerable harm to forest regeneration, as many saplings get cut with the grass.

(b) Recurring incidence of forest fires: Fire is another major cause of destruction of the reserve forests. The incidence of forest fires has increased in the recent years. Forest fires occur in Garhwal usually up to the temperate zone and are common in the summer season, when the minimum temperature rises to more than 35 degree Celsius, and there is a vast quantity of inflammable material present in the forest in the form of dry needles, twigs and branches.

Fires lead to a great deal of damage to the chir forests as also to the dry mixed deciduous and bamboo forests. Young deodar plantations are also liable to be completely destroyed by fire. Even if burning does not destroy seedlings, it bakes the ground and adversely affects the soil and moisture conditions, making it virtually impossible for forest flora to regenerate. In addition, much damage is caused by accidental fires, at times caused by failure to undertake controlled burning of fire lines. The chir forests are also subject to frequent fires mostly set by villagers to improve grazing, though some are also accidental.

The main reasons for the occurrence of these periodic fires as reported by the local people and forest officials are: (i) increase in average temperatures, due to which the moisture content is diminishing; (ii) the widely prevalent use of plastic bags to grow saplings, which are then left in the forest after plantation by forest officials leading to forest fires; (iii) dishonest practices in plantation work by forest officials; (iv) accidental fires caused by people and forest officials; and (v) alienation of people from the forests (due to government policy of curtailing their traditional rights), resulting in their non-cooperation in extinguishing forest fires.

It is ironical that while there has been an enormous increase in fund availability for plantation work (as was revealed by official records), there has been no commensurate increase in funds available for fire protection. Consequently, forest fires have been causing extensive damage to the natural vegetation; harming regeneration; increasing the problem of accelerated erosion, and even destroying the rich variety of insects, birds and animals living in the forests of the region.

(c) Commercial exploitation of the forests: Besides meeting the needs of the population for fuel and timber, the forests also provide raw materials for various industries like paper mills (Eucalyptus), matchwood industry (Semal, Gutel, Ailanthus, Poplar), plywood industry (Jhingan, Kanju, Bahera, Kharpat, Poplar), sports goods, toys and scale industry (Poola etc.), packing industry (Dhak, Gojina, Gular, Bahera) and other industries. Forests are a very important source of revenue for the hill region. The revenue obtained from the forestry sector comes from the sale of timber, royalty on resin, oilseeds, and other minor forest products, grazing, fuel wood etc.

Resin tapping has been responsible for the considerable weakening of trees, especially if the prescribed norms are not followed. This makes them prone to large scale uprooting during storms. Moreover, fire hazards increase with resin tapping as the mode of resin tapping makes trees vulnerable to fire. On account of the above, a very peculiar phenomenon has been noted in Tehri, which is that even after commercial felling of trees stopped in the region in the year 1981, the availability of timber has remained almost the same, as it was subsequently obtained, not from selective felling but from fallen and wind-blown trees. At times, felling of trees by storms had infact exceeded the felling of trees as prescribed in the working plans.

The prevalence of corrupt and illegal practices in the commercial exploitation of forests is further leading to large scale destruction and decimation of the forests. Illegal felling of green trees, instead of dead and fallen trees, with the connivance of the Forest Department and Van Nigam is widely prevalent. While the Department marks green trees together with the dead and fallen trees, the Van Nigam undertakes the felling of these trees

The involvement of the forest officials with the Forest Corporation and the Timber Mafia in the illegal felling of trees has been widely reported by the local people.

(d) Grazing by animals: Much damage is done to forests by grazing. As per estimates of the Forest Department, in the year 2001, Tehri district had an estimated 179913 cows, 120666 buffaloes, 25682 sheep and 123273 goats. Thus, there was considerable pressure of heavy grazing incidence on the forests of the region.

Moreover, in the winters, large flocks of sheep of graziers and buffaloes of gujjars come down to the lower altitudes and wreak considerable harm to the low altitude forests. Due to the heavy pressure of grazing, the natural vegetation in the vicinity of villages is invariably retarded. Grazing in the oak forests is harmful to the seedling or coppice regeneration. It also does great harm to chir regeneration. Overgrazing also leads to gully formation, which in turn leads to accelerated soil erosion. Besides, it has an adverse effect on the pasture grasses which are kept them their optimal heights for metabolic activity. Additionally, due to selective grazing of young succulent grasses only coarse and poor quality grasses are left.

(e) Transfer of forest land to other uses: The period before 1980 saw a rapid reduction in the forest area of the region due to the expansion of agriculture and human settlements. Construction of roads, canals and other infra-structure had also led to a decline in the forest area. Rich forested areas also fell in the submergence area of the, river valley projects and multiple hydroelectric power projects. An important example of this is the controversial Tehri Dam. Rich forest areas of Tehri have been submerged in the artificial reservoir which has come up as a part of the project.

The table below illustrates the extent of forest area that had been lost due to the development infrastructure being created in the region:

The illegal encroachment of forest area by people living in the vicinity of forests has been another important factor leading to a decline in forest area. As per official data, in the Garhwal Zone, 1433 ha forest area have been encroached upon illegally (as per 2001 figures).

(f) Inadequacy of protection infrastructure: The infrastructure for the protection of forests is woefully inadequate. Consequently, trees are felled

Table 4.7: Sector wise Details of Forest Area (in ha) Transferred after the Enactment of the Forest Conservation Act, 1980 (1981-82 to 2000-2001)

Development Projects	*Area (in ha)*
Irrigation projects	437.9925
Hydro power projects	5086.4955
Road construction	2311.1987
Communication projects	1205.1619
Mining projects	8358.3240
Drinking water schemes	146.9860
Other schemes	3752.3575
Total (in ha)	21298.5161

Source: Forest statistics, Forest Department, Dehradun, Uttaranchal, 2001.

and burnt in remote areas where patrolling is practically non-existent. As vigilance is not enough, the likelihood of green trees being cut and sawn along with dead and fallen trees by petty labour (generally from Nepal) or petty sub contractors of the Van Nigam (Forest Corporation) is very high.

In the past, the Forest Department was organized into territorial divisions. Tehri district, which has been one of the most blighted sections of the hills of undivided Uttar Pradesh, was covered by a single territorial division to the extent of 53 per cent of the geographical area of the district, with another 12 per cent being administered by the Yamuna territorial division and Uttarkashi territorial division respectively. Almost 68 per cent of the total area of the district consists of Reserve Forests. Moreover, the district consists of three major catchments, viz. the Bhagirathi, the Yamuna and the Bhilangana catchments. Tehri Forest Division has 12 river catchments including four major ones. In the hills each river catchment represents a valley enclosed by high slopes and separated physically from the next valley. Trans-valley movement entails crossing of the high hills and consequently makes supervision difficult. With such a large area and a difficult terrain, the ground staff remains highly inadequate to provide any protection to the forests. At the time of the study, there were 101 forest guards for patrolling, protection, fire watch and fire extinction, guarding against theft, as also plantation and improvement work, at the beat level. In the Bhilangana range, Gangi reserve alone comprises of 33,000 ha of priceless forest wealth, but was being monitored by one forest guard only.

2. Problems of Soyam Forests

(a) Unlimited access with no specific responsibilities: The soyam forests have suffered from large scale degradation and almost complete disappearance of tree cover because these lands have been treated as 'open access' lands. People have unlimited right on these forests, but no visible authority assigned with specific responsibilities for protection or prevention of misuse.

(b) Increasing biotic stress: Due to the increasing pressure of rising human and livestock population, the Soyam forests have been recklessly exploited by the local people and vested interests, without any accompanying efforts to protect, preserve or rejuvenate them. Even in their attenuated state, some products of the village commons like grass for stall fed cattle, and small bundles of firewood from coppicer shrubs, are still sustaining the villagers and there is competition among various user groups for extracting available biomass.

(c) Encroachment by vested interests: Chunks of these areas have been appropriated by the influential persons, who have diverted them to cultivation, horticulture and other non-forestry activities. Consequently, while such portions continue to be shown as forests in the revenue records, they are essentially non-forested areas.

(d) Ambivalence in policies: Ambivalent policies of the government departments have also contributed to the plight of these forests. While the Forest Department proposes the use of soyam forests as a buffer zone, which is supposed to take the burden off the reserve forests, the Revenue department and district administration continue to see these common lands as avenues for further agriculture, horticulture and creation of community facilities.

(e) Administrative problems related to control: Many of these forest areas fall within the legal jurisdiction of various gram sabhas. But since there are multiple users from different villages, neither the de jure gram panchayat nor the Forest department has any control on them. Thus, even if the de jure owners are able to temporarily affect enclosures, they cannot enforce enclosures or protect their plantations.

(f) Increasing accessibility to the forests: Increasing urbanization, coupled with the opening of a vast network of roads has further led to a situation where the public at large is able to forage for fuel wood, grass and other forest products along the extensive open stretches of these forests located by the roadside. This has contributed to their extreme deterioration in accessible reaches.

(g) Lack of successful regeneration initiatives: No regular plans have been prepared for the rejuvenation of these areas, except the recent plantation work undertaken as a part of the social forestry programme. This has also been disappointing in terms of performance. People have tended to be unmotivated for plantation work, either because forest produce is readily accessible elsewhere, or due to disputes over tenure of plantation land, or because the land selected for plantation has already been used for other purposes and consensus for discontinuing that usage is not available. Uncertainty regarding usufruct is also a major disincentive for cooperation with forest department plantations in the area. Besides, most of these forests are in scattered patches of less than 5 ha and this increases the protection and supervision costs

3. Problems of Panchayat Forests

(a) Increasing degradation due to biotic stress: As mentioned earlier, the panchayat forests have been constituted relatively recently in the district and the block. Having been created out of soyam forests, they face the same problems of exploitation and the resultant degradation, as the soyam forests. Van Panchayats have been constituted, but have not been able to do much work towards the regeneration of these areas.

(b) Ineffective and weak Van Panchayats: Although the Van Panchayat system as an institution at the 'village' level or the 'village group' level has considerable potential for involving local communities in forest management and conservation, not much work has been done in Tehri district to develop these institutions effectively. They are behest with a number of disabilities like lack of adequate powers, indifference of officials, lack of financial and personnel resources, etc. Consequently, the forests under the Van Panchayats have not been adequately protected or regenerated (details about Van Panchayats can also be found in a subsequent section).

Having discussed the common and specific problems pertaining to the different categories of forests of the region (based on ownership and management of forests), it is important to indicate one strange and interesting phenomenon observed in many places in Tehri Garhwal. Here, the reserve forests rather than the village commons carry the greatest usage and are considered as resource pools, which the villagers identify with, not simply for exploitation, but also for protection and management, (even as de jure control remains with the Forest department). Informal village boundaries are still recognized in the reserves and were still guarded and respected by the people. Hence villagers continue to identify deeply with the reserves and this feeling has been enhanced after the Chipko Andolan and the ban on felling of trees above 1000 meters. Also, the reserves are not subject to the pressure of multiple users to the same extent as are the village commons. Local women strongly object to outsiders entering the remote oak forests above their village settlements in the reserves. They still regard these as their preserves within the state forests. It is a strange paradox therefore, that reserve forests sometimes belong more to the villagers than the soyam lands or village commons. This has significance for planning for people's participation in the region.

To summarize the discussion on the state of the forests of the region, the important observations which stand out are:

1. Forests comprise the largest and the most important land use category in the region. However, the 'actual' forest cover in the region is much less than the 'recorded' forest cover. This is much less than the minimum desirable level of 66 per cent prescribed by the National Policy guidelines of 1988 for the hill districts.

2. The forests have undergone a change in ownership and management pattern. This change has been in context of the soyam forests, which have been bifurcated into panchayat forests, keeping the needs and requirements of people in mind, together with the desirability of involving people in the protection and management of forests.
3. Other changes relate to the nature and pattern of vegetation in the forests. The nature of vegetation, especially in the reserved forests has been changing. The original vegetation of mixed, deciduous forests has continued to be replaced by the commercially viable monocultures, which yield revenue to the government, but are least beneficial to the local people. Moreover, they are actually detrimental to the cause of the environment.
4. The density of forest cover is declining, and the original 'dense' forests of the region are getting replaced by 'open' forests, which presently comprise almost 30 per cent of the total forests of the region.
5. Soyam forests have come to be increasingly regarded as villagers' forests and have gradually transformed into open access common property resources, due to multiple preserves operating on them. The different categories of forests face common problems relating to increasing biotic pressure resources, as also their own specific problems. These problems need to be countered in order to protect and promote the valuable forest resources of the region.

II. Soil

The soils of this region vary according to the, altitude and climate. On the whole, the soils are young and thin. However, considerable depth of the soil can be observed in the valleys or on the gently inclined hill slopes.

The sharp variations in geo-ecological conditions have given rise to a number of soil characteristics. The vegetal cover is one of the most influencing factors characterizing the soil types; therefore some broad soil zones can be determined on the basis of natural vegetation found on it. The following table gives a soil profile of the region, classified in various pedo-ecological zones:-

Table 4.8: Soil Types of the Region

S. No.	*Pedo-Ecological Zones*	*Altitude (m)*	*Climate-Vegetal Zone*	*Soil Types*
1.	Lower Himalayan Zone	900-1800	Warm Temperate	Brown forest
2.	Higher Himalayan Zone	1800-3000	Cool Temperate to Cold	Brown deciduous and grey coniferous forest
3.	Alpine Zone	3000-4500	Alpine	Mountain meadow and Glacial

Source: Kaushik, S.D. (1959). Climatic Zones in the Garhwal Himalayas. *Geographical Review*, 24(2-3): 29, 1959.

The table shows that the soils vary between alluvial brown forest in the lower zones, to brown deciduous and grey coniferous in the middle zones to mountain meadow and glacial soil in the high altitude alpine zone.

In general, the soils are rich in potash, medium in phosphorus and poor in nitrogen content. The stony texture, poor fertility and thin layer of soil make them hard to work upon. These soils though poor for other crops are suitable for potato cultivation and horticulture. As far as problems associated with soil conditions are concerned, the most important ones pertain to: (a) Existence of exhausted and damaged soils with low fertility; (b) Prevalence of accelerated soil erosion and; (c) Increased occurrence of landslides. A brief discussion on these follows:

(a) Existence of exhausted and damaged soils: In the region, as in a large part of the Himalayan belt, the soils are in the process of being rapidly damaged. Their fertility is reduced as is their water holding capacity. This gets reflected in low crop yields. Generally the extension of cultivation on marginal soils on steep slopes, and rocky and unstable hill sides without vegetative protection from steeper slopes above, is causing a lot of havoc as far as the condition of the soil is considered. Apart from greater demands from growing populations, commercial cultivation and horticulture have cornered the better soils, pushing food crops up to higher slopes and exhausted soils. The compacted and exhausted soils are prone to large scale erosion.

(b) Prevalence of accelerated soil erosion: The biotic pressure on the forests of the region has led to a number of adverse effects on the fragile ecosystem. One of the main problems emanating from the decline in forest cover is soil erosion. Natural soil erosion is an ongoing process, but degraded forest lands are open to accelerated erosion. It was a well known fact that the multi-tiered canopy formed by the crown of trees, shrubs and herbs breaks the force of rainwater which comes with great intensity. Thus, when rainwater falls on the earth's surface with a high velocity in areas with little or no vegetative cover, it leads to the dislocation of soil particles from the ground. Consequently, soil erosion becomes rampant and takes the form of sheet wash, rill erosion, gully erosion, and mud flows. Devoid of a network of roots to bind the soil particles, the top soil is quickly washed away. Huge chunks of unprotected soil give way to the force of rain water and this results in soil slumping. Very often, the unprotected soil acts as a catalyst in the formation of land slides. Deforestation also leads to snow erosion in the upper altitudes, as lack of adequate tree cover increases the amount of snow falling on the ground, and this melt water also causes erosion.

(c) Increased occurrence of landslides: Although landslides are a natural phenomenon of erosion, they have escalated by leaps and bounds ever since the road building process started and have now become an integral part of the landscape. They have become a major problem for the region and cases of disasters caused by landslides are reported during the rainy season every year. Some landslides defy stabilization efforts and contribute huge amounts of debris annually. Besides, the valuable loss of human life and livestock, the extent of damage in terms of loss of productive land and property, siltation of reservoirs, loss in tourist trade due to failure of communications etc. is quite significant. Some of the major landslides which have occurred in the region are the Bhagirathi landslide, Kauntha landslide, Kalagad landslide, and Saknidhar landslide.

The exploitation of the forests to meet the needs of the population and the industries and the direct extraction of shrubs and medical plants for commercial use has contributed greatly to the deforestation of the Himalayan slopes. The outcome of this is that a large proportion of the region is bereft of the protective cover of vegetation, thereby leaving the soil exposed to degradation, large scale erosion and landslides.

III. Water

Apart from land, water is the other most important environmental resource. It plays a very important role, not only for the ecology and economy of the region, but also for the ecology and economy of the entire Northern India. As is well known, major rivers like the Ganga and the Yamuna emanate from the Himalayas and provide valuable water resources to a significant part of the country. Indeed they are the life lines, not only for the region, but for the country as a whole.

This section initially provides a description of the water resources of the region and then proceeds to highlight the important problems pertaining to the water resources.

1. Water Resources

The Himalayas, as the name implies are the "abode of snow" A very large number of glaciers exist above the snow line and these provide water to the major rivers of the region. Glaciers are formed from the accumulated snow which survives melting; for a glacier to exist, the snowfall should exceed the quantity of snow that melts in a summer.

The glaciers are therefore, the source of water to all major river systems. The rivers which drain the Tehri region also have their source in the snow caps and the glaciers, and hence are perennial.

The district is drained by rivers like the Ganga, Alakhananda, Bhagirathi, Bhilangana, and Yamuna. The confluence points of the rivers known as 'Prayag' like 'Deoprayag' and 'Ganesh Prayag' are more important from the point of view of religion and culture. The drainage system of the area can be classified in the following systems:

(i) The Ganga system
   (a) The Bhagirathi sub-system.
   (b) The Alakhananda sub-system.
(ii) The Yamuna system

The Bhagirathi and the Alakhananda sub-systems form the Ganga system, which drains the whole district, excepting the western border which is drained by the Bhagirathi-Bhilangana systems. Both the rivers have formed deep and broad valleys with extensive river terraces like Chham, Pilkhi, Chamiyala and Sirain. The total length of the Bhagirathi in Tehri district is 159 kms. The Bhilangana, the only sizeable tributary of the Bhagirathi takes its origin from the Bharti Kantha in the North East part of the district and join the Bhagirathi at Ganesh Prayag near Tehri. The Balganga is the main tributary of Bhilangana and it meets the latter near Pilkhi. The Bhilangana system drains the major parts of the blocks of Bhilangana, Jakholi, Pratapnagar and Jakhnidhar.

The region is therefore rich in water resources with numerous rivers and rivulets (locally known as gad and gadhera). However, most of the water sources are found at the lower altitudes, and a good number of villages are located in the higher ranges of the hills. Thus, river water alone cannot fulfill the needs of the local inhabitants. About 60 per cent of the population of the hills is still dependent on natural springs for its water supply. Unfortunately, these springs are also suffering on account of environmental degradation.

In the hilly region, the subsoil water cannot be tapped, so the total dependence of people is on surface water. Apart from the network of rivers and rivulets, rainfall is a major source of water, especially for the crops. The yearly average rainfall in the area is about 150 mm. It is not uniform through the year. The maximum downpour takes place during the months of July-August. Despite heavy rainfall in these two months, the area suffers from a severe scarcity of water due to: (i) the uneven distribution of rainfall during the year; (ii) a high run-off; (iii) an inadequacy of storage; and (iv) the low moisture retention capacity of the soil. Problems impacting the water resources of the region include: (a) changes in the water/hydrological cycle; (b) diminishing regulatory effect of glaciers; (c) frequent occurrence of flash floods; and (d) incidence of water pollution.

These have been discussed briefly:

(a) Changes in the water cycle: As mentioned earlier, forests have a direct relation with the other environmental components or natural resources. They are, to a large extent responsible for maintaining the water cycle in the hills. The rain water that seeps into the soil on a forested slope adds to the reservoir of underground water, which in turn feeds the springs and streams. This water also replenishes the moisture present in the soil.

The capacity of the soil to absorb water depends on its permeability. On steep slopes, where the soil is shallow, the forest floor litter plays a major role and absorbs more water than ordinary soil, and by easy decomposition adds to the depth of the soil. The heavily forested areas are by and large covered with litter which slows down the velocity of the run-off water. Here, soils being rich in organic matter have high water retention and infiltration rates.

Within the context, apart from the widespread prevalence of deforestation and overgrazing, the burning of leaf litter and its removal from manure has become the common practice in almost all the broad leaved and chir pine forests of the region. This naturally results in low soil moisture retention. Infiltration studies in the hilly watersheds in Tehri district clearly indicate that the average infiltration capacity of a broad leaved natural forest is much more than that of a conifer forest (246 mm). In comparison the average infiltration capacity of an eroded area is significantly less. The conversion of the original mixed forests of the region into monocultures of pine has dented the infiltration capacity of the soil, leading to drought like conditions in many areas of the region. Over the past few decades, the biotic pressure on forests has enhanced significantly, also leading to the water table declining. This has contributed to an exaggerated drudgery for the local population, especially women and children, who have to traverse huge distances to procure water, as the nearby sources of water have either dried up or are in the process of drying up due to fall in the water table. There has been a considerable decline in the discharge of many streams and it is common to come across springs which have been reduced to a mere trickle or have completely dry beds. Deforestation, grazing, trampling by livestock, erosion of top fertile soils, forest fires and development activities like road cutting, mining, building, construction work and others have reduced the "sponge action" of land and have created a hydrological imbalance in the fragile watersheds of the region.

(b) Retreat and diminishing effect of glaciers: Another important development pertaining to the water resources is related to the retreat of the various Himalayan glaciers. Glacial melt water and natural springs are the main sources of water in the region. A large part of the total water supply is contributed by the snow and glacial melt, especially during the crucial summer seasons. Glaciers also have a significant influence on the local and global environment on various time scales. Due to climate change, world over, the glaciers are known to be receding. However, fluctuations of Himalayan glaciers differ from glaciers in other parts of the world on account of their existence in a different geomorphic regime and in a tectonically active environment. Due to the global environmental changes and the regional pattern of resource use, glaciers are experiencing an extreme recession in the Uttaranchal Himalayas. Changes in the rate of retreat of various glaciers also reflect the influence of local conditions. A relatively higher rate of retreat of the Pindari, Gangotri, and Khatling glaciers indicates a larger contribution by way of human intervention in the ecosystem. It has been estimated that the Pindari glacier and the Gangotri glacier are retreating at alarming rates. If glaciers continue to recede at the present rate, it is not too far in the future that the Himalayan rivers, which are perennial sources of water for a major part of the country would face the repercussions of this irreversible phenomenon.

(c) Flash Floods: Flash floods are another manifestation of environmental tampering by man. Large scale deforestation in the Tehri region has led to the preponderance of frequent flash floods. When rainfall is received in huge amounts by the hill slopes which are increasingly devoid of a vegetative cover, instead of seeping into the soil, the rainwater drains away as surface flow and causes considerable erosion on the side. The natural channels of the mountain streams and rivers are then unable to contain the huge volume of water flowing into them from the degraded uplands. This results in devastating flash floods, as water overflows the banks of streams and rivers and inundates a large area. Large areas along the rivers or streams are destroyed and there is usually an extensive damage to life and property. Although flashfloods are not a new phenomenon in Garhwal, there has been an abrupt increase in their intensity in the recent past. This has been due to: (i) the widespread degradation of the forest cover, due to an increasing biotic pressure on the forests that lie in the catchments of various rivers that drain the area is the prime reason behind the recurring flash floods; and (ii) an enhanced rate and levels of siltation has raised the beds of rivers and streams, reducing their capacities to contain the highly enhanced water run-off during the rainy season. The worst-recorded flash floods in this region occurred in the catchment of river Alakhananda in the year 1970. Subsequently, many such flash floods have caused heavy losses and misery to the people of the area. Subsequent to the 1991 earthquake, there have been recurrent floods in river Jalkur, Bhagirathi, Bhilangana, Dharamganga and Balganga. A massive flood occurred in August 1997, in the Dharamganga in the Bhilangana block. A number of small bridges were washed away and there was immense loss of valuable agricultural land, livestock and dwellings, as the river overflowed its boundaries. It also led to a major disruption in the supply of electricity to large areas of the block for months, due to the washing away of electric poles and transmission wires. Shrigarh, Dabar and Bhigun, etc, the villages which were the worst affected.

Experts say that rapid deforestation and construction work in the hills are the main reasons behind the frequent floods and landslides. A number of hydropower projects and mining projects are being undertaken in Uttarakhand. The blasting work carried out during the construction of tunnels and mining is contributing to landslides. Several rivers are being diverted through the tunnels for these projects, leading to an enhanced vulnerability to disasters. When blasts and their resultant landslides occur, the debris often falls in the rivers leading to a rise in the water level in the river which leads to flash floods when it rains heavily. Large scale deforestation, to accommodate the projects also creates soil erosion and massive landslides.

(d) Water Pollution: The water resources of the region are also facing a huge problem of pollution. Although there is no recorded data to prove the incidence of water pollution, the same is being recognized as an important problem in the region, and the local people have expressed their deep concern with it. With an increase in the human population and livestock, requirements for water are also increasing. Water sources are becoming polluted due to the increased pressure exerted on them. The practice of dumping carcasses of dead animals as well as disposal of human bodies in the rivers is leading to rising levels of water pollution, even while the rivers are in the mountainous terrain only. Other activities like washing, bathing, as well as use by cattle have rendered the water dirty and even unfit for human consumption. The increased damming of the rivers by the multiple hydro electricity projects also prevents the rivers from their natural self purifying regimens. Furthermore, pollution is also caused by the heavy inflow of silt and sediments from the adjoining mountain slopes. The problem of water pollution is assuming alarming proportions, especially on the banks of the Bhagirathi River at Tehri.

IV. Wildlife

For long, the region has witnessed a rich faunal wealth. Inaccessibility to most parts of the high altitude region, and of course, the religious dicta and traditional sentiments have together played a significant role in safeguarding the fauna of the region. The forests of the region are home to thousands of interesting species of mammals, birds, reptiles, and amphibians. Amongst the prominent mammals are the Leopard, Tiger, Panther, Brown bear, Himalayan Black Bear, Sambar, Hog Deer, Spotted Deer, Himalayan Musk Deer, Barking Deer, Wild Boar, Oxen, Sheep, Goat, Antelope, Pigs, Gazelles, Bharal or the Blue Sheep, Himalayan Tahr, Indian Hare, Indian Porcupine, Squirrel, Indian Fox, Jackal, Kog (Wild Dog), Red Fox, Mongoose, Goral, Common Langur etc.

Both resident and migratory birds are found in the region. The main species of birds are Hill Partridge, Green Pigeon, Red breasted Parakeet, Woodpecker, Broadbill, Yellow Bulbul, Browneared Bulbul, Parrotbill, Babbler, Laughing Thrush, Bush Warbler, Sunbird, Green Magpie, Greenbilled Malkoha, Crow Billed Drongo, Cheer Pheasant, Cuckoo, Nutcracker, and Gold Crest.

The region is also endowed with riverine resources. Since a majority of rivers and streams are perennial, they are abound with many varieties of fish like Schizothorax, Tor, Labeo, Barilius, Puntius, Danio, Garra, Channa Gachua, Crosscheilus, etc. Many species of reptiles including snakes and lizards are also found.

As far as the state of the wildlife is concerned, the ever increasing rate of population growth is exerting pressure on the remaining wildlife habitats. As against the minimum requirements of 66 per cent forest area prescribed for the hill region, the forested area is much less, due to which the wildlife habitat is considerably reduced. Unscientific felling and lopping of trees and the collection of minor forest products is a common phenomenon. Forest fires are frequent. Development activities are exerting pressure on wild lands. Overcrowding of domestic livestock is yet another root cause of habitat decay, apart from exposing the wild animals to a direct and tough competition. The high altitude meadow zone, which is universally recognized as a very fragile and sensitive area and which abounds in many unique and threatened plant and animal species, is the worst sufferer of the excessive grazing pressure. Selective eradication of important plants/herbs and uncontrolled tourist activities are also exposing the meadows to further degradation.

All the above and many other activities are also leading to more and severe incidents of landslides, soil erosion, floods and other environmental calamities. Poachers use shooting, trapping and poisoning methods to kill wildlife and the already threatened or endangered species are their priority victims. As a result, many species have either reached the brink of local extinction or have become threatened or vulnerable. Faunal wealth like the Red Fox, Chukor Partridge, Cheer Pheasant and Indian Peafowl, are threatened. Snow Leopard, Fishing Cat, Pangolin, Monal Pheasant, Hornbill, Indian Python, Indian Wild Dog among others are some members of the endangered species.

V. Other Environmental Concerns

Besides discussing the state of the environment in terms of the environmental components of land, water and fauna, it is also important to focus on certain other phenomena which are occurring in the region, as a result of the environmental degradation. Primary among them are: (i) the climatic changes, which are being brought about mainly due to the degradation of the forests, and (ii) the increasing incidence of natural calamities or disasters.

(i) Climatic Variations

The most pronounced effect on climatic conditions, arising out of the degradation of vegetation and soil erosion is the variation in diurnal temperature. There is a marked rise in the average maximum temperature, whereas the average minimum temperature is falling. This is primarily due to the fact that while a good vegetative cover exerts a moderating physical and physiological effect on the climate, with a loss of vegetative cover, this effect is diminished, leading to climate changes. Besides temperature changes, a drop in local relative humidity and precipitation has also occurred due to the degradation of the forest cover, leading to instability in rains. This in turn has led to recurrent drought like situations and periodic floods, which have been experienced by the region in the last few years. Besides, an increase in the average temperatures is also linked to the increasing frequency of forest fires in the region, due to which vast stretches of forests have been destroyed within hours.

(ii) Natural Disasters

Increase in the frequency of natural disasters is another matter of concern for the region. Natural processes like earthquakes and avalanches cause a lot of damage to the environment of the region. There is increasing evidence which suggests that they have been created due to excessive tampering with the environment.

As far as earthquakes are concerned, the Himalayan chain lies in a seismologically active belt. There have been thousands of earthquake shocks, of which quite a few of the recorded ones have been very destructive. The Uttarkashi Earthquake in 1991 was an extremely destructive earthquake, which struck Uttarkashi and the adjoining Tehri Garhwal. There was widespread loss of life and property. Thousands of people were rendered homeless and standing agricultural crops were completely destroyed. For months, relief operations had to be carried out to alleviate the sufferings of the people. Another massive earthquake hit the region on 28th March, 1999 (the 30th in terms of number of earthquakes in the Central Himalayas). This earthquake was more powerful in terms of intensity than the 1991 one, but caused less damage as its epicenter was located at a greater depth. A number of big cracks had appeared in the mountains, which continue to present a continuous threat to the villagers, especially those living in villages located below the cracks.

Avalanches are another type of natural phenomena which are becoming a cause of concern for the ecology of the region. In terms of the frequency of occurrence, mass, energy and magnitude, the snow avalanches are showing an increased presence. They cause damage to the environment as they scour the hill slopes, particularly when boulders and rocks move with the mass of snow. After the snow melts, the gullies formed by avalanches are exposed to accelerated erosion. Avalanches also cause considerable damage to human life and property in forested areas. They damage large chunks of forests, thus destroying valuable forest resources.

Environmental Policies, Legislations and Programmes

Having examined the state of the environment of the study locale, it is now essential to describe and analyze the initiatives of the governmental and non-governmental agencies and groups, in dealing with the problems and issues discussed in the earlier section.

This section highlights the important policies and legislations relevant for the environmental conservation of the area. It also describes and analyses the important environmental programmes in terms of their objectives, thrust, and scope for people's participation. The policies, acts, rules and regulations promulgated by the central and state governments related to environment shall provide the context for peoples' participation in environmental action.

I. Policy Framework

Although efforts are being made by the government as well as the voluntary sector, a comprehensive policy framework covering all areas of environmental concern which may enable taking an integrated view of all environmental issues and formulating an 'Environmental Plan' for the country has not emerged. It has been so, partly because 'environment' is all pervading, and almost every sector of the economy has an environmental component and environmental problems peculiar to it. Moreover, there has been an apparent failure to clearly conceive and comprehend the comprehensiveness of the concept of environment which has resulted in the absence of a comprehensive 'environmental policy' even after six decades of planned development.

An attempt has been made here to present the important policy parameters relating to specific sectors which emerged from various documents. The sectors which had a direct bearing upon environmental preservation were—Forestry, Water Resources, Land use and Wildlife. A brief description of the policies pertaining to these sectors is presented here.

1. National Forest Policy, 1988

The first National Forest Policy was announced in 1894, in which forests were declared state property and they were considered important from the environmental and commercial point of view.

By the year 1952, the population had increased by 40 per cent and the biotic pressure on forest was increasing. It was in this year that the second National Forest Policy was announced in which emphasis was laid on regulated use of forest; control of soil erosion in the catchment areas in the hills; benefit for the local people; protection of the forests; meeting the raw material requirements of industries; etc. This policy also stated that one-third of the geographical area should be under forests of which two-thirds should be in the hills.. This policy also laid emphasis on wild life protection, and, as a result the 'Wild Life Protection Act, 1972' came to be enacted. To put on effective check on the conversion of forest land into non-forest land the 'Forest Conservation Act, 1980' was enacted. However, the increasing demand for fuel and fodder, insufficient conservation efforts and the continued demand for forest land for non-forestry purposes led to the formulation of the third 'National Forest Policy, 1988'. In this policy, environmental protection and ecological balance had been given emphasis. It also brought into focus the National parks, Sanctuaries and Protected Areas. Besides, adequate emphasis was given to ecological balance; soil conservation; water conservation; wildlife protection; social forestry; agro-forestry, forest research and education.

This policy, for the first time mentioned the importance of the involvement of people in the protection and management of forests. In 1988, the, erstwhile state of undivided Uttar Pradesh also announced its 'State Forest Policy'. The Policy seeks to protect and enhance the yields of non timber forest products in order to generate employment and income for forest and village communities.

Subsequently, the Uttaranchal government (initially the official name of the state was Uttaranchal) drafted its own 'Uttaranchal State Forest Policy, 2001', to achieve the objectives of the National Forest Policy. The main objectives of the state policy were: (i) To ensure the environmental stability of the region and to prepare and implement suitable plans for the conservation of the rich bio-diversity in flora and fauna of the region; (ii) To protect the forest, forest land and promote afforestation in vacant and degraded lands, as also in catchment areas of rivers, lakes and water bodies; (iii) To develop programmes of soil conservation and water conservation to ameliorate drought conditions and the siltation of water bodies; (iv) To provide of the meeting of fuel, fodder and small timber needs of the rural poor and to promote and encourage non-conventional energy sources to relieve pressure on forests; (iv) To promote people's participation in the protection and management of the forest through the strengthening of Van Panchayats, Joint Forest Management, and to provide a special focus on women's participation.

2. National Water Policy, 1987

Recognizing water as a precious natural resource, the policy embodied the nation's resolve to plan and develop water resources, keeping the national perspective in mind. Water being a scarce resource, its use needed to be planned, and the resource needed to be developed and conserved, in an integrated and environmentally sound manner. Various measures had been recommended which included: (i) primacy of preservation of the quality of the environment and ecological balance in the planning and implementation of projects and minimization of adverse impact on environment; (ii) monitoring of quality of surface and ground water, and improvement in the same; (iii) sound watershed management through extensive soil conservation, catchment area treatment, preservation of forests, increasing the forest area, and the construction of check dams (to reduce the intensity of floods); and (v) promotion of conservation consciousness through education, regulation, incentives and disincentives.

3. National Land Use Policy (1988)

This policy aimed at the development of land resources and the promotion of appropriate land use. The main objectives of the policy were: (i) to prevent deterioration of land resources; (ii) to restore productivity of degraded lands by an appropriate package of practices; (iii) to involve the community in the adoption of proper land use, by ensuring the meeting of their energy needs; (iv) to restructure livestock production programme so as to prevent degradation of grasslands and; (v) to coordinate the formulation and implementation of water resource management policies and forest management policies with overall resource allocation needs.

4. Wildlife Conservation Strategy, 2002

The Wildlife Strategy adopted by the country aims to protect wildlife and wildlife habitat. The main provisions of the strategy include: (i) declaration of wildlife and forests as priority areas at the national level; (ii) enforcement of law for the prevention of poaching, illicit trade in wildlife and wildlife activities, by provision of quick and deterrent punishment; (iii) protection of interests of the poor and tribals living around protected areas, by ensuring access to minor forest produce in the forest outside protected areas and employment, and encouraging their participation in afforestation and conservation; (iv) provision of societal recognition and support to the non-governmental organisations engaged in wildlife conservation; (v) prohibition on diversion of forest land for non-forest purposes from critical and ecologically fragile wildlife habitat; (iv) declaration of eco-fragile zones under relevant sections of the Environment Protection Act and associated Rules; (vii) prevention of the introduction of monocultures to replace natural forests; (viii) removal of encroachments and illegal activities from within forest lands and protected areas; (ix) mitigation measures for human-animal conflicts and mechanism for crop insurance; and (x) setting up of a Forest Commission to look into restructuring reform and strengthening the forest set-up and affiliated institutions.

5. National Resettlement and Rehabilitation Policy, 2007

Prior to this policy evolution, there was no uniform approach adopted by states towards the project affected population, as there were no safeguard policy to deal with resettlement and rehabilitation of displaced persons in the country. In the absence of such policy, ad-hoc administrative instructions, in conformity with the Land Acquisition Act were in practice. This policy was developed and promulgated by the Government of India during October 2007 and takes into consideration the safeguard policies of international development bodies like the World Bank, Asian Development Bank etc. The salient features of this policy are: (1) Makes SIA mandatory for all projects involving displacement of four hundred or more families, en-masse in plain areas, or two hundred or more families, en-masse in tribal or hilly areas etc.; (2) Public hearing co-ordination with EIA done in the project affected area shall also cover issues related to SIA; (3) Consultations with affected people and disclosure of relevant information to them at various stages of resettlement planning; (4) Assistance to affected people without legal rights; affected people categorized as landless agricultural workers, forest dwellers, tenants and artisans who are critically dependent on the acquired assets for their subsistence/livelihoods; (5) Preparation of resettlement plans that are disclosed to the affected people in draft form, and reviewed and approved by competent authorities; (6) Collection of socio-economic base line information of the project affected households; (7) Vulnerable project affected people to get extra cash/kind assistance; (8) The Grievance Redress Cell shall have representatives of women, Scheduled Castes, Scheduled Tribes residing in the affected zone. The Cell shall have the power to consider and dispose of all complaints relating to resettlement and rehabilitation against the decision of the Administrator/R and R Committee at Project level; and (9) Each project affected family comprising of rural artisan/small trader and self-employed person shall get one-time financial assistance for construction of working shed/shop for livelihood support.

II. Legislative Framework

The policy framework lays the foundation for the enactment of laws and rules for the protection and promotion of the environment. In the post-independence period, the decade of fifties and sixties did not see any significant movement pertaining to environmental legislation in India. This was primarily because the realization of the significance of the environment and its two-way linkage with development was slow in coming. It was only in the early seventies that the 'UN Conference on Human Environment' in 1972 led to the establishment of the National Committee on Environmental Planning and Coordination, which in turn led to recommendations for legislative measures and administrative machinery for environmental protection. Consequently, a spate of legislations relating to forests, water, air, and wildlife were formulated/ amended.

As far as the hill region under study is concerned, the relevant environmental legislation pertained primarily to forests, wildlife and water.

1. Legislation pertaining to Environment

As forests occupy the most important position in the environment of the country in general, and hill regions, in particular, a number of legislations and rules pertain to the forests. At this time, there were around 42 Acts and Rules related to the forests. They comprise of both Central and State Laws. The primary legislative framework for the control, protection and use of forest land and forest resources in Uttarakhand was provided by the two main Central laws which applied to the state of Uttarakhand (and earlier to undivided Uttar Pradesh) or had been adopted by the state for implementation. Besides the central legislation, the state of Uttar Pradesh had also enacted a number of state legislations for the control, protection and use of forests, which continued to apply to the state of Uttarakhand. The new state had also enacted a few new laws and enactments to replace the earlier laws applicable to its areas (when they were a part of U.P. State.) Table 4.9 presents a list of environmental legislations applicable to Uttarakhand:

Table 4.9: Main Environmental Legislations Applicable to the Region

Category	*Nomenclature of Legislations*
A. Central Acts	The Environment Protection Act, 1986.
	Water and Air (Prevention and Control) of Pollution Act, 1974 and 1981.
	The Indian Forest Act, 1927.
	The Forest (Conservation) Act, 1980.
	The Wildlife Protection Act, 1972.
	EIA Notification of MoEF 2006.
	The Ancient Monuments, Archaeological sites and Remains Act, 2010.
	Biological Diversity Act 2002, Biological Diversity Rules 2004.
	The Land Acquisition (LA) Act of 1894.
	The Scheduled Tribes and Other Traditional Forest Dwellers (Recognition of Forests Rights) Act, 2006.
	The Right to Fair Compensation and Transparency in Land Acquisition and Resettlement Act, 2013.
B. State Legislation (enacted by undivided U.P. State and applicable to Uttarakhand State)	Uttar Pradesh Forest Corporation Act. 1974.
	Tree Protection Act, 1974.
	U.P. Resin and Other Forest Produce (Regulations of Trade) Act, 1976.
	U.P. Tendu Patta (Vyapar Viniyaman) Adhiniyam.
	U.P. Establishment and Regulation of Saw Mills Rules, 1978
	U.P. National Parks Act, 1935.
	U.P. National Parks Rules, 1935.
	U.P. Transit of Timber and Other Forest Produce Rules, 1972.
C. State Legislation (enacted by the state of Uttaranchal, later called Uttarakhand)	The Uttaranchal Amendment to Indian Forest Act, 2002
	Uttaranchal Panchayati Forest Rules, 2001
	The Uttaranchal Village Forest Management Rules, 2001.

The scope of the important environment regulations and their implications are briefly furnished in the following section:

1. *The Environment (Protection) Act No.29 of 1986*: Under this Act, the central government is empowered to take measures necessary to protect and improve the quality of the environment by setting standards for emissions and discharges; regulating the location of industries; management of hazardous wastes, and protection of public health and welfare. This encompasses all legislations providing for the protection of environment in the country. It includes the power to direct the closure, prohibition or regulation of any industry, operation or process by the government.
2. *Water and Air (Prevention and Control of Pollution) Act, 1974 and 1981 (Central Act 6 of 1974) as amended in 1988*: This Act provides for the prevention and control of water pollution and the maintaining or restoring of the wholesomeness of water. The Act empowers the Central Government to appoint and constitute a Central Pollution Control Board, and the State Governments to appoint and constitute the State Pollution Control Boards for the prevention, control and abatement of water pollution. The legislation encompasses detailed provisions related to the constitution of the Boards, powers, duties and functions of the Boards and special provisions dealing with the prevention, control and abatement of water pollution.
   This Act prohibits the discharge of pollutants into water bodies beyond a given standard and lays down penalties for non-compliance. Water act includes the maintenance or restoring the wholesomeness of the water. Air act restricts the operation of any industrial plant in an air pollution control area without a valid consent.
3. *The Indian Forest Act, 1927:* This Act empowers the state Government to constitute any forest land or wasteland, which is the property of the Government or over which the Government had proprietary rights, as a reserve forest. It also prohibits alienation of rights accrued by way of grant, sale, lease, and mortgage or otherwise, without the sanction of the State Government. It empowers the Forest officer and prohibits acts like making clearings, felling, lopping, girdling, tapping or burning etc. in the forest. The Act also provides for the formation of 'Village Forest' by the State Government, as also to declare any forest/wasteland (not included in a reserve forest), as 'Protected forest'.
   The State of Uttaranchal enacted 'The Uttaranchal Amendment to Indian Forest Act 2002, for the implementation of the Indian Forest Act, 1927 in the state of Uttaranchal. This Amendment provides for

more stringent punishment for offenders in certain offence cases like: increase in maximum penalty, both in terms of fines and imprisonment; enhanced powers to DFOs to confiscate vehicles, tools, arms etc. used in the commission of crime and to order vacation of encroachment.

4. *The Forest (Conservation) Act, 1980, and amended in 1988*: This Act provides for the conservation of forests and provides restrictions on the de reservation of forests by any State Government or other authority, except with the prior approval of the Central Government, as also on the use of any forest land for any non-forest use. The Central Government is empowered to constitute a committee to advice the government with regard to the grant of approval for the above. The latest Amendment to the Act, in 1988 deemed it illegal for any agency, other than the State Government, to engage in afforestation projects without permission from the Central Government.
5. *Joint Forest Management, 1993*: Joint Forest Management induces peoples' participation in forest management sharing mechanism, in order to distribute the benefits of interventions carried out on the common resources property, government lands, and wastelands. Benefits are categorized into two: ecological benefits and economic benefits.
6. *The Wildlife (Protection) Act, 1972, Amendment 1991*: This Act provides for protection to listed species of Flora and Fauna in the declared network of ecologically important protected areas such as wild life sanctuaries and national parks. The wildlife protection act has allowed the government to establish a number of national Parks and Sanctuaries, over the past 25 years, to protect and conserve the flora and fauna of the state. This Act provides for the protection of wild animals, birds and plants, with a view to ensuring the ecological and environmental security of the country. It prohibits hunting of wild animals and provides protection for specified plants. It deals with protected areas and empowers the state governments to declare the constitution of national parks and prohibit a person from destroying, exploiting or removing any wildlife from the same.
7. *EIA Notification of MoEF 2006*: All projects listed under Schedule-I of the Notification require environmental clearance from the MoEF. The list of project categories under Schedule I of the Environmental Impact assessment Notification is available on the MoEF Website.
8. *Biological Diversity Act 2002, Biological Diversity Rules 2004*: The Biological Diversity Act, which came into force in February 2003, aims to promote conservation, sustainable use and equitable sharing of benefits of India's biodiversity resources. It provides for

establishment of a National Biodiversity Authority at national level, State Biodiversity Boards at state level and Biodiversity Management Committees at the level of Panchayats and Municipalities.

9. *The Land Acquisition (LA) Act of 1894*: The Land Acquisition (LA) Act of 1984 is commonly used for acquisition of land for any public purpose. It is used at the State level with State amendments made to suit local requirements. Expropriation of and compensation for land, houses and other immovable assets are carried out under the Land Acquisition (Amendment) Act, 1984. The Act deals with compulsory acquisition of private land for public purpose.

   The 1984 amendments to the LA Act addressed the matter of compensation and delays in payment. As regards, the level of compensation, the rate of solatium was increased from 15 per cent to 30 per cent. For delays, the amendment requires that a time of one year be fixed for completing all formalities between the issuance of Section 4 and Section 6; and that the compensation award must be determined within two years of the issuing of section 6 notification. Interest is payable at a rate of 12 per cent per year from the date of preliminary notification to the date of dispossession. These changes apply to cases before the Civil Courts even for awards made before the enactment of the amendments.

10. *The Scheduled Tribes and Other Traditional Forest Dwellers (Recognition of Forests Rights) Act, 2006*: The Scheduled Tribes (Recognition of Forest Rights) Bill, 2005 which was re-christened as "The Scheduled Tribes and Other Traditional Forest Dwellers (Recognition of Forest Rights) Act, 2006" was passed in the parliament, lower house of Indian parliament, on 13 December 2006. The Ministry of Tribal Affairs is the nodal agency for implementing the provisions of the Scheduled Tribes and Other Traditional Forest Dwellers (Recognition of Forest Rights) Act, 2006. The Act seeks to recognize and vest the forest rights and occupation in forest land in forest dwelling Scheduled Tribes and other traditional forest dwellers who have been residing in such forests for generations but whose rights could not be recorded. The Act was notified for operation with effect from 31.12.2007. The Scheduled Tribes and other Traditional Forest Dwellers (Recognition of Forest Rights) Rules, 2008 for implementing the provisions of the Act have also been notified. As per the provisions of the Act and the Rules framed there under, the onus of implementation of the Act lies at the level of the State/UT Governments. The Act seeks to recognize and vest certain forest rights in the forest dwelling Scheduled Tribes and other traditional forest dwellers. To ensure that the intended benefits of

this welfare legislation flow to the eligible forest dwellers, comprehensive guidelines to the State/UT Governments on for better implementation of the Act have been issued

11. *The Right to Fair Compensation and Transparency in Land Acquisition and Resettlement Act 2013*: This is an act which has replaced both the Land Acquisition Act 1894 and National Resettlement and Rehabilitation Policy 2007. This act has ensured, in consultation with institutions of local self-government and Gram Sabhas established under the Constitution, a humane, participative, informed and transparent process for land acquisition for industrialisation, development of essential infrastructural facilities and urbanisation, with the least disturbance to the owners of the land and other affected families. It intends to provide a just and fair compensation to the affected families whose land has been acquired or proposed to be acquired or are affected by such acquisition and strives to make adequate provisions for such affected persons, for their rehabilitation and resettlement and for ensuring that the cumulative outcome of the compulsory acquisition should be that affected persons become partners in development leading to an improvement in their post acquisition social and economic status and for matters connected therewith or incidental thereto.

Besides the aforementioned main legislations, The Mines and Minerals Act, 1982; and, The Cattle Trespass Act, 1871, also apply to the region.

As far as state legislations are concerned, a number of Acts pertaining to undivided Uttar Pradesh continued to apply to Uttaranchal. These include: the U.P Forest Corporation Act, 1974, providing for the establishment of a Forest Development Corporation to departmentalize the commercial harvesting and working of the forests. Subsequently, the state of Uttaranchal established its own Uttaranchal Forest Corporation, in the year 2001 in line with the Act. This Corporation had assumed work related to commercial harvesting and working of the state forests with effect from its year of establishment. The Tree Protection Act, 1974 was enacted to prevent individuals from felling marketable species of trees for timber (classified as protected species by the Forest Department) on their own land without obtaining permission from the Forest Department. The U.P Fruit Nurseries (Regulation) Rules, 1976, provided for licensing and regulation of fruit nurseries in the state. Another important legislation, The U.P Resin and Other Forest Produce (Regulation of Trade) Act, 1976 provided for the carrying on by the state for the trade of purchase and distribution of resin to the exclusion of others, and for the regulation of manufacture and preparation of various articles based on forest produce. The U.P. Tendu Patta (Vyapar Viniyaman) Adhiniyam, 1972 provided for the creation of state monopoly in the purchase and distribution of tendu leaves. Besides these state laws, the ban on commercial felling of green trees above 1000 meters in 1980 was one of the most important restrictions (which are in operation even today).

It is important to note that almost all of the aforementioned state laws applicable to the state have led to the creation of state monopoly in forest management and in the purchase and distribution of a number of forest products, together with the objective of providing protection to the forest. The other State Laws applicable to the State are: U.P Establishment and Regulation of Saw Mills Rules, 1978; U.P. National Parks Act, 1935; U.P National Parks Rules, 1935; and U.P Transit of Timber and other Forest Produce Rules, 1972.

Besides these Acts, the state of Uttarakhand had also enacted new laws and enactments to replace the earlier laws applicable to its areas (when they were a part of U.P. state). These were: (1) Uttaranchal Panchayati Forest Rules, 2001, which regulate the formation and functioning of Van Panchayats in Uttaranchal. The Uttaranchal State Government notified these Rules on 3rd July, 2001, by making amendments to the Van Panchayat Rules of 1976. The Uttaranchal Panchayati Forest Rules, 2001, originated from the Indian Forest Act, 1927. The constitution and composition, term, power, and duties, budget and accounts and all other aspects related to the functioning of the Van Panchayats are now entailed in the provisions of these Rules; and (2) The Uttaranchal Village Forest Management Rules, 2001, which have replaced the U.P. Village Forest Joint Management Rules, 1997. The Rules provide for joint management of 'Village Forests' by the Joint Forest Management Committee (JFMC) and the officers of the Forest Department. The Rules aim to devolve forest management through restructuring of the state-community roles within the stipulated land use and forest policy framework for nurturing democratic, gender-equal, self-governing community institutions.

Van Panchayats and Van Panchayat Rules

The central Himalayas of India are renowned not only for their natural resources, but also for natural resource based agitations and their indigenous traditional forest management system. The State of Uttarakhand (formerly Uttaranchal) has been a precursor in participatory management of common natural forest resources and the traditional Van Panchayat system can be credited with deepening the bond between the people and their forests. The Van Panchayat system originated out of conflicts and compromises that followed the settlement and reservation of forests in the region at the turn of the 19th century. The history of Van Panchayats in the central Himalayas dates back to the beginning of British colonial rule in the early 1800s. After the defeat of the Gurkhas in 1815, British occupation of central Himalayas was complete. The British rulers progressively curtailed the area of forests under the control of local communities (Guha, 1991). At the same time, they also enacted elaborate rules specifying strict restrictions on the logging of fodder trees and grazing rights, prohibited agricultural extension, sought to regulate the use of fire that villagers believed led to higher grass production, and strengthened the number of official forest guards (Pant, 1992). These rules sowed the seeds of discontent among local people. The curbs on the rights of local people to use forest products resulted in opposition to the government in the hills of Kumaun and Garhwal. These social protests culminated in the summer of 1921, when a wide-ranging campaign to burn forests controlled by the government virtually paralyzed the administration in these hills. This forced the government to appoint the Kumaun Forest Grievance Committee to look into the demands of the local population. More than 30 recommendations were made by the committee (Aggarwal, 1996).

On the basis of these recommendations, the State Government passed the Forest Panchayat Act (Forest Councils Act) of 1931. This Act empowered villagers to form relatively autonomous (at local level) management committees for hill forests. This devolution of powers to control and manage forest for subsistence purpose is the earliest example of comanagement of natural resources by the state and local communities in India. Since then, Van Panchayats or Forest Panchayats have been incorporated under Section 28(2) of the Indian Forest Act, 1927. Their objectives are to protect and develop forests and distribute their produce among stakeholders in an equitable manner. Till the year 2011, about 12,064 Van Panchayats had been established in Uttarakhand. These Van Panchayats manage a forest area of about 5,23289 hectares forming about 14 per cent of the total area of the state in eleven hill districts (administrative units) in the State of Uttarakhand: Chamoli, Pauri, Tehri, Uttarkashi, Dehradun, Rudraprayag, Nainital, Almora, Pithoragarh, Champawat and Bageshwar (Forest Department, 2011). Most of the Panchayat forests provide the villagers with important subsistence benefits such as fodder, leaves for animals bedding, grazing space for their animals, fuelwood, and timber for house construction and agricultural implements.

As per the Van Panchayat Rules, villagers themselves make the rules for day-to-day management. These rules relate to monitoring, dispute resolution mechanisms, selection of guards for enforcement of rules, fines for rule breakers, management of finances, equitable distribution of usufructs, and use of surplus earnings for the community. However, the Van Panchayat Rules, while making Van Panchayats responsible for proper management of the forests, deny them the necessary authority and financial autonomy, which is vested with revenue and forest officials. The Forest Department is responsible for providing technical help to the villagers and it must be consulted before harvesting forest produce such as resin and timber. The officials of the Revenue

Department are consulted for the enforcement of rules and sanctions if recalcitrant villagers refuse to follow local directives. However, there has been continuous decline in the authority of Van Panchayats since their inception in 1931. A number of forest officials have been assigned the task of looking after the affairs of Van Panchayats under the Van Panchayat regulation 2005, thus reducing the power of elected committees of Van Panchayats and handing control of management of Panchayat forests to the Forest Department. Similarly, the Divisional Forest Officer (DFO), who sits far away from the real situation, has been given the responsibility of formulating the management plan where the Panchayat forest exists. As a result, Van Panchayat does not play any role in the management plan. As per the Van Panchayat regulation 2005, the DFO must approve every rule made by the Van Panchayat committee. During the last 80 years, there have been three major changes in Van Panchayat rules-in 1976, 2001 and 2005—which have changed the original concept of formation of Van Panchayats. It has therefore become imperative to compare the successive rules. This study attempts to review the policy implication of decline in the authority of Van Panchayats in light of the successive Van Panchayat rules made during 80 years of their existence.

Analysis of Legal Framework

1. An analysis of the existing central and state legislations shows that in terms of number, a multitude of enactments exist. While some main acts are centrally enacted, the rest, (especially those pertaining to forests) are state enacted legislations. Most legislation, however, caters to forests and forestry, either directly or indirectly. Six central acts cater to 'non-forest' environmental components like wildlife, land and water. This centrality of forest-related legislation is however, quite expected as forests form the backbone of environmental management in this region.

2. As far as the nature of forests related legislation is concerned, there are more state enacted legislations emphasizing the commercial use of forests and forest resources. Thus, besides promoting the objective of protection of forests, most state laws lead to the creation of state monopoly in forest management, and in the purchase and distribution of a number of forest products.

3. Most forest related acts also push for progressive restrictions on the local use of forest resources. For example, 'The Indian Forest Act', 'The Forest Conservation Act', the ban on felling, monopoly controls over timber and commercially valuable NTFPs all pose restrictions on the rights of the local people to procure usage of forest products. Large scale livelihood and resource displacement has been caused by the expansion of the protected area network. Laws have also led to the reduction in area eligible for inclusion under 'village forests' due to class I reserves being taken out of the village

boundaries. The classification of natural grasslands as 'forests', under the management of the Forest Department, have changed the land-use and the nature of forests. The resource base available for sustaining livelihoods has diminished greatly, even while population has increased manifold. Thus, it is quite evident that the main thrust of forest legislation has been on centralized forest management based on a conservationist ideology. They have led to changing people's attitudes towards forests and undermining the incentives for community forest management.

4. The central level enactments are few in number and are wider in terms of perspective, as compared to state legislations which are more specific in terms of objectives and scope.

5. A changing pattern is emerging in the orientation of legislations in the more recent context, as legislations focusing on the provision of a greater scope for community participation in the protection and management of the forests is being introduced. The 'U.P. Panchayati Forest Rules, 1972,' and subsequently the 'Uttaranchal Panchayati Forest Rules, 2001' provided for the system of Van Panchayats and ' Village Forests' (due to selective implementation in certain areas only, these community-based institutions were non-existent in Tehri Garhwal till as late as 1997-98, in spite of the fact that this district had a significant forest cover). Uttar Pradesh State (undivided) was a late starter of Joint Forest Management and only passed its JFM Resolution in the year 1996. The 'Uttaranchal Village Forests Joint Management Rules, 2001' aim at the decentralization of powers to the communities and providing a sound legal foundation for community participation in forest management and protection.

6. Intensive interaction with the environmentalists and functionaries of voluntary organisations however revealed a contradictory perspective. They feared that there were hidden dangers in the state driven devolution in the form of the new Van Panchayat formation and JFM Rules. They felt that in the name of devolution, VFJM had empowered the Forest Department to reassert control over Van Panchayat Forests and Civil/Soyam lands, the only surviving village commons. Instead of validating the rich diversity of indigenous knowledge of the local people to manage their forests, VFJM Rules reinforce the monopoly of the Forest Department, in many ways.

Programmes of Environmental Protection and Promotion

In this section, a description and analysis of the environmental programmes and initiatives of the government, voluntary organisations, women's and youth groups, local activists and Van Panchayats shall be undertaken.

1. Governmental Programmes

There were three broad categories of government programmes. These were:

(i) Central Sector Programmes/Schemes and Centrally Sponsored Schemes; (ii) State Sector Schemes; and (iii) District Level Schemes.

A list of the important programmes and schemes under the central, state and district sectors is provided by Table 4.10.

Table 4.10: Governmental Environmental Programmes Being Implemented in the Region

S. No	*Category*	*Name of Scheme/Programme*
A.	Central Schemes/ Programmes	The National Wasteland Development Programme (NWDP), which consists of two Schemes:
		Rural Fuel wood Plantation Scheme.
		Integrated Soil, Water and Tree Conservation in the Himalayas. (Operation SOILWATCH).
		Integrated Watershed Development Project (IWDP).
		Area-Oriented Fuel wood and Fodder Projects Scheme.
		Plantation/Afforestation in the Catchment of Tehri Dam.
		Afforestation under 20 Point Programme.
		Uttarakhand State Action Plan for Climate Change
		Integrated Afforestation and Eco-Development Projects Scheme (IAEPS).
		Samanvit Gram Vanikaran Samirdhi Yojana (SGVSY) and creation of Forest Development Agency (FDA).
		Sindhughati Pariyojana
		Modern Forest Fire Control Programme.
		Integrated Watershed Management in Catchments of Flood-Prone Rivers.
		Sampoorna Grameen Rojgar Yojana (Total Rural Employment Scheme):
		National Rural Employment Guarantee Scheme (NREGS):
		Promotion of Non-Conventional Energy *Sources*.
B.	State Sector Programmes/ Schemes	Uttar Pradesh Forestry Project.
		Forest Protection Programme.
		Creation of Van Chetna Kendras.
		Mahila Vikas Yojana.
		Development of Soyam Forests.
		Uttarakhand Rural Water Supply and Environmental Sanitation Project (Swajal).
		Uttarakhand Disaster Recovery Project
C.	District Level Schemes and Activities	Multipurpose Plantation Scheme.
		Natural Regeneration Scheme by Biotic Fencing (Pandit Deendayal Upadhyay Biotic Fencing Scheme).
		Van Sanchar Sadhan Scheme.
		Conservation and Development of Medicinal Plants.
		Wildlife Protection Scheme
		Production of Bio-Fertilizers
		Celebration of Environment Day, Wildlife Week, Fire Protection Week.

An analysis of the government environmental Programmes operational in the area reveals the following important points:

1. The governmental programmes are mostly Central Schemes, that is, either Central Sector Schemes or Centrally Sponsored Schemes (eleven ongoing Schemes). Besides, there are six State Sector Schemes. Out of these, two schemes are externally-funded schemes. viz. Swajal Project and 'Uttar Pradesh Forestry Project'. Only six schemes and environment related activities like celebration of Environment Day, Wildlife Week etc. are district level programmes. This indicates that most of the environment initiatives of the government have been conceived and planned at the central level and followed a top-down approach. Decisions are taken at far away centers, and local concerns, problems and priorities are rarely taken into account. The state level schemes also follow a similar approach. Furthermore, the two externally funded schemes being sponsored by international organisations have been determined and designed by the external agencies, which are even more far removed from the ground reality situation than the central and state governments.

2. The programmes have been planned and implemented by a multitude of government ministries and departments, like: Forests, Agriculture, Horticulture, Soil Conservation, and Minor Irrigation. Consequently, the lack of an integrated approach to environmental planning and implementation was quite apparent. Moreover, there is a poor coordination between the different departments. This is evident from the lack of information available at different state/district level departments about each other's programmes.

3. Most governmental programmes are programmes of afforestation and tree plantation. Forest protection and natural regeneration is not given much importance, except in case of fire protection and a few other schemes. A due emphasis on the promotion and encouragement to the non-conventional energy sources has been found to be lacking. According to the people and the environmentalists, this component really needs to be focused upon, as only the development of suitable alternatives would greatly contribute towards saving the valuable forests from destruction.

4. Most programmes have little/no scope for community participation and are exclusive government initiatives. The programmes fail to integrate the traditional people's organisations and groups into their programmes. They are mostly based on a beneficiary-oriented approach.

5. In those government programmers which do incorporate an element of community participation, the emphasis has been on the creation of new people's institutions like VFMCs, FDAs etc. from time to time, instead of relying on the traditional and already available groups/organisations.

6. The externally funded programmers have been time bound programmes with no assurance of continuity. For example, the JFM programme was funded by the World Bank and was planned for a period of four years. Subsequently, a review of the programme determined the future of funding and hence the continuity of the programme.

2. Programmes of People's Groups and Organisations

Before studying the contemporary environmental initiatives of the people's groups and organisations, it is necessary to develop a broad understanding of the rich history of voluntary action in the region. This includes a study of the traditional community management of natural resources, especially forests in the Pre-Independence period; people's action to resist the commercial exploitation of their forests in the form of peasant uprisings; as also the broad-based people's movements viz. Chipko and Anti-Tehri Dam Movements in the Post-Independence period. This is attempted in the following section.

A. Traditional Community Management of Forests

The primary thrust and focus of environmental initiatives in the region has been on forests, since they comprise the main environmental component. Protection and management of the forests has always been a prime consideration for the people, even during the pre-British times. At that time the forests were the property of the monarch, but people enjoyed full rights over their usage. People show a high degree of dependence on the forests, but are also aware of the need to protect them and use them sustainably. Culture accords a high value to nature, and rituals related to them are zealously followed. A love for nature forms the very basis of the sub-conscious of the Garhwali society at large, and forests form an integral part of the socio-cultural ethos. Through religion, folklore and tradition, the village communities have drawn a protective ring around the forest. There exists a highly sophisticated system of conservancy that takes various forms, thereby keeping the resource-base intact. One such dominant form is the prevalence of 'sacred groves'. Often hill tops are devoted to local deities and the trees around the spot regarded with great respect. These sacred groves have a major functional role in stabilizing water flows and preventing land slides. In these groves, no villager can injure the vegetation in any way. Infact, planting a grove is regarded as a work of great religious merit.

While the traditional religious values contribute to the preservation of nature, often informal practices regulate the utilization of forest produce by the community. Customary restrictions on the use of forests operate over large areas, although no formal management exists. For example, in many oak forests, rules prohibited the lopping of trees in the hot weather. In these forests, within village boundaries called 'banjanis', branches of trees are cut only at specific times, and even then with the permission of the entire village community. Even the grass cut by each family is strictly regulated, and the penalty for the infringement of rules includes social boycott and/or exclusion of the offender from the forest.

Every village in the hills has fixed boundaries existing from the time of the pre-Gurkha rulers (and recognized subsequently by G.W. Traill in the settlement of 1823, also called sal-assi boundaries). Within these limits the villagers exercise various proprietary and other rights of grazing and fuel, secured by long usage and custom. Traditionally speaking, many villages have fuel reserves even on 'gaon sanjait' (common land), which the villagers cut in regular rotation by common consent. They amicably graze their flocks and fetch wood from the common forest and pasture land without any dispute, thus exhibiting cooperation of a very high order.

The existence of collective action among the hill communities is mainly due to: (i) the absence of serious economic differences and presence of social solidarity (due to ties of kinship and caste shared by villagers). The diluted caste system, absence of sharp class divisions and strong community solidarity make the hill society an exception to the pattern of social hierarchy elsewhere in India; (ii) The institution of panchayat has been stronger here and these deal with social disputes and all other matters, with every adult member having a voice in its affairs; and (iii) The ecological constraints and extreme reliance on natural resources for this mountain society has resulted in a close regulation of the common properly resources, so crucial for the subsistence economy of individual households. Thus, the system of resource use has become an integral, seemingly permanent part of the social fabric.

B. Early Peasant Uprisings: Resistance to Commercial Forestry

A new phase in the economic life of Garhwal started in 1851, when following the victory of the British in the Gorkha War, Garhwal was divided into two parts. The western part, comprising of what currently constitutes the Tehri-Garhwal and Uttarkashi districts, came to be identified as the princely state of Tehri. The eastern part comprising of the present Chamoli and Garhwal districts, came to be known as British Garhwal and became a part of British India. The British annexation led to the beginning of the commercial exploitation of Garhwal's forests marking an absolutely new phase in the socio-economic history of Garhwal, and ultimately leading to the emergence of forest conflicts.

Despite being in the hands of the local ruler, the condition of the Tehri forests worsened. One Mr. Wilson, an enterprising Englishman, obtained the lease for exploiting all the forest of Tehri Garhawal in 1950, from the Tehri state for a paltry annual fee of ₹ 400. By using the rivers Bhagirathi and Yamuna to transport timber downstream to the Indian plains, he enhanced the accessibility of the hitherto inaccessible Tehri forest. Thereafter, the British government entered directly into a contract with the Tehri state in 1865 for long term felling rights. In 1885, the Raja of Tehri leased large tracks of rich deodar forest to the British for a period of 40 years. This led to the construction of forest roads and bridges and brought large area of forests in the catchments of Bhagirathi and Yamuna rivers under commercial exploitation. Having realised the commercial value of the forests, the Raja began to use them for his own benefit. The Tehri state, in 1895, started its own forest department and declared as 'reserved' or 'protected' most good quality forests and severely curtailed the traditional rights of the villagers and their access to them.

As over time the greater part of the revenue of Tehri durbar came to be realized from its rich forests, the Raja steadily introduced a policy of stricter forest conservancy modeled on the system prevailing in the British territory Gradually several new forest divisions were constituted and the entire forest of the state came to be managed under working plans with revenue orientation becoming more marked. Reservation of large tracts of forest meant an effective loss of control over their habitat for forest-based communities. An increased pressure was felt on the forest that remained open to villagers, hastening their destruction. The result of the curtailment of their 'Haq Haqooq' (traditional rights) to their natural resource base was people's active opposition to this marginalization and alienation from what they considered to be their common property. But the overt manifestation of this resentment did not take place until after 1900 A.D. when cases of organised resistance against authority took place.

Traditionally, peasant protest in the entire Uttarakhand region took the form of individual and collective resistance to tyranny by officials with a simultaneous call to the monarch to restore justice. This concept of peaceful protest was known as 'dhandak' and it played an important role in building the non-violent character of the average Garhwali.

A number of dhandaks ensued, the main ones being: (i) the Dhandak of 1906 to protest against the reservation of forests surrounding the Chandrabadani temple to which villagers claimed full and exclusive rights; (ii) the Rawain Dhandak of 1930, which was marked with bloodshed as it to led the brutal killing of many protesters in Tilari by the king's army. These intermittent and localized protests crystallized into a widespread movement known as Tehri Kisan Andolan (1944-48), which was a response to the almost complete loss of control of the local peasantry over their forests and the near total curtailment of their traditional rights (Haq-Haqooq). The latter protest culminated in the merger of Tehri Garhwal with the Indian Union in 1949.

C. Chipko and Tehri Dam Agitation

The post-independence era continued to be marked by an extractive forest policy, primarily due to the preoccupation of the Indian planners to fuel the large scale industrialization model opted by them for achieving development. The new National Forest Policy framed in 1952 was on colonial lines and endorsed the monopoly of the state over forests. The major aim was to maximize revenue by encouraging commercial forestry. Oak and other multi-purpose trees were discouraged as was the supply of various non timber forest products (NTFPs) on which the life and livelihood of the people depended. This era was also marked by a rapid increase in human and livestock population in the region (a growth rate of almost 2.6% per annum for human population). But life supporting system failed to keep pace with this increase.

The local people's aspiration to change the forest policy and to hand over the forest felling to local cooperatives, led in due course to the world famous Chipko movement. It is however important to note that the Chipko Movement, as also the forest conflicts prior to Chipko were not necessarily based on a consciousness of ecological stability, as modern literature often tends to project. These remained for a long time basic economic struggles over access to resources and right to survival. It was only later, that is, between 1974 and 1977 that some important cognitive developments took place which infected a strong ecological sensitivity into the Chipko Movement. Prominent among these developments were: (i) heightened awareness of the hill women about the significance of the forest in sustaining their life and the eco system. In fact this was used by women to mobilize their sisters into the Chipko fold. Forests were referred to as the women's 'Maika' (parents' abode) on which they could depend, in good times and bad; (ii) the Report of Virendra Kumar Committee, highlighting widespread deforestation as the major reason behind the Alakhananda disaster; (iii) the role of the Chipko leadership, especially Sunderlal Bahuguna in articulating local concerns through global opinions and the media attention that the movement attracted. As a result, Chipko metamorphosed from a peasant movement to a global campaign, focusing on the sustainability of forests. As evidence of ecological damage of deforestation started mounting, the Government had to impose a moratorium on green felling in 1980, ultimately endorsing Chipko as a conservationist movement. The role played by Chipko in the subsequent phase in creating and sustaining grassroots activism, especially among the women of the region, as also in influencing the methodologies of action of people's groups and voluntary organizations of the region will be examined to some extent in the later sections of this study.

It is however ironical that while Chipko started with the objective of reviving local forest management through participatory mode of action; it implicitly appointed the government as the custodian of forests. The traditional rights of the local population, as also the indigenous ecological knowledge of the people to sustainably manage their forests were again bypassed. The state used the environmental concern to centralize forest management rather than decentralizing it. Moreover, the ban on tree-felling stopped even primary development work on the region, as they entailed tree felling. Since 1988-89, some 4,500 development schemes in the hills had not been cleared due to environmental reasons. In fact this fuelled the "Ped Kato Andolan" (Fell trees Movement) in 1988-89, an antithesis of Chipko, by a group of youth activists of the Uttarakhand Kranti Dal.

The movement against Tehri Dam also emerged as another example of the growth of ecological consciousness among the people of Tehri Garhwal in particular, and the entire hill population in general. Amongst the strongest opponents of the controversial Tehri Dam were the residents of Tehri town and the thousands of people of the villages in the submersion area. With them were the most renowned and articulate environmentalists, who disproved the economic and ecological utility of the dam. Located in the same area and involving almost the same activist groups, both movements made different contributions to the advancement of popular consciousness about sustainable mountain development. While Chipko was a success, the completion of the Tehri project and its operationalization, on the other hand, has been an indicator of the lack of success of the anti-dam movement. However, both movements have made significant contribution to raising the ecological consciousness of the local people.

(D) Contemporary Programmes of People's Groups

(i) Programmes of Voluntary Organisations

All voluntary organizations selected for the study acknowledged environmental protection and promotion as a primary objective. They had been undertaking diverse environmental programmes. The important programmes and initiatives were:

(a) *Afforestation/plantation*: All organizations are undertaking plantation/afforestation work in their target villages. Emphasis is mainly on the plantation of fruit trees, as also those trees which provide fodder and fuel wood to meet the needs of the local people. All organisations support plantation of mixed, people-friendly species of trees. In fact three organisations are taking a lot of initiative to pressurize the forest department to stop creating monocultures, especially of chir-pine and to promote mixed forests, which are the traditional vegetation of the region. Broad-leaved trees like oak and other local varieties like Bhimal, Moru etc., are promoted by these organisations, both through generating awareness among people for planting such trees, as also taking up plantation of such trees exclusively.

Plantation work is undertaken, both through the distribution of saplings to people for plantation and by undertaking mass plantation programmes on community/panchayati lands by involving village groups. Training for plantation work and after care, as also the incentives to ensure survival of saplings, are provided to support people's efforts. The rate of survival of such plantations has been found to be very good and the researcher witnessed several such plantations in target villages.

(b) *Nursery development*: In view of the fact that procurement of healthy saplings and local indigenous varieties of species is difficult, organizations prefer developing their own nurseries. While four organisations have small nurseries on their own premises, the other three provide appropriate training to enable interested persons to set up their own nurseries. There are also instances of women's group collectively taking initiative of setting up village-based nurseries. Availability of local nurseries serves a dual purpose viz. as a source of income derived by individuals/groups from sale of saplings) as also ensuring local availability of saplings for plantation. These show better survival rates as they are suited to the soil and climate of the area. Moreover, long distance transportation from government nurseries can be avoided. Nurseries are also used for demonstration purposes to encourage interested persons to set them up.

(c) *Forest protection:* This is a major component of the environmental action programme of all voluntary organisations. Forest protection work is undertaken by means of: (a) formation of village groups like Mahila Mangal Dals, Nav Yuvak Mangal Dals, Van Samitis etc. to afforest, protect and manage their forests; (b) support to Van Panchayat and Gram Sabha/Village Panchayat to take up protection and management of forests; and (c) mobilisation of village communities/groups into action to stop/prevent illegal felling/commercial felling of trees. The latter initiatives are called by different names like Vriksha Chetna, Van Andolans, Rakshasutra Andolan, Van Bachao Andolan etc. by different organisations. In the past there have been several instances when the voluntary organisations have successfully prevented private contractors, forest mafia and even Van Nigam/Forest Department from illegally felling trees from the reserve forests.

(d) *Formation and support to village groups*: Six organizations have actively undertaken the responsibility of mobilizing community persons, especially women and youth into organizing themselves into groups. A multitude of women's groups (Mahila Mangal Dals) and youth groups (Nav Yuvak Mangal Dals) have been formed in many villages of the region due to the active effort of voluntary organisations which act as catalysts and facilitators. The organisations have provided training inputs to women, and financial and material support. They have also enabled many groups to register themselves. They have helped the groups, particularly women's groups to revive the traditional values associated with conservation. The researcher had the opportunity to see numerous forests, (both village forests and patches of reserve forests) which are being protected by the active efforts of the women's groups. These forests have regenerated due to the women's efforts towards saving them. The groups are also provided with inputs on nursery development, plantation work, improving soil fertility, water conservation, plant pests/diseases etc, and provided saplings/seeds for plantation work. Besides environmental related work, the groups are also supported to involve themselves in the larger social issues of child marriage, polygamy, women's illiteracy, preference for boys and addressing the needs and problems of womenfolk.

(e) *Conservation and development of medicinal plants/herbs*: Five organizations are involved in this work and groups are motivated to take up herb cultivation at the village level. Two particular voluntary organisations are predominantly involved with conservation of medicinal herbs, especially those which are fast disappearing, due to uncontrolled commercial exploitation. While one organisation has set up a nursery of medicinal plants/herbs, for demonstration purposes, the other is in the process of setting up a botanical garden to enable people, especially women to set up nurseries and utilize them for income generation. Another organisation has set up a small scale unit to prepare basic medicines/supplements (like Trifala, churans etc.) and herbal products like Vajradanti tooth powder, soaps etc. and is providing income generation opportunities to the local people. Awareness generation among people about the commercial and utility value of herbs, as also scope for income generation from their conservation and propagation is also undertaken.

(f) *Soil conservation programmes*: Six organizations have been undertaking programmes directed towards soil conservation. This is done by taking up plantation work in open, degraded forest lands, and also by means of gap filling and patch filling plantations. Pasture development work is also taken up to prevent soil erosion. Construction of check dams, spurs, gully plugging, etc. are also undertaken with the participation of local people. Retaining walls are built to stabilize landslides in landslide prone zones. People are also made aware of the dangers associated with overgrazing, tree felling, forest fires etc. and their role in loss of vegetative cover leading to erosion, and loss of soil fertility.

(g) *Water conservation and management*: This is also one of the more important areas of work undertaken by almost all the voluntary organisations (five of them). The Chals or Chahals (as they are popularly called) are traditionally well known water conservation structures, which not only check the run-off of rainwater, but also harvest rainwater. The storage of water leads to moisture retention, which in turn leads to natural regeneration of vegetation in the area. This is also seen to recharge groundwater and revive/recharge natural sources of water. Two organizations have taken up construction of ferro-cement tanks. The activity is also used to generate wage employment for people. Villagers also contribute by way of voluntary contributions or free labour (shramdan).

(h) *Environmental sanitation*: All the voluntary organisations are involved with programmes of environmental sanitation in their target villages. Four organisations work through the women and youth groups, which assume work related to sanitation, cleanliness, etc. Three of them mobilize community people to undertake cleanliness drives, cleaning of Chals etc. on a periodic basis. Many mahila mangals are doing pioneering work in the area of village sanitation. Apart from cleaning of village roads and public places, proper garbage disposal, sanitation and cleanliness in and near water sources is also emphasized. The commonly followed practice of disposal of animal carcasses and dead bodies in water is being discouraged by these organizations. Awareness generation on the link between sanitation and health is also undertaken.

Five organizations assist the communities in the construction of low cost latrines in individual households, and 'Mahila Complexes' (group/community toilets). Besides, training in the construction of compost-pits and soak-pits is also provided to community groups. Four voluntary organisations have also launched programmes for the promotion of pollution free or smokeless chulhas, and fuel efficient cooking devices like pressure cookers. These have been supplied at subsidized rates. A new and emerging area of work in the realm of prevention of land pollution relates to the popularization of organic farming techniques among people and making them aware about the negative effects of using chemical fertilizers and pesticides on the fertility and productivity of soil. Two organisations have taken up this work.

Another relatively new area of work chosen by two voluntary organisations relates to dissuasion of people from using non-biodegradable materials like plastic in daily life and reverting back to their traditional ways of life. In fact, polythene has been banned in Tehri through the initiative of the previous D.M. of the district.

(i) *Awareness generation*: All organizations are involved in creating environmental awareness among people through the use of multiple for like Van Shivirs, Van Sammelans, Vichar Goshthies (discussion meetings) and Eco-Development camps. These play a very important role in creating awareness, information and new ideas. Sometimes, interaction sessions with agricultural experts from universities, and forest officials are also organised. Special programmes are organized for groups, like farmer's groups, women's groups and youth groups. Apart from shivirs and camps, awareness generation is undertaken through the use of innovative methods like padyatras (walking tours), cycle tours, street plays, puppet shows, songs, poems, theatre/drama and other such interactive media called variously as Chetna Jagran, Jan Jagran etc. These have relied on indigenous and traditional methods of awareness generation. A very innovative approach used by a few organisations to gather and mobilize people, especially women pertains to the holding of a weekly/ fortnightly satsang, religious sermons, and rendition of epics/Bhagwat Geeta. These were followed by discussions on different environment related and other relevant issues.

(j) *Promotion of non-conventional alternate energy sources*: Four organizations have been working towards popularization of non-conventional sources of energy in order to reduce the biomass related pressure on forests. Efforts are made to enable women, especially from villages located on the roadside to benefit from the government scheme of subsidized cooking gas connections. As per the people, this has really worked but the charges of the cylinder remained steep for most people to afford. Training on the construction of Deshbandhu gobar gas plant had been undertaken by two organisations, but these were not found to be very successful. This was due to the fact that livestock being limited, animal wastes were not sufficient to run a biogas plant for the village. Moreover, people use animal wastes as a natural manure to enhance soil fertility. Demonstration and training in the use of solar cookers and solar lights is also routinely undertaken. Two organizations have made special efforts to promote microhydels and water mills to utilize the ample river resources of region in order to generate electricity and provide energy for running small scale units like grinding/milling machines, electrical tools/ machines etc. A few committees of villagers have been formed to promote water mills.

(k) *Training and capacity building*: Five organizations have been organizing training programmes focusing on different aspects of environmental action, like environmental sanitation, water conservation techniques, and traditional water conservation systems, watershed management, forest management, nursery development, horticulture and food processing, organic farming, use of alternate energy, herb cultivation, plantation etc.

(ii) Programmes of People's Groups

(a) Village councils/Samitis

The area demonstrates widespread community management of common property resources, mainly forests, outside any formal legal framework within or near villages. This is particularly so in villages located away from the roads, where commons are still crucial for sustaining the local subsistence economy. Informal user and protector groups like Van Samitis, Van Suraksha Samitis, even a few traditional Lath Panchayats, and Mahila Mandals are found to be regenerating and regulating use of all categories of forest lands, within or near villages, including reserve and soyam forest tracts (although the former category are more commonly protected). Although the system of protection and management of forests by village groups/councils possesses commonalities, the work of the women's groups (Mahila Mangal Dals) remains slightly distinct and will be considered separately in the subsequent section.

Some important observations about the initiatives of the village councils/ samitis are:

(i) In most villages covered by the researcher and which possess community management systems, the focus, of people's protection is the village settlement, which operates on the basis of consensus, and is distinct from elected panchayats. Protected areas are based on traditional village boundaries (which have never been documented) and are only occasionally co-terminus with panchayat boundaries. In fact, more than one community management system often exists in a single panchayat area.

(ii) Over 80 per cent of the forests protected by informal community groups fall in the reserve forests. Thus, community groups are collectively protecting those forest tracts, where they have limited user rights, as compared to civil/soyam tracts where they enjoy unlimited rights. This is mainly because the latter are degraded, having been treated as common access lands, and also because the dependence of people on reserve forests is much greater.

(iii) 'Protection for regeneration' is the main strategy behind most eco-management practices, People, by and large feel that regeneration is cheaper and affordable, as compared to plantations, and also generates more income for the poor, due to proliferation of undergrowth in the form of shrubs, bushes, creepers and grasses.

(iv) The concept of 'social fencing' is operative in a few cases, where villagers take their village devata (Temple Deity) around the area to be protected, thus automatically sealing the boundaries of the forest tract. These are construed as de facto protected areas, and no villager dares to enter the plot thereafter. The significance of religious belief and tradition in forest protection is evident here.

(v) In most 'protected areas' however, villagers appoint a full time chowkidar (forest watchman) who is paid in cash or kind through contributions shared equally by all households. This annual contribution by households is commonly known as 'phant' This practice of voluntary 'watch and ward' is the most commonly found eco-management practice found prevalent in the area. Chowkidars are given powers to seize the sickles and other tools of the offenders and scold or disgrace them. In several places, fines are imposed, which could be realized from offenders by the chowkidar. Payment is ensured because failure to comply often leads to debarment from the forest. The people's chowkidar enjoys authority due to his power to impose fines, seize sickles, and disgrace offenders. Due to active consensus for protection, the chowkidar also founds support from the women's groups, Panchayats and the village assembly support him against habitual offenders (as against the people's chowkidars, the forest department chowkidar was mostly sidelined by the villagers and had minimal role in protecting the forests).

(vi) Most samitis follow the system of annual or biannual meetings to decide on the appointment of chowkidar and other rules for closure and opening of forests; regulations of extraction; and controlled exploitation of the biomass. Closure of forests is mainly dependent on the state of the forests. Degraded forests are completely closed and are opened only once or twice a year and that too only for harvesting of grass. In forests, which are in a better condition, entry with any kind of sharp instrument is forbidden, while harvesting of leaves and twigs is permitted. Rotational lopping of trees is also followed in a few protected areas. The rules are worked out carefully to ensure an equitable distribution of forest products.. The leaves, twigs, branches and grass loads brought down from the forest are usually weighed at the entrance and only equal measures allowed to be taken out free. The rest are sold or auctioned and usually the women themselves busy the excess. The villagers usually inspect their forests before they are opened and if trees are found damaged or felled, the chowkidar is fined. The samitis meet more frequently in case of conflict resolution or for other important issues (as per need).

(vii) Protection of forests from forest fires is another important component of work of the samitis. However, this is usually limited to the community owned forests. Besides, forest protection and management, the samitis or councils are also involved in other programmes like environmental sanitation programmes, afforestation, and soil and water conservation. Most programmes are functional through voluntary contributions of time, labour, and money, as also the support of voluntary organisations and local activists.

(b) Mahila Mangal Dals

Women's groups or women's associations called Mahila Mangal Dals are found to be playing a very important role in environmental protection and promotion of the area. Although the study covered only registered Dals, numerous other Dals are working as well, or even better, in trying to protect and promote their natural resource base. Some of the registered Dals covered by the study are: Kandersyun, Silyara, Kothiara, Gangar, Thati Budhakedarnath, Mandara, Khawada, Saunph, Ragari, and Kothiara.

The main programmes of these groups are:

(i) *Forest Protection and Management*: Most settlements in Balganga and Bhilangana valley have protection mechanisms for forests and a number of them are managed by women's groups. The women Dal members have taken over the functions of the traditional Van Panchayats (which were conspicuous by their total absence, in Tehri Garhwal, till 1997-98). They are functioning autonomously, unlike the elected Van panchayats, which are bound by various legal provisions. The Dal members either keep guard of their protected forest areas themselves through a system of rotational duty (examples:-Kandersyun, Sendul, Saranshgaon, Saruna, Syura, Pedokha) or follow a system of appointing chowkidars (Silyara, Kothiara, Gangar, Thati, Ragari, Mandara, Khawada etc.).

The women hold annual or biannual meetings for closure of forests and select the chowkidar (although Dal members otherwise met twice a month for meetings). They meet more frequently when there is a conflict to be resolved. On occasions of inter-village conflicts the members often guard the forest themselves and apprehend offenders. The members make rules about controlling grazing, felling, lopping, catching violators, prosecuting and imposing fines on them and settling disputes over forest produce, and these are found to be strictly enforced and adhered to by the villagers. Rules also govern extraction of forest products and are made so as to ensure equitable distribution of the same. Often the chairpersons of the Dals take initiative to consult and involve men folk, especially present and past pradhans in their work. Women are also involved in protecting forests from fires. In fact, they are found to be more active than men folk, of the area.

(ii) *Afforestation/Plantation*: Dal members also undertake plantation work in community village forests. Emphasis is on plantation of various broad leaf species, like Kachnar, Sandan, Semla, Aonla, Banjh, Moru, Bhimal etc, which yielded fuel and fodder. Members mainly rely on voluntary organizations (if existent locally) to provide seeds and saplings and on 'shramdan' (free, voluntary labour) for plantation activities.

Afforestation and protection of forest tracts have led to a number of favourable consequences, which were witnessed by the researcher personally. Apart from yielding nutritive biomass and organic manure, ground water has been recharged and village 'gadheras' (water channels) have become activated. Moreover, people also report improved soil fertility in agricultural fields downhill.

(iii) *Nursery development*: A few Mahila Mangal Dals have collectively taken up nursery development. (eg. Silyara, Khawada). These are being utilized by the groups to acquire desirable saplings for plantation. The money derived from sale of saplings is put in the village fund and used for village programmes.

(iv) *Environmental sanitation*: This is an important programme undertaken by almost all Mahila Mangals. This involves cleanliness campaigns wherein cleanliness of the village, village paths, water harvesting structures like chals, etc. is undertaken jointly by the Dal members. It also involves evolving commonly agreed upon rules for keeping the water sources clean, keeping animals in separate enclosures, and disposing off garbage properly. A few Dals are also involved in the construction of compost pits, soak pits, low cost latrines etc. through 'shramdan', in liaison with local voluntary organizations.

(v) *Environmental awareness generation*: Dals are actively involved in holding programmes for awareness generation on environmental issues. They hold meetings once or twice in a month and discuss problems pertaining to forests, water, biomass, farming, etc. and also probable solutions to the same. Many a times, meetings are held at site (that is, within the forest or near the water source, as the case may be), so as to gain a firsthand understanding of the problem and its likely solutions. Dal members also mobilize other womenfolk through the organisation of religious and cultural programmes.

(vi) *Social action programmes*: Many Mahila Mangal Dals, like those of Silyara, Budhakedar, Kothiara, Khawada, Chamiala and Sarasgaon are involved in opposing illegal tree felling/commercial felling of forests through collective movements, adopting confrontationist approach. As mentioned earlier, many Dals were constituted during the time of the Chipko Andolan and have carried the legacy of peaceful, non violent confrontationist mode of opposition to commercial exploitation of their natural resources by outsiders. Many Dals have actively participated in Anti-liquor campaigns and Tehri Dam Agitation under the leadership of their leader Shri Bahuguna. Many of them have also been active participants in the Rakshasutra Andolan, during which they tie kinship strings (rakhis) to trees and vow to protect them from being felled.

(c) Programmes of Van Panchayats

As the Van Panchayats functional in the block were being governed by the State Van Panchayat Rules, 2001, they have compulsory duties and powers accorded by the Rules. The main programme/function of the Van Panchayats is Forest Management and Protection. This includes: (i) Protection of forests from damage and using only those trees which were marked for felling; (ii) Protection of forests from encroachment, illicit felling, lopping, fire and other damages and to conserve them; (iii) Promotion of natural regeneration through management of forest fires, and controlled grazing; (iv) Maximization of rainwater conservation by afforestation and protection of forests in catchment areas; (v) Ensuring of preservation of wildlife and (vi) Utilization of the forest produce to the best advantage of the right holders, keeping in view the silviculture health and sustainable resource management.

In context of the fact that the Van Panchayats were constituted in the year 1997, they were found to have initiated work in the land allotted to them. They hold meetings once in two months and a general meeting of all users/ right holders. Measures have been taken by the Panchayats to detect and guard against the illicit use of the forests. Since the Van Panchayats do not have adequate financial resources, they have taken on the responsibility of guarding the forest themselves, with each household taking turns. The Van Panchayats have also adopted various precautionary measures, mostly informal to prevent encroachments and illegal felling. They have framed rules and regulations pertaining to equitable and fair distribution of forest produce and penalties/ punishments for violators.

At the time of data collection, the Panchayats were attempting to improve the condition of their allotted forests by undertaking plantation through voluntary contributions and 'shramdan'. It was early for them to become fully functional, as per the provisions of the Panchayati Rules.

A review of the two categories of programmes viz. government programmes and programmes of the people's groups reveals the following differences:

Table 4.11: Comparison between Government Programmes and Programmes of People's Organisations/Groups

Government Programmers	*Programmes of People's Organisations/Groups*
1. Majority of the schemes/programmes were central schemes, conceived and planned at the centre. Thus, they followed a top-down approach	1. People's programmes were decentralized and site-specific programmes, conceived and planned at the local village or group of villages level.

(*Contd.*)

Table 4.11 (*Contd.*)

Government Programmers	*Programmes of People's Organisations/Groups*
2. Being central schemes, they worked under a uniform policy framework and guidelines.	2. Programmes were flexible, and as per needs of target groups/target areas.
3. Decisions were taken at faraway centers viz. Central ministries or State departments, so they rarely took into account local concerns and problems. Programmes were merely implemented at different places.	3. Decision making units were small and local, and programmes were mostly based on local issues and concerns. Decision-making was mostly transparent and open to local population.
4. Programmes mostly did not cater to the socio-economic needs of the people; not focused on women specific problems pertaining to a degraded environment.	4. Programmes were suited to the socio-economic and other needs of the local people, and there was some focus on gender issues, especially pertaining to the environment.
5. Environmental programmes, mostly focused on `conservation' aspect, and were alienated from other community development or rural development issues.	5. People's programmes, (especially those of voluntary organizations) were integrated into other developmental initiatives. Also emphasized meeting of basic needs of people first.
6. Most governmental programmes were programmes of afforestation, tree plantation.	6. Programmes were multifaceted and varied.
7. Plantation undertaken by the Forest Department mainly involved commercially viable species of trees and focused on creation of mono-cultures. Little regard for needs of people in species selection.	7. Plantation by people involved broad leaved varieties of fuel, and fodder yielding trees species and emphasized mixed forests. Full regard for people's needs in tree species selection.
8. Programmes were organized in highly compartmentalized manner, with different government ministries and departments handling different environmental programmes, and at times even different aspects of the same programme. There was poor coordination between the state forest department and other departments concerned viz. Agriculture, Horticulture, Soil conservation, Minor Irrigation, Rural Development etc., contributing to inadequacies in planning and implementation.	8. Programmes were handled by people themselves, either directly or through the organization of broad based people's committees and groups. Also significant cooperation and collaboration between different people's groups and organizations in environmental action at village level.
9. Little or no scope for the vast store of traditional knowledge that local people, especially women possessed about the natural resource base.	9. Programmes based on people's own traditional wisdom about their environment and environmental practices.

(*Contd.*)

Table 4.11 (*Contd.*)

Government Programmers	*Programmes of People's Organisations/Groups*
10. Programmes used standard methods/ strategies of implementation.	10. Programme implementers relied on indigenous and traditional, culturally specific strategies and approaches.
11. Most programmes had no scope for community participation and were exclusive government initiatives. Government failed to meaningfully integrate the traditional village-based people's institutions into their programmes. Recent emphasis was on creation of alternative mechanisms like Village Forest Management Committees, FDA etc; leading to potential conflict between the traditional institutions and 'imposed', government promoted institutions.	11. Programmes presented full scope for community participation. People relied on their own traditional community resource management systems existent for a long time.
12. Government has not realized the potential of people-led conservation efforts. Emphasis on external funding has led to dictates of foreign funding organizations being included in programmes. Also little role envisaged for women who are prime users of forest produce.	12. People's programmes based more on voluntary contributions, and Shramdan. Programmes based on rich traditions of local conservation initiatives and experiences of people themselves Programmes had immense scope for women's participation.
13. Programmes were based on beneficiary-oriented approach, and tended to create dependence on local bureaucracy for saplings, funds, timber, and NTFPs, rather than building the confidence and capacity of local institutions.	13. Programmes based on participatory approach, and oriented towards building confidence and capacity of local people and people's institutions.

5

People and their Environment

Awareness and Interrelationships

Prior to understanding the various aspects pertaining to the participation of respondents in specific programmes, it is essential to develop an understanding of their different categories, their organisational/group affiliation, and their background features. The same has been undertaken in this chapter. Additionally, since awareness of the respondents with regard to the environment, environmental issues and problems, and environmental programmes is deemed to have a bearing on their participation, the same has also been examined in this chapter.

The chapter has consequently been divided into two parts. The first part deals with the background of the respondents and includes a description of their organisational/group affiliation. The second part examines and analyses the nature and extent of awareness of the respondents with regard to the environment.

The Respondents: Their Background

1. Categories of Respondents

While a brief description of the different categories of respondents covered by the study has already been covered in Chapter II, a category-wise profile of respondents is presented below, along with a brief description of their organisational or group affiliation.

These six categories of respondents, who were the participants in environmental programmes of the study area were:

(a) Members of Village Councils, including Panchayat members: A total of 180 members belonged to this category. As mentioned earlier, the researcher had come across many village communities in villages like Thatikathod, Kepars, Mandara, Lasyalgaon, Dalgaon, Silyara, Saruna, Devath, Sayura, Saunph and others, which had been protecting and managing their natural resource base for the past many years (at times even 50 years) independently and without any external support. 90 members of these village councils, who had been participants in the environmental initiatives, were covered. Out of this group, 59 members were male and 31 were female. Another 90 members were gram panchayat members belonging to the village settlements covered by the study. This group comprised of 30 Pradhans (Chairpersons), 30 Up-Pradhans (Vice chairpersons) and 30 members of panchayats. While 60 panchayat members were male, the rest, that is, 30 of them were female.

The duration of membership/association with the work of the group or organisation was different for panchayat members and other members of village councils, as the duration of membership of the former was based on their tenure as elected representatives. The tenure varied between four years (for 82 members who had been elected for the first time) to nine years for the 8 members (who were serving a second tenure). The duration of association of other members with environmental work of village councils showed a wide variation. It varied between four years to over forty years.

The members reported multiple motivations for their participation. The important ones were: (i) self inspiration/desire to serve the people (65.55%); (ii) concern about local issues and problems (51.66%); (iii) personal interest in environmental issues (32.22%); (iv) association with voluntary organisations (18.33%); (v) inspiration from Sarvodaya leaders/Chipko leadership and other local activists (20%); (vi) association with Chipko Movement/Anti-Liquour Andolan and other local movements (30%); (vii) political ambition (5%); and (viii) reservation of seats (15%). It is important to note that 15 out of 27 respondents who mentioned 'reservation of seats' as an important motivational factor were women and 12 were male members belonging to Scheduled Caste category

(b) Members of Mahila Mangal Dals: Comprising about 18.8 per cent of the total respondents (60 in number), this was an all female category. Mahila Mangal Dals of the block had been working on programmes related to environmental action; women's welfare and development (like literacy, income generation, health, nutrition, recreation/leisure, social issues/problems, awareness generation etc); prohibition of alcohol in the region; and agricultural improvement, among others.

Classified on the basis of posts/designations, the members included 6 'Adhyakshas' (Chairpersons), 6 'Up-Adhyakshas' (Vice-Chair persons) and 48 'Sadasyas'(members) of Mahila Mangals Dals (MMDs).

The duration of membership varied for different members. A majority of the members had a medium term (i.e. 5-10 years) or long term (more than 10 years) membership in their groups, i.e. 40 per cent and 43.3 per cent respectively. It was interesting to note that all twelve chairpersons and vice-chairpersons had a long-term association with their Dals. This indicated that the senior or more experienced members were occupying the leadership positions in the Dals. Members showed multiple motivations for association with the Dals. The main ones included: (i) motivation by local voluntary organisations (46.6%); (ii) inspiration from Chipko leaders/local activists (23.3%); (iii) self inspiration to work for women's issues (15%); (iv) motivation by Mahila Samakhya workers (15%); and (v) motivation by other Dal members (11.7%). It is important to note that since a number of Mahila Mangal Dals were established by Chipko/Sarvodaya leaders, voluntary organisations and Mahila Samakhya workers, they were acknowledged as the main source of motivation. Two-thirds of the MMDs operated at the level of one village settlement only, while the rest comprised members from two or more smaller settlements.

(c) Members of Nav Yuvak Mangal Dals: This category comprised of 24 male youth members. While 3 of them were Chairpersons, 2 were Vice-Chairpersons, and the rest, i.e. 19 youth were members of Nav Yuvak Mangal Dals (NYMDs).

Apart from environmental programmes, NYMDs also took up other programmes, mainly pertaining to youth welfare and development (like employment generation, sports and recreation, etc) as also general programmes like prohibition of alcohol, awareness generation about social problems etc.

An analysis of duration of membership revealed interesting data. Most members showed medium term (9 members) or short term membership (10 members). The main reason for this related to the high degree of outmigration among youth, mostly for employment and at times for education.

Again multiple sources of inspiration/motivation for membership were cited. These included: (i) encouragement by voluntary organisations (12 members); (ii) self inspiration (6 members); (iii) inspiration from local activists/leaders (3 members); and (iv) political aspirations (3 members). Most youth groups covered one village settlement only.

(d) Functionaries of Voluntary Organisations: This group comprised of 20 respondents, out of which 7 members were chief functionaries, who were all male members, and 13 of them were workers/mobilizers employed with voluntary organisations covered by the study. Out of the latter category, 8 workers were female and 5 were male.

A variety of programmes were being undertaken by the seven organisations. The main programmes included: Environmental protection and promotion; Adult Literacy; Education (Pre School, Formal and Non-Formal); Balwari and Day Care; Health, Nutrition and Immunization; Vocational Training; Income Generation; Programmes against alcohol and other social issues.

As far as the duration of association with voluntary organisations was concerned, 5 out of the 7 chief functionaries showed a long-term association, while the other 2 had a medium-term association. Among the workers, 6 had a short-term affiliation and 7 had a medium-term association with their respective organizations.

The main sources of motivation for joining voluntary organisations varied from: inspiration by founder members (8 members); inspiration by other local activists/Chipko leaders (8 members); self inspiration to serve the community (4 members); monetary reasons (5 members); and family tradition of community service (2 members).

(e) Local Activists: This category included 20 local activists, who were involved in environmental programmes, at their own level. They were all working with/through different informal village groups and sometimes seeking involvement of formal groups like panchayats also.

While 15 activists were working in context of environmental initiatives like 'Rakshasutra Andolon', 'Beej Bachao Andolan', 'Meera Van Bachao Andolan' and 'Balganga Shiksha Prasar Samiti', 5 of them were erstwhile Chipko activists, who were working on different environmental issues in the contemporary period. While 14 activists were male, 6 of them were female. The work of the activists differed as per the objectives of their environmental initiatives.

An analysis of the duration of association of members with environmental programmes revealed that half of them, i.e. 10 activists showed a long-term association, while 7 of them showed a medium-term association. The rest, i.e., 3 activists had a short-term association. The five Chipko activists showed a very lengthy association, dating back almost three decades. All of them had been involved with environmental issues/concerns on an intermittent basis.

The main sources of motivation included: influence of Sarvodaya leaders/ Gandhian ideology (8 activists); self inspiration (5 activists); concern about deteriorating state of the environment (11 activists); inspiration from other local activists and voluntary organisations (4 activists).

(f) Members of Van Panchayats: 16 members from the four Van Panchayats existing in the block were included. All four Van Panchayats (V.Ps) were headed by female Sarpanchs. On the whole, the groups comprised of 6 female members and 10 male members. As far as designations of members were concerned, the groups included two chairpersons, two vice-chairpersons and twelve members of Van Panchayats. Duration of membership was short-term for all members (as V.Ps had been constituted in 1997-98 only). The main sources of motivation for them to join and participate in the initiative included: pressure from community members/panchayats (6 members); prior experience in forest protection (6 members); and self inspiration and interest (4 members).

2. Places of Residence

Table 5.1: Distribution of Respondents According to their Places of Residence

S. No.	*Name of Patti/Revenue Zone*	*Respondents (Percentage)*
1.	Basar	16.56
2.	Gongarh	9.06
3.	Argarh	10.63
4.	Thati Katod	12.81
5.	Kotifaigul	13.13
6.	Bhilang	26.88
7.	Kemar	10.93
	Total	100.00

The Patti-wise distribution of respondents was in line with the sampling plan adopted by the study. Bhilang patti comprised the maximum number of villages and thus more Gram Sabhas were selected from this patti. Resultingly, more than one-fourth of the respondents belonged to Bhilang. Gongarh patti was the smallest in terms of number of villages and thus only about 9 per cent respondents belonged to this Patti.

3. Religion and Caste

All the respondents were Hindu. This was due to the fact that almost the entire block population (that is 99%) followed the Hindu religion. As far as the caste-wise distribution is concerned, a majority of them were Kshatriyas or Rajputs (almost 50%), followed by Brahmins (28%). These two categories comprised the upper-castes. Table 5.2 reveals that a dominant majority of the respondents (i.e. 71.2%) belonged to the upper caste groups. The scheduled castes comprised 16.9 per cent of the respondents and included the Chamars, Anjees, Lohars, Kumbhars, Kolis, etc. These constituted the lower castes. Although the 'Vaishyas' were not a traditional caste group of the region, they were migrants from other regions, who had settled in the area and were mainly pursuing trading, small businesses etc. These comprised 5.6 per cent of the respondents.

Table 5.2: Caste-wise Distribution of Respondents

S. No.	*Caste*	*Respondents (Percentage)*
1.	Brahmins	28.12
2.	Kshatriyas/Rajputs	49.38
3.	Vaishyas	5.62
4.	Scheduled castes	16.88
	Total	100.00

4. Sex and Age Distribution

As far as the sex-wise distribution was concerned, almost 56 per cent of the total respondents were male, while the rest were female. Table 5.3 provides the sex distribution of respondents arranged category-wise.

Table 5.3: Sex-wise Distribution of Respondents (as per Categories)

S. No.	*Categories of respondents*	*Sex of respondents*		
		Males	*Females*	*Total*
1.	Members of village councils	119 (66.11)	61 (33.89)	180 (100.0)
2.	Mahila Mangal Dal members	—	60 (100.0)	60 (100.0)
3.	Nav Yuvak Mangal Dal members	24 (100.0)	—	24 (100.0)
4.	Functionaries of voluntary organizations	12 (60.0)	8 (40.0)	20 (100.0)
5.	Local activists	14 (70.0)	6 (30.0)	20 (100.0)
6.	Van Panchayat members	10 (62.5)	6 (37.5)	16 (100.0)
	Total	179 (55.94)	141 (44.06)	320 (100.0)

Note: Figures in parentheses indicate percentages.

While all other categories of respondents comprised of both male and female members; two categories viz. Mahila Mangal Dals and Nav Yuvak Mangal Dals comprised of only females and only male respondents respectively. A majority of the respondents of the other four categories, viz. village council members (66%); functionaries of voluntary organizations (60%); local activists (70%) and Van panchayat members (62.5%) were males. This could be due to the traditional dominance of men in the formal groups like Panchayats and Van Panchayats. Although more women were coming forward and were breaking the traditional barriers, but the process was gradual. Reservation of seats for women in Panchayats and Van panchayats was a first step in this process.

As far as the age distribution was concerned, the respondents were classified into six groups in terms of their age. The age-wise distribution of respondents revealed that the majority of the respondents belonged to the age group of 30 to 39 years (30.6%), followed by the age group 20 to 29 years (26.6%) and 40 to 49 years (19.4%). Only a very small proportion i.e. 5 per cent belonged to the 'very young' category (below 20 years) and about 6 per cent fell in the 'old' category (60 years and above). Thus, the respondents predominately belonged to the young and middle age groups.

The average age of the respondents was 38 years. The village council members showed a mean age of 40 years, while the members of Mahila Mangal Dals had an average age of 36.5 years. While the functionaries of voluntary organisations were relatively younger, with an average age of 29 years, the van panchayat members had a mean age of 34 years. The Nav Yuvak Mangal Dals were youth groups and members mean age was only 22 years. Although the local activists belonged to different age categories, they were the senior most, with their average age being 50 years.

5. Marital Status

As is indicated by the table below, a majority of the respondents (almost 80%) were married. In the region, there was comparatively early marriage, especially for girls, and they were usually married before they reached the age of 20 years.

Table 5.4: Marital Status of Respondents.

S. No.	*Marital Status*	*Respondents (Percentage)*
1.	Unmarried	15.00
2.	Married	80.31
3.	Widowed/Separated	4.09
	Total	100.00

6. Educational Standard

The distribution of respondents by their educational background is depicted in Table 5.5.

Table 5.5: Distribution of Respondents by Educational Standard and Sex

S. No.	*Educational Standard*	*Respondents*		
		Males	*Females*	*Total*
1.	Illiterate	20 (11.17)	32 (22.69)	52 (16.25)
2.	Literate	31 (17.32)	47 (33.33)	78 (24.38)
3.	Below primary school	29 (16.20)	23 (16.31)	52 (16.25)
4.	Below middle school	30 (16.76)	15 (10.64)	45 (14.06)
5.	Below high school	20 (11.17)	7 (4.96)	27 (8.44)
6.	High school pass	36 (20.11)	14 (9.93)	50 (15.63)
7.	Graduate	8 (4.47)	2 (1.42)	10 (3.13)
8.	Post Graduate	5 (2.79)	1 (0.71)	6 (1.88)
	Total	179	141	320

The Table revealed that almost 16 per cent of the respondents were illiterate. While the rest, that is, 84 per cent were literate. This, when contrasted with the block literacy figures revealed a stark contrast, as almost 60 per cent of the block population was illiterate. Further, a gender based classification showed, that about 22.7 per cent of the female respondents were illiterate, and the rest, i.e. 77.3 per cent were at least literate. At the block level, female literacy rate was as low as 16.9 per cent. This indicated that a majority of the participants of environmental programmes were better placed in terms of literacy status and belonged to the small proportion of the literate block population.

Further, almost one-fourth of the respondents were merely literate, thus signifying that almost 40.6 per cent of them had no educational background whatsoever. Almost 38.7 per cent respondents had undertaken different stages of schooling but had dropped out before completing matriculation. Only 16 per cent of them had completed high school and a miniscule proportion (i.e. about 5%) were graduates and above. Although the aforementioned figures were not very impressive in terms of literacy status and educational attainment of the respondents, nevertheless they indicated that this group had a better literacy and educational background as compared to the total block population.

A sex-wise distribution of respondents in different educational categories revealed that females tended to fare worse than males in terms of both literacy and educational background. Almost 22.7 per cent of the females were illiterate and 33.3 per cent of them were merely literates. Moreover, a big proportion of them had dropped out from schooling at different stages, that is, almost 32 per cent. Only about 10 per cent females had completed high school and 3 of them (or 2.1%) were graduates and above. However, as was the case with the combined groups of respondents, the females too showed a better literacy status and educational background as compared to the total female population of the block.

The high rate of illiteracy and low educational attainment among females was reflective of their relative lack of access to educational opportunities. Many factors had contributed to this trend. Apart from the fact that the traditional, male dominated, patriarchal society discouraged female education, a number of local constraints also existed, making girls' education a difficult proposition. Some of these were: (i) lack of female school teachers, making parents hesitant to send their daughters to school; (ii) fewer number of girl's schools; (iii) migration of men folk, forcing girls to drop out of school and work even before they attain 15 years of age (Thus education was relatively brief for girls and ended before that for boys); and (iv) distant location of schools, discouraging attendance of girl children.

Apart from gender-based differences, there were also caste based differences, with lower castes manifesting a lower level of educational attainment. Out of the 54 Scheduled Caste respondents, as many as 22 were illiterate; 20 of them were merely literate; 8 were below primary school and 2 were below middle school level. Only 2 of them were high school pass.

Thus, gender and caste based differences in literacy and educational attainment were observed within the group. Out of the total respondents, 34 of them (10.6%) reported having received some form of training. This varied from carpet making, sewing, motor mechanics, electrical wiring, food preservation, basket making, nursery development, mushroom production, and fisheries.

7. Family Structure and Size

Data on family structure revealed that as many as 217 or approximately 68 per cent of the respondents lived in joint families. A comparison with block situation also showed the same trend with a majority of the families being joint families.

It is also important to note that joint families were more prevalent among the upper castes. Almost 85 per of the upper caste respondents (Brahmins and Kshatriyas) lived in joint families. The main reasons for their living in joint families were provision of physical, emotional and economic security, as also support to womenfolk and elders due to large scale out migration of men.

As far as depicts the size of the families of respondents was concerned, for a majority of the respondents (about 50%), the family size varied between six to ten members. Another 30 per cent families comprised up to five family members and 68 families (21.3%) were still bigger in terms of family size, with members exceeding eleven.

The size of the family was linked to its structure. Since joint families were more prevalent, the average family size was bigger, as compared to the relatively smaller nuclear families. It was interesting to note that the average family size for the block was 5.5 members.

8. Occupational Background

The distribution of respondents according to their occupational background is presented in Table 5.6. The data revealed that more than half the respondents (i.e. 54.7%) were engaged in agriculture. Animal husbandry was an allied activity and out of the 175 respondents engaged in agriculture, almost 77 per cent also undertook animal husbandry. Thus, a big majority of respondents (55%) were engaged in primary sector occupations of agriculture and animal husbandry. Only 7 per cent were into secondary sector occupations, while about 22 per cent were in the tertiary (services) sector. Almost 9 per cent of the respondents were engaged in social work/social service on a full time, voluntary basis. This group was distinct from the functionaries of voluntary organizations, who were included in the category 'private service'.

The gender-wise occupational distribution showed that a substantial majority of the female respondents (more than 70%) were engaged in primary sector occupations, as compared to only about 40 per cent of the male

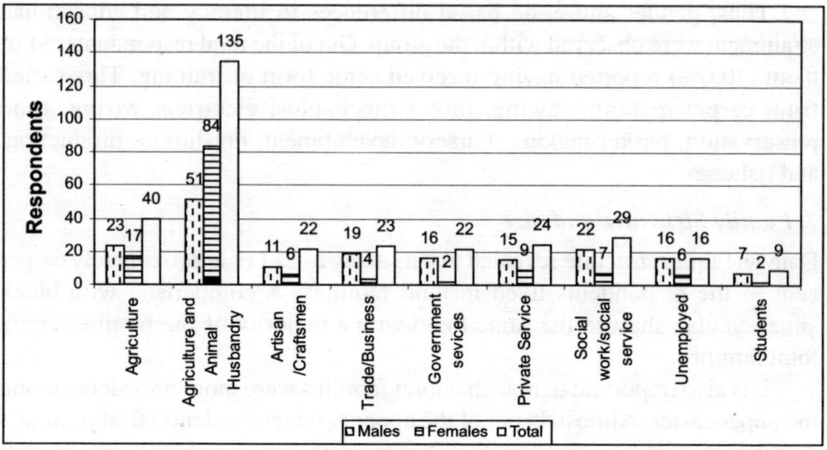

Fig. 5.1: Distribution of Respondents according to their Main Occupations

respondents. Thus, more women than men were engaged in the primary sector. The role of women work force in the agriculture sector could be explained on account of the high out-migration of males and lack of alternate means of livelihood in the hilly terrain. In fact, Tehri Garhwal district, along with four other hill districts showed a very peculiar trend, i.e. more than 95 per cent of its female workers were cultivators (as against 47.83% for undivided U.P and 33.2% for the country as a whole). On the other hand, only 4.3 per cent and 13.5 per cent of the females were engaged in secondary sector and tertiary sector occupations respectively. The comparable figures for male respondents were higher i.e. 89 per cent and 28 per cent respectively in secondary and tertiary sector occupations. The smaller proportion of respondents (both male

Table 5.6: Distribution of Respondents according to their Main Occupations

S. No.	*Occupation*	*Respondents*		
		Males	*Females*	*Total*
1.	Agriculture	23 (12.8)	17 (12.0)	40 (12.5)
2.	Agriculture and Animal Husbandry	51 (28.5)	84 (59.6)	135 (42.2)
3.	Artisan/Craftsmen	16 (8.1)	6 (4.3)	22 (6.9)
4.	Trade/Business	19 (10.6)	4 (2.8)	23 (7.2)
5.	Government service	16 (8.9)	6 (4.3)	22 (6.9)
6.	Private service	15 (8.4)	9 (6.4)	24 (7.5)
7.	Social work/social service	22 (12.3)	7 (5.0)	29 (9.1)
8.	Unemployed	10 (5.6)	6 (4.3)	16 (5.0)
9.	Students	7 (3.9)	2 (1.4)	9 (2.8)
	Total	179	141	320

Note: Figures in parentheses indicate percentages.

and female) being engaged in secondary and tertiary sectors was primarily due to an almost total lack of employment opportunities available in the block and a substantial over-dependence on agriculture. Approximately 12 per cent of the males and 5 per cent of the females were also engaged in social work/social service and about 8 per cent of the respondents were either studying or were unemployed.

As far as family occupations were concerned, a predominant majority (i.e. 81.2%) of the respondents belonged to agricultural families, as is depicted by Table 5.7:

Table 5.7: Distribution of Respondents according to Family Occupation

S. No.	*Family Occupation*	*Respondents (Percentage)*
1.	Agriculture and Animal	81.25
2.	Artisan/Craftsmen	7.50
3.	Trade/Business	4.06
4.	Services	5.31
5.	Social Work/service	1.87
	Total	99.99

The rest, that is, 18.8 per cent of the respondents reported other family occupations like crafts, trade, business, services etc. An analysis of the caste background and family occupation of respondents revealed that all the 24 families engaged as craftsmen/artisans belonged to the scheduled caste groups. The rest of the 30 scheduled caste respondents belonged to agricultural families.

9. Family Income

Data on family income is presented in Table 5.8. The table shows that 22.5 per cent or more than one-fifth of the respondents' families lived below the poverty line, i.e. had an annual family income below ₹ 11,000. Out of this category, almost 70 per cent were scheduled caste families (i.e. 50 out of 72 families). A majority of the respondents had an annual family income between ₹ 11,000 and ₹ 22,000 (i.e. 43.7%) with the mean annual family income being ₹ 19095. While the economic background of the Brahmins and Rajputs was almost the same (with mean annual family incomes being ₹ 21327 and ₹ 21870 respectively, the Vaishyas were the most economically well off community with an average annual family income of ₹ 25666. The scheduled caste families were economically very poor with the mean annual family income being only ₹ 5804.

Thus, a close relationship was observed between caste groupings and economic background, with scheduled caste respondents showing a poor economic status (92.6% of them fell below poverty line). A majority of the Rajput respondents, (i.e. almost 67%) had family incomes falling above

Table 5.8: Distribution of Respondents according to Annual Family Income and Caste

S. No.	Annual Family	Respondents				
		Total	Rajputs	Brahmins	Vaishyas	S.Cs
1.	Less than ₹ 5,500	28 (8.75)	—	—	—	28 (51.85)
2.	₹ 5,501- ₹ 11,000	44 (13.75)	14 (8.86)	8 (8.89)	—	22 (40.74)
3.	₹ 11,001- ₹ 16,500	71 (22.18)	45 (28.48)	19 (21.11)	3 (16.67)	4 (7.40)
4.	₹ 16,501- ₹ 22,000	69 (21.56)	38 (24.06)	26 (28.89)	5 (27.78)	—
5.	₹ 22,001- ₹ 27,500	48 (15.0)	23 (14.56)	20 (22.22)	5 (27.78)	—
6.	₹ 27,501- ₹ 33,000	22 (6.88)	12 (7.60)	9 (10.00)	1 (5.55)	—
7.	₹ 33,001- ₹ 38,500	17 (5.31)	13 (8.22)	3 (3.33)	1 (5.55)	—
8.	₹ 38,501- ₹ 44,000	14 (4.38)	10 (6.33)	3 (3.33)	1 (5.55)	—
9.	More than ₹ 44,001	7 (2.18)	3 (1.89)	2 (2.22)	2 (11.11)	—
	Total	320 (99.99)	58 (99.99)	90 (99.99)	18 (99.99)	54 (99.99)
	Mean Annual Family Incomes (X)	19095	21870	21327	25666	5804

Note: Figures in parentheses indicate percentages.

the poverty line income ceiling of ₹ 11, 000 but below ₹ 27, 500 per annum. A majority of the Brahmin respondents (i.e. about 72%) also fell in the same income bracket. Almost 24 per cent of the Rajput respondents and 19 per cent of the Brahmin respondents had annual family incomes falling in higher income brackets (i.e. ₹ 27, 500 and above).

Thus, it was seen that the economic status of the respondents was generally middle or low, with the average annual family income being ₹ 19095. The scheduled caste respondents showed a very low economic status with most of them falling below poverty line, and having an average annual family income of ₹ 5805 only.

10. Ownership Pattern

The ownership pattern of the respondents was analyzed in terms of ownership of land and house.

(a) Land ownership: All the families of the respondents owned some land, either in the form of agricultural land or homestead land or both. Almost

92 per cent of them possessed agricultural land. The agricultural land ownership pattern of these 295 families is given in Table 5.9 below:

Table 5.9: Land Holding Pattern of Respondents

S. No.	*Size of land Holdings*	*Respondents (Percentage)*
1.	Less than 1 acre	36.27
2.	1-1.5 acres	26.44
3.	1.5-2 acres	15.93
4.	2-2.5 acres	8.47
5.	2.5-3 acres	5.42
6.	3-3.5 acres	3.73
7.	3. 5-4 acres	3.05
8.	Above 4 acres	0.68
	Total	99.99

Data revealed that a big majority (about 87%) of the families owning agricultural land were marginal farmers, (that is, owning land less than 2.5 acres). The rest, that is, 13 per cent of the families were small farmers, (owning more than 2.5 acres but less than 5 acres of land). So, the average agricultural holdings owned by the respondents were fairly small. This could be partly explained by the economic background of the people and partly by the complex topography and limited availability of cultivable land.

Again, a relationship was observed between the ownership pattern, income levels and caste background. All 25 families not owning agricultural land belonged to the lower castes and had a family income of less than ₹ 11,000 per annum. The rest of the 29 scheduled caste families owned less than 1.5 acres of agricultural land and for all of them the annual family incomes were less than ₹ 20, 000 per annum. Thus, in the absence of alternative occupations there was tremendous dependence on land and agriculture. Moreover, lower castes faced a paucity of agricultural land and were thus, economically poorer than other castes.

(b) Housing: Families of all the respondents possessed a house/dwelling. The houses were either pucca, kutcha or semi-pucca.

While about 70 per cent of the families lived in pucca houses, the rest resided in semi-pucca or kutcha houses.

People's Awareness about the Environment

In this section an attempt has been made to examine the environmental awareness of the respondents in terms of certain parameters, which included: (1) awareness about the importance of environment on life and living; (2) environmental problems, and changes therein; and (3) environmental programmes (both government and people's programmes) in terms of their nature, goals, activities, time frame and effectiveness.

1. *Importance of Environment*: All respondents acknowledged the very important place that environment occupied in their lives and the impact it exercised on their life and living. All of them showed an awareness of the direct relationship between a healthy and well conserved environment and good life and living conditions.

When asked to identify specific reasons for which the environment was perceived as important by them or elaborate upon the nature of importance of the environment, ten main areas of importance were identified. These are:

(a) 'All respondents acknowledged the overriding importance of the environment in their life and living through its impact on the availability of food, fuel, fodder and timber/wood which were all imperative for their basic survival.
(b) A significant majority (almost 92%) perceived the importance of the environment for their livelihood, as the income and economic subsistence in the hill area were determined by the environment, either directly or indirectly.
(c) A big majority of respondents (about 89%) also highlighted the direct relationship between environment and the availability of water for various purposes.
(d) A dominant majority (about 81%) also felt that the state of the environment had a significant impact on the life and living conditions of the womenfolk as they depended on the environment for provision of the basic requirements of food, fuel, fodder and wood for their household. Their work load varied with the state of the environment.
(e) A number of respondents (almost 61%) mentioned the importance of the environment for soil fertility, which in turn affected crop yields.

Environment was perceived as important for a number of other reasons too, like: for supply of clean air (19%); for conducive climate (49%); for safety of life and property (18%); for good health/less morbidity (37%); and for settled life (14%). The latter was mentioned, as a deteriorating environment led to migration, displacement and such other problems.

While the above description revealed the composite perception of the entire group of respondents, a gender-wise and a category-wise analysis revealed some differences in perception in between sexes and categories of respondents.

Gender-wise distribution of responses revealed the gender orientation to the importance of environment. For example, (1) while almost all female respondents (98%) reported a basic linkage between environment and their own lives and living, a relatively smaller proportion of males (68%) showed an awareness and sensitivity of the same (2) Although both groups showed a good awareness of the importance of the environment for an adequate supply of water, more females (97%) than males (83%) acknowledged the same. This was due to the rural women's primary involvement with the provision of water (besides food, fuel, and, fodder) for the household (3) More women (45%) than men (30%) showed an awareness of the relationship between environment and health. This was due to the greater involvement of women with the day to day health problems of their families as compared to men (4) More men (7%) perceived the importance of the environment for soil fertility/productively as compared to women (46%). This could be due to the relatively greater commercial/economic orientation of men towards the natural resource (5) Both men and women showed an excellent awareness of the importance of the environment for their livelihood/ sustenance (approx. 93% and 91% respectively). This was understandable, in view of the perceptible dependence of the subsistence based hill economy on the natural resource base and the almost equal, if not greater involvement of the hill women in the economic life of the region.

A category-wise analysis of the responses also revealed interesting trends. Although all categories of respondents demonstrated a reasonably good awareness about the importance of the environment, the members of voluntary organizations showed a better understanding of the same. This could be concluded from the observation that all 20 respondents belonging to this category had identified the five main areas of importance of the environment. This difference could be explained on the basis of the organizations' day to day involvement with the environmental issues, as also exposure of their staff to relevant literature/training inputs.

Mahila Mangal Dals and local activists also showed a relatively good awareness of the importance of the environment. While the Mahila Mangal Dals comprised of women who showed an active involvement/interaction with environment and thus a greater awareness, the local activists had a greater exposure and experience of working on environmental issues. For example, the erstwhile Chipko activists had a rich experience of working on environmental concerns with environmental stalwarts like C.P. Bhatt or S.L. Bahuguna. Four of them had also been active participants in the Anti-Tehri Dam Movement launched by Shri S.L. Bahuguna in this very area. The other group of local activists comprised of relatively young, educated persons who showed good networking with local and regional voluntary organizations and consequently had a good exposure and awareness of the field.

2. Problems in the Environmental Domain

Table 5.10 elucidates the awareness and understanding of the respondents about the issues, concerns and problems related to their environment.

As is evident from the above, the respondents had identified eleven main environment problems prevailing in the region. These have been briefly described below:

Table 5.10: Perception of the Respondents about the Environmental Problems of the Region

S. No.	*Environmental Problems*	*Respondents (Percentage)*
1.	Deforestation	100.00
2.	Decline/Disappearance of local or indigenous species of flora and seeds.	19.06
3.	Spread of monocultures/Decline in mixed forest.	57.19
4.	Increase in frequency of forest fires	60.63
5.	Drying up of water sources/decline in water supply.	69.06
6.	Water pollution	20.00
7.	Increased incidence of soil erosion/land slides.	59.06
8.	Decline in soil fertility	16.88
9.	Land pollution/lack of sanitation	26.25
10.	Increased occurrence of natural calamities.	50.00
11.	Climatic changes	58.13
12.	Any other changes	10.31

A. Problems Related to Forests

(a) ***Deforestation:*** All the respondents had described deforestation or decline in the extent of tree cover as an important problem. Many instances of them quoting earlier times, when thick, forested belts could be found in the vicinity of their villages, and in the upper belts, came to the attention of the researcher.

(b) ***Changes in nature of vegetation:*** More than three-fourths of the respondents highlighted the changes pertaining to the nature of vegetation of the region. Two main changes highlighted were: a decline in the indigenous varieties of flora/seeds and an increase in monocultures at the cost of mixed-forests. Most respondents expressed their concern over these two changes, as also that the eco-friendly and people-friendly varieties like oak were being replaced by commercially viable monocultures of chir pine. Most of them showed a good awareness of the disadvantages of the present trend and its impact on their own lives, as also on the environment as such.

(c) ***Forest Fires:*** Almost 60 per cent of the respondents identified the recurring forest fires as a main environmental problem of the region. They reported that forest fires, especially in the summer months had become more frequent and were leading to the destruction of vast stretches of the rich reserve forests.

B. Problems Pertaining to Water Resources

Two main problems were identified. These were:

(a) ***Drying up of water sources:*** Almost 69 per cent of the respondents mentioned a decline in water supply due to the drying up of water sources as an important environmental problem confronting them. Many of them also showed an awareness of the link between deforestation and drying up of water sources.

(b) ***Water pollution:*** Almost 20 per cent respondents identified water pollution as an environmental problem. The main reasons attributed for this included dumping of dead bodies and animal carcasses into the rivers; pressure of increasing population and heavy siltation. Some of them also mentioned that the present trend of damming free flowing rivers of the Himalayas was leading to the problem of river pollution.

C. Problems of Land/Soil

Almost 60 per cent of the respondents felt that soil erosion and land slides had become rampant and almost 17 per cent of them reported depletion in soil quality. More than one fourth of the respondents also pointed to the unhygienic conditions and lack of sanitation as important environmental problems. Lack of proper garbage disposal facilities, as also lack of toilets led to insanitary conditions in the villages. It is important to note that as many as 42 respondents showed an awareness of the increasing use of the non-biodegradable plastic material and its adverse impact on the environment.

D. Other Environmental Problems

Almost half of the respondents pointed to the increasing incidence of natural calamities like flashfloods, droughts, and earthquakes as important environmental problems of the region. Many of them mentioned about the recent spate of flash floods which caused immense damage to property and loss of life. Irreversible changes like rivers changing their course, as well as inundation of fertile agricultural/habitational land were taking place, and were contributing to a lot of misery for the local population. About 58 per cent respondents also identified climatic changes prevailing in the region as important. This included changes in average temperature and the amount and pattern of rainfall. As per them, climate had become very unpredictable and varied, and this led to an adverse impact on their life. The average day temperatures had risen and summers were becoming hot, even in this hilly terrain. As far as the "other" environment problems were concerned, a very small proportion of respondents felt that the destruction of the natural habitat of the wild animals was leading to a decline in wildlife or a change in the animal behaviour. They opined that the problem of man eating leopards which had arisen in different parts of Garhwal was a consequence of this habitat destruction. Two respondents also described the destruction of the upper altitude flora, especially in the Bugyals or the alpine pastures, due to increased accessibility of the area to tourists and pilgrims and also due to overgrazing by cattle kept by Gujjars. Six respondents also showed an awareness of the recession of important glaciers like the Khatling and Pindari glaciers, and identified this as an environmental problem/change, which could lead to further problems of immense magnitude.

3. Programmes of Environmental Protection and Promotion

An attempt was made to study the awareness of the respondents about the programmes of environmental protection and promotion being undertaken at the block level. Awareness about governmental programmes and people's programmes was studied separately to determine the respondents' awareness about: (a) the number of programmes being implemented; (b) the nature of the programmes; (c) their goals/objectives; (d) years of operation; (e) target group; and (f) impact/effectiveness. A three point scale was used to study the extent of awareness of the respondents with regard to these components of the programmes.

(a) Awareness about Government Programmes

The awareness of the respondents with regard to governmental environment programmes has been briefly summarized in Table 5.11 below:

Table 5.11: Awareness of Respondents w.r.t. Governmental Environmental Programmes

S. No.	*Programme Components*	*Level of Awareness*		
		Full	*Partial*	*None*
1.	Number of programmes	18 (5.6)	142 (44.4)	160 (50.0)
2.	Number of programmes	18 (5.6)	142 (44.4)	160 (50.0)
3.	Goals/objectives of programmes	18 (5.6)	142 (44.4)	160 (50.0)
4.	Years of operation	–	73 (22.8)	247 (77.2)
5.	Target groups	118 (5.6)	184 (36.9)	302 (57.5)
6.	Impact of programmes	18 (5.6)	118 (36.9)	184 (57.5)

Note: Figures in parentheses indicate percentages.

The data was very revealing in terms of understanding the awareness of respondents about different dimensions of government environmental programmes.

It indicated that only a very small proportion of the respondents (5.6%) showed a 'full' awareness of the number, nature, goals, target groups and impact of government environmental programmes. On the other hand, almost half of the respondents showed no awareness about the ongoing programmes, in terms of their number, nature, goals and objectives, and more than three-fourths (77%) were unaware of their time frame. The rest of the respondents showed a 'partial' awareness of the different aspects of government programmes.

A category-wise distribution of the respondents showed that the panchayat members and functionaries of voluntary organisations showed a relatively better awareness of government programmes. All 18 respondents who showed 'full' awareness were chairpersons of the panchayats. Other panchayat members and all functionaries of voluntary organisations showed a 'partial' awareness of the different aspects of these programmes. This was so because panchayats were the implementing agencies of some of the government programmes, at the grass roots level (e.g., afforestation, plantation work etc. undertaken by the panchayats, though the utilization of funds of the Employment Assurance Schemes like MNREGS). Also panchayat members, specially the Pradhans had greater opportunities to interact with government officials at the block and district levels, and also the Forest Department employees. Members of voluntary organisations also showed some occasional interface with officials and were consequently more exposed to government programmes. Other groups did not show such exposure to the ongoing government initiatives. Most openly acknowledged that no government official bothered to approach them and orient them about governmental initiatives.

The main governmental programmes about which respondents showed some degree of awareness were:

Table 5.12: Awareness of Respondents with Regard to Main Governmental Programmes

S. No.	*Type of Programme*	*Awareness in Percentage (%)*
1.	Afforestation/plantation	50
2.	Forest Protection Programmers	50
3.	Pasture Development Programmes	40.6
4.	Water Conservation Programmers	31.2
5.	Soil Conservation Programmers	31.2
6.	Village Sanitation Programmers	19.37
7.	Promotion of Non-Conventional Energy *Sources*	14.4
8.	Wildlife Conservation Programmes	22.5

It is however important to note that most respondents did not know the nomenclature of the programmes and referred to them by their nature/ objectives. Afforestation/plantation and forest protection initiatives of the government were relatively better known among respondents. This was obvious, as most government programmes generally focused on afforestation and plantation work.

(b) Awareness about Programmes of Voluntary Organisations

Table 5.13 summarizes the awareness of respondents about environment programmes undertaken by the voluntary organisations functioning in the vicinity of their villages.

As is evident from the above data, almost 82 per cent of the respondents were either 'fully' or 'partially' aware of the programmes of voluntary organisations functioning in their area. About 18 per cent respondents reported that they were 'unaware' as there was no voluntary organization working in their vicinity. A majority of the respondents showed a 'full' awareness about the nature, goals, target group and impact of the programmes. However clarity about the exact time frame was lacking among the respondents other than the staff of the voluntary organisations. The main programmes of the voluntary organisations about which the respondents showed awareness were:

Table 5.13: Awareness of Respondents with Regard to Environmental Programmes of Voluntary Organisations

S. No.	*Programme Components*	*Level of Awareness*		
		Full	*Partial*	*None*
1.	Number of programmes	170 (53.13)	93 (29.06)	57 (17.81)
2.	Goals/objectives	164 (51.25)	99 (30.94)	57 (17.81)
3.	Years of operation	23 (7.9)	240 (75.0)	57 (17.81)
4.	Target groups 18	157 (49.06)	106 (33.13)	57 (17.81)
5.	Impact of programmes	148 (49.06	115 (35.94)	57 (17.81)

Note: Figures in parentheses indicate percentages.

(i) Plantation/afforestation/distribution of saplings for plantation (82.19%).
(ii) Environmental awareness programmes/Eco-Development Camps (80%).
(iii) Social action programmes for environmental conservation (75.62%).
(iv) Support/training for people's groups (65.62%).
(v) Village sanitation programmes (61.87%).
(vi) Water conservation (56.25%).
(vii) Protection of local plants including medicinal plants/seeds (53.12%).

Thus, respondents showed a greater awareness of the programmes initiated by the local voluntary organisations. The four relatively well known programmes included: Plantation; Environmental Awareness; Social Action

Initiatives (like Rakshsootra Andolans, Jan Chetna Manch and others); and Support to People's Groups. It is interesting to note that all these programmes entailed greater involvement of people as compared to others. A number of respondents mentioned social action programmes/environmental movements like the 'Chipko Movement' launched by environmental stalwarts like Shri S. L. Bahuguna and Shri Chandi Prasad Bhatt and the 'Anti Tehri Dam Movement' launched by Shri Bahuguna, as notable voluntary efforts of the past, as also contemporary programmes like 'Rakshasutra Andolan'. This was because these programmes had widespread relevance and participation of the people of the region and they could immediately relate to them. A category-wise analysis showed that respondents from all categories showed an awareness of the programmes of voluntary organizations.

(C) Awareness about Programmes of People's Groups

(a) Mahila Mangal Dals: A significant proportion of the respondents (91%) showed awareness about the environmental programmes of the local Mahila Mangal Dals. The following table depicts the details:

Table 5.14: Awareness of Respondents with Regard to Environmental Programmes of Mahila Mangal Dals

S. No.	*Programme Components*	*Level of Awareness*		
		Full	*Partial*	*None*
1.	Number of programmes	273 (85.31)	17 (5.31)	30 (9.38)
2.	Goals/objectives	273 (85.31)	17 (5.31)	30 (9.38)
3.	Years of operation	97 (30.31	193 (60.31)	30 (9.38)
4.	Target groups 18	273 (85.31)	17 (5.31)	30 (9.38)
5.	Impact of programmes	227 (70.94)	63 (19.69)	30 (9.38)

Note: Figures in parentheses represent percentages.

As far as specific awareness about the nature, goals and target groups of the programmes was concerned, almost 85 per cent of the respondents were 'fully' aware of the same. A significant majority (71%) also showed 'full' awareness of the impact of these environment programmes. But a majority of the respondents were only 'partially' aware of the time frame of the programmes. The main programmes of the Mahila Mangal Dals about which the respondents were well aware of were:

(a) Forest protection through fencing and chowkidars (91%).
(b) Plantation work (91%).

(c) Village sanitation (86.01%).
(d) Social action for environmental conservation (86.36%).
(e) Environmental awareness programmes (82%).

It is important to point out that apart from the registered Mahila Mangal Dals being covered by the study, there were many other Dals which were unregistered but working actively in these areas. They were very "visible" in terms of their work in the area of environmental conservation, apart from being involved in other village level activities. Thus, on the whole people showed a much better awareness of their work.

(b) Nav Yuvak Mangal Dals: The awareness of respondents about the environmental programmes of the youth groups was rather low. Only 46 per cent respondents showed such awareness (either 'partial' or 'full'). This was due to the small number of these groups operating in the block (especially those that were registered and functional).

Table 5.15: Awareness of Respondents about the Environmental Programmes of Nav Yuvak Mangal Dals

S. No.	*Programme Components*	*Level of Awareness*		
		Full	*Partial*	*None*
1.	Number of programmes	83 (25.94)	67 (20.94)	170 (53.13)
2.	Goals/objectives	83 (25.94)	67 (20.94)	170 (53.13)
3.	Years of operation	31 (9.69)	119 (37.19)	170 (53.13)
4.	Target groups 18	60 (18.75)	90 (28.12)	170 (53.13)
5.	Impact of programmes	60 (18.75)	90 (28.12)	170 (53.13)

Note: Figures in parentheses indicate percentages.

The above data reveals that out the 47 per cent respondents who showed an awareness about the environmental programmes of the youth groups, only 26 per cent showed 'full' awareness about the nature and goals of the programmes. Moreover about 10 per cent showed a 'full' awareness of the time frame; 19 per cent showed a 'full' awareness of the target groups and the impact of the programmes of the youth groups.

The relatively better known programmes of the youth groups included: Forest Protection and Plantation programmes. It needs to be mentioned here that the awareness of respondents about the environmental programmes of local activists and Van panchayats was not determined by the researcher separately, as both these categories operated in specific areas only. The Van panchayats were only four in number and thus, it was unrealistic to expect a wider awareness about their efforts.

Sources of Awareness

Multiple sources were used by respondents to develop an awareness of the various governmental programmes and programmes of people's groups including voluntary organisations. The most important sources used to develop awareness about governmental programmes included: (a) Panchayat pradhans; (b) Forest officials; (c) Block Development Officer (B.D.O); and (d) Village Level Workers. The main sources used by respondents to develop awareness about programmes of voluntary organisations included: (a) Direct personal involvement in programmes; (b) Village level mobilizers and workers of voluntary organisations and; (c) Meetings and camps organized by voluntary organisations.

The important sources used by respondents to develop awareness about programmes of people's self-help groups included: (a) Direct personal involvement in group programmes; (b) Observation of village level activities of groups; and (c) Word of mouth.

6
People's Participation
Forms, Nature, Levels and Methods

This chapter analyses the participation of people in programmes of environmental protection and promotion, in terms of its forms, nature, duration and level. It also highlights the methods used to secure participation. All this has been done with the objective of providing an in depth understanding of people's participation at the micro level, which is the basic thrust of this study.

Forms of Participation

The study was organised in a block wherein environmental programmes were being organised by the government and people's groups, including voluntary organisations. It is important to indicate that people's environmental action has assumed a regular character from the period of Chipko in 1975-76. Prior to that, people were involved in environmental action, but more on an intermittent basis and not on a regular and sustained basis, (as was highlighted in a previous chapter). Moreover, earlier the environmental programmes were merely perceived as afforestation or forest protection programmes of the government. But gradually, with increasing dimensions of environmental action being perceived, environmental initiatives took the shape of an ongoing programme, covering the twin dimensions of protection and promotion. And in this process, people's action started assuming significant importance along with governmental action.

It is commonly accepted that participation in any programme can be in the form of policy planning, implementing, evaluating or sharing of programme benefits. However, this distinction in terms of the forms of participation was not found to be applicable in the block. Although people participated in different forms, a diffusion or overlap of these different forms was very much evident. Consequently, it was found that the forms of people's participation were not confined to the aforementioned four forms (as will emerge through discussion, a little later in this chapter). A number of important observations were made in relation to the forms of participation existent at the block level. These include:

First of all, the recognition of the importance of the concept of evaluation as a distinct form of participation was lacking, both at the cognitive and at the action level in the area. Evaluation was yet to be accepted as an important element in the management of any programme at the micro level. Consequently, for the organisation of the environmental programmes, either of the government or of the people's groups, there was hardly any infrastructure for the performance of the role of an evaluator. Evaluation, as a distinct form of participation was consequently non-existent at the block level. The implementers or the planners of the programme did whatever little evaluation was undertaken.

Secondly, as far as benefit-sharing was concerned, there were problems related to the identification of specific people as beneficiaries of environmental programmes due to the very nature of these programmes. This was primarily because, apart from the specific benefits flowing out of these programmes to certain designated beneficiaries, environmental programmes provided benefits to all concerned. (Consequently, in a way all participants were beneficiaries). Thus, categorising people in terms of benefit-sharing was not easy, except in such cases where benefits were more tangible and had an economic value or dimension.

Thirdly, the emphasis on centralised planning in governmental programmes, did not leave scope for participation of people as planners, excepting in such cases wherein they were expected to make some alterations or modifications. An analysis of the governmental programmes in chapter IV had revealed that most ongoing governmental environment programmes were either Central Schemes or Centrally Sponsored Schemes or State Schemes, which were being implemented at the district level. Apart from centralised bureaucracies, international aid agencies like the World Bank had also started playing a role in conceiving and planning environmental programmes for the region. This had taken planning further away from the grassroots and the people. In this context it is also important to note that although the Gram Sabha had been envisaged to be the most broad-based village level body conceived to elicit participation of all adult members, but in reality it had no role to play in planning. The suggestions and recommendations of the Gram sabha were not binding on the panchayats. Therefore, at the lower levels (block and village levels), the scope of planning as a form of participation in government programmes was minimal or even absent. Respondents confirmed that they had no role in planning in these programmes. At times they were only asked to give their opinion. Hence, in government programmes, the role of people was more in the form of implementers and beneficiaries.

Fourthly, the forms and nature of participation was also seen to vary with the level of formalization of structure and hierarchical base of different agencies and groups organising the environmental programmes. It was observed that distinctive roles/forms could be seen in organisations having formalized and hierarchical structures, while the organisations/institutions which were not very much formalized and hierarchical in terms of structuring did not have specific roles for different categories of participants in their programmes. Consequently, more distinct roles and forms of participation could be seen in government organisations, which were formal and hierarchical in terms of their structure and functioning, but the same was not applicable for people's organisations. The latter were known for their members working together as a group, without much structural formalisation and segregation of roles and functions. This could be partly attributed to the smallness of the their operation, both in terms of area covered (usually one village or a cluster of 2-3 small village habitations) and their limited size (in terms of the numbers of persons comprising these organisations), and partly on account of financial constraints, and lack of infrastructural availability arising out of it.

People's organisations and groups were also characterised by a greater degree homogeneity arising on account of common interest areas and common understanding of the members, which in the first place drew most members together. There was also greater equality in terms of member's socio-economic status. This also contributed towards the existence of an informal structure and functioning of these organisations. In fact, members of these organisations/ groups commonly believed that a hierarchical structure stood in the way of their effective functioning as grassroots organisations, and it was their flexibility which gave them importance. As a result of all of the above, people's organisations showed a large degree of diffusion and intermingling of roles and forms of participation. In these organisations, persons performing the role of planners also had the responsibility of carrying on implementation. In many cases the same people also shared the benefits of the programmes.

However, it is interesting to point out that within the people's organisations, voluntary organisations showed some variability. Despite their flexibility in functioning and their pronounced emphasis on providing a greater role to the people, members were given specific duties for planning or for implementation, thus making it relatively easier to identify and classify persons in terms of their distinct forms of participation. But the same was rendered extremely difficult in the case of people's groups, like women's groups, youth groups and local activist groups, where due to multiplicity of roles, there was considerable overlapping or diffusion in forms of participation, which in turn presented difficulties in the classification of different forms of participation.

Considering all of the above, the micro level situation was different and forms of participation exhibited by the people in the environmental programmes were not as per the four recognised forms mentioned at the beginning of this section.

In spite of difficulties, some degree of classification and categorisation of roles and forms of people's participation was found possible and attempted. Data available revealed that the participation of people in environmental programmes at the micro-level takes place in three forms, plus a combination of these three forms (which arises out of the diffusion and overlap of forms), and this various according to the agencies securing involvement and participation. Accordingly, the common forms of participation at the level of the people and people's organisations were six in number and these were:

(i) Planners;
(ii) Implementers;
(iii) Beneficiaries;
(iv) Planners cum Implementers;
(v) Implementers cum Beneficiaries;
(vi) Planners cum Implementers cum Beneficiaries.

Table 6.1: Forms of People's Participation in Environmental Protection and Promotion Programmes of the Government

Forms of Participation	*Categories of Participants*						
	Village Councils	*Mahila Mangal Dals*	*Nav Yuvak Mangal Dals*	*Functionaries of voluntary organizations*	*Local activists*	*Van Panchayat Members*	*Total*
Implementers	65	—	—	—	—	—	65 (20.31)
Beneficiaries	45	60	24	9	—	16	154 (48.13)
Implementers cum Beneficiaries	35	—	—	—	—	—	35 (10.94)
Non Participants	35	—	—	11	20	—	66 (20.62)
Total	180	60	2	20	20	16	320 (100.0)

Note: Figures in parentheses indicate percentages.

In contrast, the common forms of participation in the environmental programmes of the government agencies were three in number and these were:

(i) Implementers;
(ii) Beneficiaries and;
(iii) Implementers cum Beneficiaries.

Table 6.1 and 6.2 depict the forms of people's participation in the government environmental programmes and programmes of people's organisations respectively.

Table 6.1 shows that 79.4 per cent respondents were participants in governmental programmes, at the block level. But an analysis of the different forms in which people participate in these programmes reveals that:

1. The most dominant form of people's participation in government programmes was in the form of benefit-sharing, with almost half the people (48%) participating as beneficiaries. This provides direct evidence for the contradiction of the tall claims of the government about following 'participatory' approaches. Reality situation has shown that the government primarily follows a 'beneficiary-oriented' approach. As per this approach, even the stakeholders are treated as 'beneficiaries' and not as 'partners' in environmental management and conservation.
2. People's participation in the implementation of government programmes was also limited. Only one-fifth of the people (i.e., 20.3% of the respondents) reported participation as 'implementers only'. This category mainly comprised of members of panchayat and members of certain committees/sub-committees constituted for a specific purpose. However, such committees were often more in namesake, as was the case with the specially constituted 'Fire Protection Committees'. These were formed in a few villages in the block by the Forest Department. But it was found that these committees were largely dysfunctional. People by and large, did not cooperate in extinguishing forest fires in the Reserve forest. The popular sentiment shared by the majority of the people was manifested in an often repeated statement: "*Forests do not belong to us, they belong to the 'sarkar' (government), and so let the 'sarkar' put off the forest fires*".
3. About one-tenth (or 10.9%) of the respondents participated as 'implementers cum beneficiaries' in government programmes. The category also comprised of panchayat members who along with participating in implementation, were also beneficiaries of some government programmes. It is important to highlight that the limited role of people in the implementation of government programmes could be largely attributed to the lack of suitable mechanisms or infrastructure available for eliciting participation. Apart from panchayats, no other effective mechanisms existed for this purpose. Panchayats had also tended to centralise power within them and had often worked against enabling the common people to participate in government programmes. It is however important to point out that the efforts of the government to constitute Village Forest Management Committees under the World Bank funded Joint Forest Management programme launched in the region, was seen to be a step in the

direction of providing some mechanism to the people to participate in government programmes (But since the committees were behest with multiple functional problems, their potential and scope for effective and meaningful participation in environmental action was seen to be severely curtailed).

Based on all of the above, it could be said that at the micro-level there were three dominant forms of people's participation in government environmental programmes. These were: people as 'beneficiaries', 'implementers' and 'beneficiary cum implementers'. As mentioned earlier, 'planning' and 'evaluation' as distinct forms of participation did not exist at the micro-level.

Table 6.2: Forms of People's Participation in People's Environmental Programmes

Forms of Participation	*Categories of Participants*						
	Village Councils	*Mahila Mangal Dals*	*Nav Yuvak Mangal Dals*	*Functionaries of voluntary organizations*	*Local activists*	*Van Panchayat Members*	*Total*
Planners	20	—	—	7	—	—	27 (8.44)
Implementers	21	—	13	—	—	—	34 (10.63)
Beneficiaries	18	6	—	—	—	—	24 (7.5)
Planners cum Implementers	35	—	—	—	—	20	55 (17.18)
Beneficiaries cum Implementers	41	—	3	—	—	—	44 (13.75)
Planners cum Implementers cum Beneficiaries	45	54	21	—	16	—	136 (42.50)
Total	180	60	24	20	16	20	320 (100.00)

Note: Figures in parentheses indicate percentages.

The above table reveals that:

1. All respondents were participants in the environmental programmes of the people.

2. As far as different forms of participation were concerned there was significant overlapping or diffusion of roles, as a result of which people showed multiple forms of participation. As many as six categories based on forms of participation were evident. These were:

(i) Planners cum implementers cum beneficiaries (42.5%);
(ii) Planners cum Implementers (17.2%);
(iii) Beneficiaries cum implementers (13.7%);
(iv) Implementers (10.6%);

(v) Planners (8.4%); and
(vi) Beneficiaries (7.5%)

Out of these six categories, three categories depicted combinations of different forms, signifying multiple role performance by individual participants, and three categories depicted single forms of participation, thereby signifying single role performance by certain individual participants.

Thus, as has been discussed earlier, apart from the three single and distinct forms of participation, (i.e., as planners, implementers and beneficiaries), people showed three combinations of different forms of participation. This was mainly due to the informal, non-structured and non-hierarchical settings in which people's programmes were carried out. Since people's groups were characterised by decentralized planning and management, participatory decision making, multiple need-based objectives, sustainability considerations and flexibility in approaches, individuals ended up performing more than one role, thus showing more than one form of participation (or combinations of different forms of participation).

3. It is important to note that a significant proportion of respondents showed a combination of different forms of participation or multiple role performance) as compared to those who showed single forms of participation (or single role performance) Almost three-fourths of the participants (73.4%) showed a combination of different forms of participation, while the rest, that is 26.6 per cent showed single forms of participation.

4. The most dominant form of participation shown by people was a combination of all three forms of participation, that is as 'planners cum implementers cum beneficiaries'. A majority of the respondents (42.5%) exhibited this combination of forms. This category of participants comprised of members of women's groups, and youth groups, as also members of Van panchayats. It was observed that these groups functioned democratically and informally and members were expected to share in both planning and implementation related tasks. Besides, as the women's groups and youth groups were self-service groups and Van panchayats were user organisations, members were also beneficiaries of their actions. This category also included members of village councils who were members of the various village level committees (like Forest Protection Committees). These members also performed multiple roles as 'planners cum implementers cum beneficiaries', in context of their own environment programmes.

5. The 'planners cum implementers' category comprised of 17.2 per cent respondents. This category mainly comprised of the local activists, who worked with different village level groups like women, youth, children, school students, farmers, village councils, etc. As local activists functioned very informally, they did not have specific tasks assigned to specific persons in their groups.

Thus, they were responsible for planning the programmes, as also working towards their implementation. This category also included a few pradhans and up-pradhans of panchayats who performed the dual roles of planning and implementation.

6. The category 'implementers cum beneficiaries' comprised of 13.7 per cent of the respondents. A significant proportion of members of the village councils (i.e. 41 in number) belonged to this category and exhibited a combination of implementation and benefit sharing forms of participation. Three employed members of the youth groups also belonged to this category, as they participated in the implementation of the NYMD programmes on an occasional basis (but were regular beneficiaries of their programmes).

7. The single forms of participation, viz. 'planners only', 'implementers only' and beneficiaries only' were shown by 8.44 per cent, 10.63 per cent and 7.5 per cent respondents respectively. The 'planners only' category comprised of panchayat pradhans and chief functionaries of voluntary organisations. The pradhans, as chairpersons of the panchayat and head of village councils (Gram sabha) occupied a very important position in the community. They were consulted and often relied upon by most informal village groups like Mahila Mangal Dals, Nav Yuvak Mangal Dals, Village Forest Committees, and local activist groups etc. to undertake planning/assist in decision making. The chief functionaries of voluntary organisations had the primary duty and responsibility of running their respective organisations, undertaking planning and making decisions pertaining to the functioning of the organisations.

The 'implementers only' category comprised of the other functionaries of the voluntary organisations who were given specific programmes/activities to implement. Besides, the category also included members of panchayat and village councils who associated themselves with the implementation of different programmes.

The 'beneficiaries only' category comprised of 24 respondents, out of which four were senior Mahila Mangal Dal members who were not able to partake active work in their Dal on accounts of age and ill-health. Two other members of their Dals could not participate actively in Dal programmes due to lack of time.

A few members of village councils also belonged to this category as they professed not to have time/interest in village level activities. However, they derived benefits of the programmes, along with other beneficiaries.

8. Evaluation as a distinct form of participation did not exist even in the programmes of people's organisations/groups. Some respondents, especially from the voluntary organisations and panchayats were aware of the importance of monitoring and evaluation, and mentioned that they did undertake the same in context of implementation of certain programmes, but it was done in an informal, and ad-hoc manner.

Thus, Tables 6.1 and 6.2 revealed that at the micro level, the form of people's participation, both in governmental environmental programmes and programmes of people's organisations could not be strictly examined from the point of view of the four generally accepted forms. While the role of an evaluator could not be found, a number of combinations of the remaining three forms were found, especially in people's programmes where significant diffusion of roles was found.

Difference in Forms of People's Participation between Governmental Programmes and Programmes of People's Organisations

Tables 6.1 and 6.2 also reveal important differences between the forms of people's participation in governmental environmental programmes and environmental programmes of people's organisations. These were:

1. All respondents participated in programmes of people's organisations, while one-fifth (20.6%) of the respondents were non-participants in government environmental programmes.

2. There was greater variation and diffusion in forms of participation in the programmes of people's organisations. While participation assumed three forms in government programmes, it was manifested in six main forms in programmes of people's organisations. More people showed single forms of participation (or single role performance) in government programmes, while in programmes of people's organizations more participants exhibited combinations of different forms of participation (or multiple role performance). This was evident from the fact that while 68.4 per cent participants in government programmes showed single forms of participation (as beneficiaries or as implementers), only 26.6 per cent of the participants in people's programmes showed single forms of participation (as planners, implementers or beneficiaries), and a dominant majority (73.4%) showed a combination of different forms of participation.

3. The dominant form of people's participation in governmental programmes was 'benefit-sharing' (shown by 59% participants), followed by 'implementation' (shown by 31.3% participants). On the other hand, 'implementation' was the most dominant form of participation (shown by 84% participants) in programmes of people's organisations. This was followed by 'planning' (68%), and 'benefit-sharing' (63.8% participants).

4. It is important to note that 'planning' is considered to be the most superior and empowering form of participation as it enables people to have a say in decision-making and influencing the course of events related to their own lives and living. While programmes of people's organisations provided access to almost 68 per cent participants to participate in planning and decision-making, government programmes denied any such opportunity to participants. Moreover, more people (almost 84%) were provided with opportunities to

take action based on their decisions, (through participation in implementation) in programmes of people's organisation, as compared to those participating in government programmes (31.3%). On the other hand, while almost half of the total participants (48%) participated solely as beneficiaries in government programmes ('benefit-sharing' being a relatively passive form of participation), the proportion of such participants in programmes of people's organisations was very small (i.e., 7.5% only).

5. Despite difficulties in identifying beneficiaries of the environmental programmes, it was still easy to identify them in government programmes, because most of the government programmes had an economic/tangible dimension.

6. There was greater scope of the involvement of people in all forms of participation in the programmes of people's organisations while the scope in government programmes was restricted.

7. There was also a difference in people's feelings about the programmes of the government and the people's organisations. In context of government programmes, people did not believe that they were their programmes. Quite often, during discussions, they talked of 'Sarkar's' (government's) programmes. They also added that they had no/very little idea about government programmes, and that there was an absolute lack of communication between them and the government officials. As per many of them, "*Sarkari babu to kabhi nazar nahin aate*" (we don't get to see government officials) or "*Forest wale apne ped lagate rehte hain, par hamse koi kuch nahin poochta*" (Forest officials keep planting trees, but don't consult us about any matter). Thus, people considered governmental programmes as 'outsider' programmes. They identified themselves with their own programmes and consequently showed greater participation in the same.

Nature of Participation

The nature of people's participation has been discussed in terms of two components:

Direct/Indirect Participation

As far as a comparison between the nature of people's participation (direct/indirect) in environmental programmes of the government and those of people's organisations is concerned, people's participation in governmental programmes, as 'implementers' was predominantly direct (91%). Only 9 respondents participated in implementation indirectly, that is, through family members (5 of them were women panchayat members who had young children and were often represented by their husbands/fathers in law and 3 were elderly panchayat members, who could not participate on a day to day basis and hence were represented by other family members). As beneficiaries, the participation of people was both direct and indirect (75% and 25% respectively). Indirect participation included participation through family members. It is important to note that most programme benefits were given in the names of heads of families, unless programmes were directed at specific target groups. Grants/funds to affiliating groups/organisations also constituted indirect benefits.

As far as nature of participation in programmes of people's Groups is concerned the following trends emerge:

1. People's participation as 'planners' in the programmes of people's groups was direct (97.3%). 'Planners' played a direct role in planning and decision making process in people's programmes. Only 3 scheduled caste women members of Van Panchayats and 3 female panchayat members were represented by their husbands in the meetings of their groups.

As far as scope of functioning as 'planners' in the people's programmes was concerned, most of the 'planners' reported a broad scope of functioning in terms of roles and functions performed as planners. 'Planners' in voluntary organisations reported sufficient opportunities and scope for planning, as they were responsible for formulation of plans, policies and strategies of action, as also resource mobilization. The scope was facilitated by the higher educational status of this group, their experience, exposure, and training in planning (6 out of the 7 chief functionaries had undertaken some form of training in project formulation, resource mobilization and planning). Chairpersons and vice chairpersons of women's and youth groups also enjoyed greater scope of functioning as 'planners' on account of their relatively higher status in the group, and initiative expected from them during planning and decision making. In case of youth clubs, the chairpersons had a higher educational experience (they were all matriculates and above), as also exposure of interaction with other groups. Women chairpersons were facilitated in their functioning as planners, due to their long work experience with the Dals, age and exposure. (As was revealed in chapter V, chairpersons were the senior most members, both in terms of age and experience of working). All of them mentioned that interaction with panchayat members, NGO functionaries, government officials etc. during the Block Development Committee meetings, as also training cum orientation sessions organised by voluntary organisations and groups like Mahila Samakhya, had enhanced their ability to function as 'planners' and 'implementers' of their programmes.

Local activists working with informal groups also enjoyed sufficient freedom and scope as 'planners'. Like the chief functionaries of voluntary organisations, their prior experience and exposure, as also association with voluntary organisations facilitated their scope of functioning as planners. Sixteen out of the twenty local activists had been actively working on different issues/problems of the area for over 8 years. Van Panchayat and panchayat members also reported sufficient scope of participating as planners in the people's programmes. They had sufficient freedom to formulate their plan of action, rules/regulations for the protection of the common property resources, including village/panchayat forests. This was primarily due to the fact that panchayat and Van Panchayat members had the advantage of their statutory position and was thus given importance by people's groups.

2. The participation of people as 'implementers' in environmental programmes of people's groups was also predominantly direct and almost 97 per cent of the 'implementers' participated in these programmes directly. The 9 respondents who participated indirectly included 3 female Van Panchayat members and 6 members of village councils/panchayats who were often represented by their family members in programme implementation.

The scope of functioning of the implementers was almost the same for all categories of people's groups, except for minor variations. Almost all of them opined that they got sufficient opportunities to express their views and opinion w. r. t. programme formulation and implementation. They also had sufficient freedom to plan strategies of action and implement them, with due consultation with other members/co-implementers. This was more so with functionaries of voluntary organisations, local activists and members of women's and youth groups. Members of voluntary organizations were facilitated in the performance of their roles as 'implementers' by training inputs provided to them through their agencies. 12 of them also acknowledged that they were given the responsibility of evaluating programmes informally on an occasional basis.

Implementation of programmes entailed working on individual tasks and responsibilities, but most often working in teams/groups. It is worth mentioning that apart from the settings, the scope of functioning as 'implementers' was linked to their educational background and exposure. Out of the 204 respondents who expressed their views freely and associated themselves with planning strategies of action, 133 were either middle/high school passed and had a longer duration of affiliation with their groups or organisations (more than 5 years), as compared to those who performed their roles 'in the usual manner' or 'as per expectations of the group' or 'followed standard procedures for implementation'.

3. The nature of participation of people as 'beneficiaries' in the environmental programmes of the people's groups was also direct (97%). Scope of functioning as 'beneficiaries' was greater than under government programmes, as a majority of the 'beneficiaries' opined that they had a greater say in choosing benefits and in expressing their satisfaction/dissatisfaction with the amount/nature/regularity of benefits (182 respondents or 89%).

Regularity of Participation

As far as regularity of people's participation in government programmes was concerned, it varied with the forms of participation. People's participation as 'implementers' was 'intermittent', and participation depended on the availability of a relevant programme, in which the participation of people could be elicited. Participation of people as 'beneficiaries' varied between being 'intermittent' (47.6%) and 'occasional' (52.4%). Benefits under certain programmes, like MNREGS, and other programmes like afforestation, soil conservation, village sanitation, non conventional energy sources/fuel efficient devices were 'intermittent', while benefits like training/orientation to registered MMDs and NYMDs, funding to people's groups, etc. were 'occasional'. On the other hand, regularity of people's participation in people's own programmes presents a different picture.

In terms of regularity of participation, people's involvement in programmes of people's organisations was either 'ongoing'/'regular' or assumed an 'intermittent' nature for all forms of participation. Two thirds of the planners put in 'regular' participation in environmental programmes, while the rest of the one-third participated on 'intermittent' basis. Planners belonging to voluntary organisations, Mahila Mangal Dals, Van Panchayats and Panchayats showed a 'regular' participation, whereas members of Nav Yuvak Mangal Dals, Local activists and members of Village Councils contributed planning inputs on a more 'intermittent' basis.

Again, almost two thirds of the implementers participated in environmental programmes on a 'regular' basis. They included Mahila Mangal Dal members, Nav Yuvak Mangal Dal members, and functionaries of voluntary organizations and members of Van Panchayats. The rest, i.e., 32 per cent of the implementers participated on a more '*ad-hoc*' basis.

All beneficiaries reported a 'regular' participation in benefit sharing (arising out of some or the other environmental programmes of the people's groups/organisations). It is however note worthy that categorisation of beneficiaries in terms of regularity of participation in people's own programmes was difficult, on account of the fact that not all environmental benefits stemming out of their programmes were perceived as tangible benefits. Most beneficiaries generally felt that efforts of the people to protect and promote the environment yielded ongoing benefits to them. Moreover, participation in benefit-sharing was not understood by people as a specific form of participation (like planning or implementation) and this also contributed to their confusion.

Comparison between Nature and Scope of Participation in Governmental and People's Programmes

A comparison of the nature and scope of people's participation in government programmes and programmes of people's groups revealed that:

1. People's participation in government programmes as 'implementers' and 'beneficiaries' was mainly 'direct' (91% implementers and about three-fourths of the beneficiaries participated directly). There was no participation of people in planning of government programmes. People's participation in their own programmes existed in all three forms and was almost totally 'direct', with almost 97 per cent planners, 97 per cent implementers and 97 per cent beneficiaries showing 'direct' participation.

2. People's participation in government programmes as 'implementers' and 'beneficiaries' varied between being 'intermittent' or 'occasional'. This was mainly due to: (i) people perceiving government programmes as 'outsider' programmes; (ii) the sporadic availability of government programmes; (iii) lack of appropriate mechanisms for eliciting people's participation and (iv) almost no direct contact between government officials (other than panchayat members) and local people. On the other hand, a majority of the people (66% planners, 68% implementers and all beneficiaries) participated in their own programmes on a 'regular' basis, while the rest showed 'intermittent' participation. Due to predominance of personal relationship, face-to-face contact and interest of participants in their own action programmes, nature of participation often becomes 'regular' till the need of the situation, which was not the case in government programmes.

3. The scope of participation of people in their own programmes was more than that in government programmes. People's programmes provided greater opportunities and freedom to think, plan, and act and share benefits. This flexibility was absent in government programmes, due to the nature of their bureaucratic functioning and emphasis on following procedural norms, rules and regulations. Moreover, government officials were seen to be averse to devolving roles and responsibilities to people due to their own vested interests, leading to more or less mechanical performance of tasks by people in government programmes.

Duration of Participation

As far as duration of people's participation was concerned, it varied with the nature and duration of programmes as also the organisational structure of the agency seeking participation. The participation of people whether as 'implementers' or 'beneficiaries', in governmental programmes was determined by the time frame of the programme. The situation was different for participation in people's programmes. In this case, it was not only determined by the time frame of the programmes, but also by the continuity of efforts. This continuity of efforts could suffer on account of several factors like loss of interest of leaders or organizers, resistance of vested groups, lack of adequate resources (whether in terms of funds or manpower), etc. Apart from Van Panchayat and Panchayat members, whose duration of participation was determined by their tenure, that is five years (after completion of which they could be re-elected), the duration of participation of people affiliated to other people's groups/organisations was long-term oriented. For example, participation of Mahila Mangal Dal members was long-term oriented, as these groups had continued to function for a long time. Data related to organisational affiliation had revealed that 43 per cent members of MMDs had been participating for more than 10 years and another 40 per cent for between 5 and 10 years. In fact a few chairpersons of these Dals had been participating in the Dal programmes ever since the Chipko Movement in 1973-74. Participation in Nav Yuvak Mangal Dals was also long-term oriented and depended on the duration of existence of the NYMDs. However, it was seen that since the groups comprised of youth members, their participation was limited or curtailed on account of employment, out migration for education/work etc. Data on NYMD members had revealed that 9 youth members had a medium-term and 10 members had a short-term participation in the environmental programmes of the groups.

Duration of participation of functionaries of voluntary organisations was certainly long-term oriented. They could expect to function till the continuance of their organisations. It had been seen that 5 out of 7 of the chief functionaries (planners) of these organisations had shown a long-term participation in programmes, while other functionaries had also been participating for 3 years to 9 years. Participation in programmes organised by local activists/activist groups could expect to continue up to the time the programme/action continued. For the local activists covered by the study, participation had been long-term oriented as for sixteen of them; their programmes had been operational for more than 8 years. For members of village councils, participation was again determined by the continuance of the programmes and interest of members. Most of them had been participating in their programmes for a long period of time, as the various Forest Protection Committees had been functional for a long time.

Level of Participation

The level of participation of the planners, implementers and beneficiaries had been determined with the help of a scale (described in the chapter on 'Methodological Considerations' and presented in Appendix). This was worked out separately for government programmes and programmes of people's groups. Tables 6.3 and 6.4 present the levels of people's participation in government and people's programmes respectively.

The table on levels of participation of people in government programmes was very revealing. It was very interesting to observe that:

1. None of the implementers or beneficiaries participating in government programmes could be categorized as 'active' in terms of the levels of participation.

Table 6.3: Level of Participation of People in Government Environmental Programmes as per Forms of Participation

S. No.	*Type of Participation*	*Levels of Participation*			*Total*
		Active	*Average*	*Passive*	
1.	Implementers	—	58 (58.0)	42	100 (100.0)
2.	Beneficiaries	—	34 (18.0)	155 (82.0)	189 (100.0)

2. As far as implementers were concerned, while 58 per cent of the implementers were 'average' in terms of level of participation, as many 42 per cent of them were 'passive' participants. It was also observed that while a majority of the implementers put in 'active' or 'average' participation in terms of certain indicators like 'regularity in attending meetings', and 'carrying out assigned tasks satisfactorily', many of them were 'passive' or 'average' in terms of the other indicators.
3. A majority of the beneficiaries were 'passive' participants in government programmes, (i.e. 82% of the beneficiaries). The rest of the 34 beneficiaries (or 18% of them) were 'average' in terms of their level of participation. While most beneficiaries reported an 'average' participation in terms of 'selection of self as beneficiaries', they were 'passive' in terms of indicators like: 'decision/choice on nature of benefits', 'grievance redressal' as also in terms of 'action undertaken in case grievances were not met'. This indicated that beneficiaries were 'passive' participants in government programmes. Benefits from government programmes were mainly perceived as the domain of the government and beneficiaries did not perceive much of a role for themselves with regard to them. Thus, beneficiaries, by and large, did not perceive the importance of 'active' participation in benefit sharing.

Table 6.4 presents the level of participation of people as planners, implementers and beneficiaries in the programmes of people's organisations. The results show that:

(a) A majority of the planners showed 'active' participation (61%) or 'average' participation (28%) in planning the environmental programmes. Only 23 planners could be categorized as 'passive' participants.

(b) A similar trend was depicted by the implementers, as a majority of them showed an 'active' level of participation (59%), followed by those who were 'average' in terms of their participation (29%).

Table 6.4: Level of Participation of People in Programmes of People's Groups, as per Forms of Participation

S. No.	Forms of Participation	Levels of Participation			Total
		Active	Average	Passive	
1.	Planners	133 (61.0)	62 (28.4)	23 (10.6)	218 (100.0)
2.	Implementers	158 (58.7)	79 (29.4)	32 (11.9)	269 (100.0)
3.	Beneficiaries	135 (66.2)	59 (28.9)	10 (4.9)	204 (100.0)

Note: Figures in parentheses indicate percentages.

(c) Almost two-thirds of the beneficiaries (66%) were 'active' in terms of their participation in benefit sharing, followed by beneficiaries who put in an 'average' level of participation (29%).

Comparison between Levels of Participation of People in Government Programmes and Programmes of People's Organisations

A comparison of Tables 6.3 and 6.4 brings out the important differences between levels of people's participation in government programmes, and in the programmes of their own groups and organisations. It showed that the level of people's participation in government programmes ranged between 'average' and 'passive', (a majority of implementers showed 'average' participation while a majority of the beneficiaries were 'passive' in terms of their level of participation), the same for people's programmes was mainly 'active' for all three forms of participation, viz. as planners, implementers and beneficiaries, followed by an 'average' level of participation for another sizable proportion of the people.

This difference was mainly due to a lack of sense of identification with the government programmes, which led people into becoming average or casual participants in the same. Most of them perceived the government or 'sarkari' programmes as afforestation/plantation programmes, in which they had no constructive role to play, or as programmes wherein some benefits were just made available to the people on conditional terms. This confirmed to the broad view that people all over held about the government and its programmes. On the other hand, people identified with their own programmes and felt a sense of responsibility towards them. It was revealed through group discussions that, people by and large felt that they had a greater stake in the well being of their natural habitat and that necessitated their personal efforts to protect and promote the same.

Methods of Securing Participation

Both governmental agencies and people's groups and organisations make use of multiple methods to secure people's participation in their environmental programmes. While some methods are common, that is, relied upon by both government and people's groups, some are specific methods, used by particular agencies and groups. These common and specific methods used for securing people's participation are:

Common Methods for the Securing Participation

1. Provision of Organisational Structure: It is a well-established fact that if people can be brought into some form of organisational structure, their participation can be ensured. Local organisations are needed so that they can act as channels through which the local people can participate in the development and implementation of any rural development programme. In case of governmental programmes, the local organisations act as intermediaries between the bureaucracy and the local people, to provide suitable mechanisms/framework for involving people around areas of common needs and problems. Both governmental agencies and people's groups and organisations of the area have tried to secure people's participation in their environmental action programmes through the creation and strengthening of suitable organisational framework at the local level.

As far as the government is concerned, the three-tiered panchayati system is by far the most important and broad-based mechanism that has been created to secure people's participation in rural development at the grassroots level. Besides, through the provision of reservation of seats in the panchayats, the government makes efforts to secure the participation of the disadvantaged and weaker sections, like women, S.Cs and S.Ts, who otherwise are usually sidelined.

Thus, the government has primarily relied on the panchayats to elicit people's participation in its environmental programmes too. Additionally, certain committees and subcommittees have been constituted at the level of the Gram Sabha to implement government programmes and distribute benefits, as and when required.

Although the government had realized the importance of self-help groups in securing people's participation and had also contributed towards the organisation and registration of many such groups in the block, it was not able to use them meaningfully on account of lack of sustained support and a long term perspective of involving them in its various initiatives. As a result, a few government departments had made a sparing use of these groups, as and when needed. In the more recent context (i.e. in the period subsequent to data collection by the researcher), the government agencies, notably the Forest

Department was in the process of making renewed efforts to broaden and strengthen the organisational base for securing people's participation in the environmental conservation programmes. Subsequent to the introduction of the Joint Forest Management Rules, the government had initiated a process of establishing 'Forest User Groups' and 'Village Forest Committees', comprising of elected village representatives for involving people to share responsibilities, products, control and decision-making authority over forestlands. (However, since the World Bank funded the project, foresters themselves were skeptical whether the process would sustain once the funding stopped after its stipulated period of operation). The government was also trying to integrate the Van panchayats into the programme. As per government sources, this was in line with the National Forest Policy and was intended towards broadening the scope of people's participation in natural resource management.

On the other hand, the presence of people's own organisations and groups in the localized context represents a genuine and appropriate indigenous response of the people towards carrying forth their symbiotic relationship with nature. The people themselves have been more active and successful in creating and sustaining a diverse institutional structure for securing a wider grassroots participation in their own initiatives. In fact, the relative isolation of mountain communities and the need for adaptation to a harsh and fragile environment has led to the emergence of strong collective action strategies. Being far from the centres where government officers preside or even manage to reach, these communities have formed their own informal and formal institutions to administer their programmes and even to formulate social and legal 'laws' by consensus. The many village communities (names mentioned earlier), which have been traditionally protecting and managing their forests and other Common Property Resources since the past many years without any outside support, by constituting their own indigenous institutional mechanisms, bear ample testimony to the existence of strong, informal community-based institutions. Called by different names like *Van Samitis* or *Van Suraksha Samitis* or *Van Sansadhan Samitis*, these committees have been eliciting wide participation of people in people's own environmental initiatives. Moreover, the traditions of reciprocity, shared labour, and mutual help form the basis of survival for the mountain communities and has been instrumental in the accumulation of the rich social capital that people possess even in the contemporary context. All these traditions have led to the formation of strong informal institutions. However, it is unfortunate that the government has singularly failed to tap these rich traditions of peoples' organisations to intermediate between the governmental initiatives and the communities. Efforts to create newer structures to propel governmental programmes are futile in a context where strong, vibrant and self-motivated groups and structures already exist.

Many Mahila Mangal Dals (MMDs) and Nav Yuvak Mangal Dals (NYMDs) have been in existence for a long time and have provided a well-accepted and effective institutional mechanism for the participation of women and youth members. Voluntary organizations have also placed great reliance on these groups for securing participation of people in their programmes. On account of their sustained support, local presence and personal contact with the MMDs and NYMDs, the voluntary agencies have developed strong linkages with them, and have used these groups as effective mechanisms for enlisting people's participation. Additionally, a few voluntary agencies have also delegated responsibilities to the people through the constitution of committees like *Vanikaran Samities* (Afforestation Committees), *Gram Swatchata Samities* (Village Sanitation Committees) and others, at the village level.

The local activists have also, relied upon the formal and informal, village –based organisations and groups like village committees, women's/youth groups, panchayats, etc., to execute their environmental programmes. It is important to mention that because of their basic dependence on people and people's participation, the people's groups/organisations have relied upon local institutions to a much greater extent than government agencies.

Moreover, institution-building by people and people's organisations has led to the creation of institutions, which are free from statutory obligations and political considerations. On the other hand, the reliance of government agencies on the local institutional framework has been much less, primarily on account of the fact that the government is yet to incorporate people's participation in most of its environmental programmes. Besides, institution-building by the government agencies has usually led to the creation of institutions with statutory obligations and political considerations, thus creating obstacles in the path of effective people's participation.

However, the mere provision of institutional mechanism does not automatically lead to people's participation. It has to be made functional, through active inputs of the agency seeking participation.

2. Organising meetings and discussions/Establishing contact: Both government agencies and people's groups and organisations use interactive fora like meetings to establish and maintain contact with people, and also to make them aware of their programmes and initiatives. The government agencies were found to use this method more sparingly as compared to the people's organisations, as the government officials rarely visit the village communities themselves. Grassroots workers and block level functionaries are expected to establish contact with the local people. Panchayat members, especially the pradhans are relied upon to organise meetings at the level of the village/groups of villages. Certain other fora like Tehsil Diwas, and Kisan Seva Kendras, exist to also provide for interactive sessions with the people, but relevant officials were found to be irregular in attending the same.

On the other hand, this method was seen to be very popular with people's groups. Voluntary organisations were found to be using this method very frequently, both among their own staff as also with village communities/target groups, for different purposes like creating awareness about environmental problems/programmes, as also for delegation of implementation tasks, and discussing benefit sharing and other agenda. Village councils also use the system of bi-annual meetings and resolutions (wherein procedures about forest protection and management are laid down and enforced) as also other meetings to circulate information about the closing/opening of forests. Special meetings for conflict-resolution are also organized occasionally. Meetings of committees and sub-committees are undertaken as per need. The Gram Sabhas also meet twice in a year (during Kharif and Rabi agricultural seasons) to discuss problems and issues, forward suggestions, approve programmes, budgets etc. Besides, panchayats also conduct periodic meetings to take up relevant local issues.

The women's and youth groups normally organize two meetings every month for the purposes of planning, and implementation of their programmes, as also for discussion on relevant issues. Village leaders, especially panchayat pradhans, ex-pradhans and others are also invited to the meetings as per need for consultation or approval. Van panchayats also organize at least two meetings per month to discuss relevant agenda pertaining to forest management. Local activists rely upon meetings and discussions as the main avenue for mobilizing people's participation.

3. Provision of technical, financial and/or material support: Both government and voluntary organisations provide technical, financial and material support to people/people's groups as a means of securing their participation. The government uses the medium of schemes and programmes to garner people's involvement. Funding and material help under different environmental schemes like afforestation programmes, water conservation, Swajal, village sanitation etc, as also support to self-help groups is provided by occasional financial and material help. The Forest Department also provides technical inputs to Van panchayats and village councils for various environmental initiatives. Three voluntary organisations were also being provided grants and technical inputs by the government on an occasional basis.

Voluntary organisations, although constrained viz. a viz. resources also provide technical and material support to self-help groups and village councils. Inputs in the form of saplings, seeds (free and subsidized), smokeless chulhas and pressure cookers, construction material, as also technical advice have been provided. However, a notable difference was found in the approaches of the government agencies and voluntary organisations pertaining to the provision of support to people. While the voluntary organisations by and large enable people to play an active role as implementers or even beneficiaries by expecting matching contributions from the people (through voluntary contributions, shramdan etc), the government mainly followed a beneficiary-oriented approach, whereby people are 'encouraged' to be dependent on government agencies for financial and material support.

4. Information Dissemination and Awareness Generation: In order to participate meaningfully in any programme, people clearly need sufficient and objective information at hand in a form, which is clearly understood by them. Government agencies mainly rely on panchayat members and block officials to communicate relevant information about government programmes to people. (However, people were found to be quite critical about the lack of contact between government agencies and them. Even block officials hardly ever went to the villages, especially those in the interiors, while higher officials were most conspicuous by their absence).

On the other hand, voluntary organisations emphasize face-to-face contacts, both with individuals and groups. In fact, a multitude of fora are used to attract the attention of the people and provide them basic information about the environmental problems; to conscientise them; and to seek their participation in their programmes. These include religious gatherings like bhajans and kirtans, rendering of epics, festivals, religious fairs etc. for establishing and renewing contacts and to keep people updated about their efforts. Special cultural programmes like puppet shows, drama/theatre, folk songs by local musicians called Bajgis, and folk stories, and poems written by famous poets like Gaurda are held by most voluntary agencies/activist groups to stimulate the flow of information.

A very novel method developed by the voluntary agencies is the concept of Eco-Development Camps. These camps are held regularly to enhance people's understanding of environmental problems and create sensitivity for and knowledge of possible cost-effective solutions to environmental problems. These camps are reported to be extremely effective in awareness generation, as also empowering people with specific skills of undertaking environmental action. Another important method used by voluntary organisations, women's groups and local activists for awareness generation and social action pertains to the holding of on-site meetings like Van Sammelans, Van Goshthis etc. to discuss problems and initiatives pertaining to forest, water etc. The researcher attended many such meetings and observed that these were very effective in stimulating the collective participation of people.

5. Use of community organisers/socials mobilizers: Government agencies claim to have an extension network to act as an intermediary between the government and the village communities. However, in practice the use of extension workers/community level workers seeking support and cooperation for government environmental programmes is extremely limited. A few lower rung functionaries of the Forest Department (forest guards and rangers) were found to be active in mobilizing communities especially into participation in 'Fire Control/Prevention Programmes'.

On the other hand voluntary agencies use social mobilizers and community organisers extensively to create awareness and seek the involvement of people. Most agencies pick up local women volunteers, train them and use them as community mobilizers. The efforts of grassroots groups like Mahila Samakhya have been commendable in this direction. They have trained local women and girls and have empowered them by providing them the opportunity and freedom to work out locally tailored solutions for locally perceived problems. The social mobilizers play an important role in the organisation of people's groups, enabling them to articulate their problems, network with other groups, meet, talk and come up with need specific plans for managing their micro-environment.

6. Creation of stakes and incentives: Creation of personal stakes in the maintenance and sustainable use of natural resources is another method employed by the different agencies and groups to facilitate participation. This is justifiable in context of the fact that people of the region are too poor and are faced with immense pressure to subsist under difficult circumstances. In such a context, they can not be expected to cooperate or give priority to natural resource conservation for future use, when they have to make a survival choice today. Thus, the provision of sustainable livelihood security through the equitable sharing of benefits is an approach used by the government and some people's groups. The government is encouraging organisation of people into different user groups like Van panchayats, Mahila Mangal Dals and cooperatives. That people should be able to perceive 'benefits' as a concrete reality or that the benefits should be "visible" to people is the premise on which this approach is based. The government has also introduced schemes of afforestation, through which people are rewarded for their participation in plantation. Moreover, incentives are given to people for aftercare, as saplings which survive beyond a certain period are given a financial remuneration. Similarly, people's groups like village councils, Mahila Mangal Dals, Van Panchayats and others also work on the principle of 'benefit-sharing' or 'usufruct-sharing'.

7. Training, orientation and demonstrations: The mere possession of knowledge does not automatically lead to popular participation. A more conscious and sensitive strategy of human resource development is required. Skill development to undertake sound environmental management is emphasized by different agencies but operationalized to varying degrees by them. The government agencies reported organising training programmes for environmental conservation like forestry, nursery development, horticulture, soil conservation etc. on an intermittent basis. Voluntary organisations are in fact known to give primary focus to the provision of training to different groups for effective participation in environment conservation programmes. A few of the Mahila Mangal Dals also reported a lot of initiative in enabling their members to develop expertise in certain areas related to natural resource management, like plantation, nursery development, conservation of medicinal herbs etc. Both government agencies and voluntary organisations also use demonstration projects (to varying degrees) to prove the viability of certain environmental initiatives like nursery development, plantations, non-conventional energy sources, herb cultivation, etc.

Specific Methods Used by People's Groups and Organisations

It was interesting to note that apart from the methods mentioned so far, people's groups and organisations rely on certain other methods as well, to secure people's participation on a more ongoing basis, as also on a wider level. A number of reasons lead to the usage of these specific methods by these groups/ organisations. These included: (a) These groups/organisations are more 'people-centric'. Consequently, they attribute more importance to people's involvement, as compared to government agencies. They function on the basic premise that people's participation is central to all developmental efforts; (b) People's groups and organisations are highly dependent on community participation for the success of their programmes. Therefore, there exists a sense of urgency for them to seek the wider participation of people; (c) These groups and organisations are dependent on people for their very existence. They cannot not exist without people and people's support; (d) Being constrained by resource-availability, these groups and organisations have to primarily rely on relatively cheaper, locally available and indigenous methods to garner the support of maximum number of people; and lastly; (e) Being a part of the same socio-cultural context, the voluntary organisations and people's groups have a special understanding of, and a greater affinity to the usage of certain culture-specific methods and approaches, as they emanate out of their own belief systems. Moreover, since these methods find wide acceptance among the local people, they are used effectively to create a wider support-base for these organisations. Some such specific methods that are used by people's groups and organisations are:

1. Use of local knowledge and indigenous technology: Voluntary organisations, local activists and people's groups primarily rely on the use of locally available and indigenous knowledge held by the community. The traditional wisdom possessed and used by the people is integrated into these programmes in order to enhance acceptance and people's participation. For instance, the nature of tree species to be planted, use of local varieties of seeds, type of water harvesting structures, forest management approaches, and fire management practices are all consolidated around local knowledge and indigenous and simple technology.

2. Integration of culture and religion in environmental conservation: People's participation is institutionalized through a variety of social and cultural mechanisms. Since the people of the area are highly religious, tradition bound, and possess a reverential attitude towards nature; some people's groups use religion, folklore, and tradition to elicit people's participation in environmental programmes. Traditional resource management practices like sacred groves, sacred trees, worship of nature and natural resources in the form of deities and such other practices are especially used by village councils, Van Suraksha Samitis, and Mahila Mangal Dals to elicit wider participation of people, as also adherence to commonly approved rules/norms related to forest protection. Women rely on indigenous practices like 'Parikrama' (circumambulation) of the area with the Temple Deity; and the offering the forest collectively to the devata (Deity) –'*devata ko chadhana*'*;* establishment of a '*devsthal*' (abode of the Diety) within the forest; and such other practices to elicit people's participation in forest protection and management endeavors.

Most groups rely on the deep sense of identification that the people possess with regard to their forest and rivers to mobilize participation. Local activists also use cultural symbolisms like the 'Chipko' practice of hugging trees, 'Rakshasutra' (tying a goodwill thread around trees to pronounce a vow for protection), and such other practices to revive memories of local and regional movements for mobilizing widespread participation of village communities for environmental action.

3. Use of traditional mass media for information dissemination: People's groups, especially voluntary organisations and local activists utilize traditional mass media like street theatre, drama, puppet shows, songs and poems (especially those composed by Chipko activists and local leaders), traditional drum beating (dhols), etc. to create awareness and to disseminate relevant information about environmental issues among people. Use of padyatras, cycle tours, and re-enacting of 'dhandaks' (traditional, non-violent protests in the times of the Tehri rulers) is also common. Besides, some voluntary organisations also adopt hunger-strikes, marches, and other sarvodaya methodologies to mobilize people into action.

4. Use of Confrontationist Approaches: Voluntary organisations and local activist groups make purposeful use of 'confrontation' and 'social action' as stimulation to participation. Special social action programmes like Rakshasutra Andolan, Van Andolan, and Van Raksha Andolan, are also organised to mobilize people's collective participation in order to oppose illegal tree felling, commercial exploitation of forests by the Van Nigam and to redress other such concerns. These methods are fairly successful, as they revive memories of earlier movement like Chipko, Anti-Liquor movement, and Tehri Bandh Virodh Andolan. Moreover, such methods enable people to reaffirm community solidarity to resist unjust official action and to press for local rights and benefits.

5. 'Common Interest' as incentive for participation: Different people's groups and voluntary organisations purposefully hold 'activities of common interest' for specific groups to mobilize their participation. For example, one particular voluntary agency has made it a practice of organising weekly 'satsangs' (religious discourses) for the community women. These 'satsangs' are usually followed by discussions on pertinent local issues, including environmental issues. Mahila Mangal Dals tend to organise programmes/activities related to nutrition, health, child care and other issues relevant for members to elicit wider participation of women. Bhajans/kirtans, and Bhagwad Gita paths (citation of the religious texts/epics) are also organized to mobilize women's participation. During agricultural seasons, Dal meetings are organised around women's work schedules and are even held at the fields for the convenience of women. Meetings are also held in the village forests to get a firsthand idea about the issue/problem and discuss solutions. Known variously as 'van sammelans' or 'van goshthis', these fora also possess the advantage of being 'on site' and thereby facilitate a more concerted and site specific deliberation and planning with regard to presenting problems. Sports, competitions, cultural and recreational programmes are organized for mobilizing the involvement of the youth in programmes of Nav Yuvak Mangal Dals and Voluntary Organisations.

6. Capitalizing on traditional ways of self-help and mutual aid: People's organisations place a greater reliance on people's own self-help initiatives. Voluntary contributions by people in the form of locally determined 'phants' (subscriptions for village protection), creation of village forest funds, and shramdan (voluntary labour) evoke a sense of ownership of the programmes among the people, leading to a greater and more sustained participation of the village communities. Thus, people's groups and organisations incorporate these traditional forms of self-help and contributions to enlist participation.

7. Establishing a more personal dialogue/contact with non-participating individuals and social groups: The local presence of people's groups makes it possible for members to establish personalized contact with those individuals and groups who are hard to involve due to work pressures, social barriers, or cultural values, which inhibited their participation.

7
Women and their Participation

Women's Participation: Nature and Forms

Recognising the key role that women play in managing the environment, women's participation in programmes of environmental protection and promotion becomes imperative. An elaborate discussion on the significance of women's participation in these programmes has already been undertaken in the introductory chapter.

This section focusses on the forms, nature, duration, scope and level of women's participation in environmental programmes, both of the government as well as of the various people's groups.

Forms of Participation

Tables 7.1 and 7.2 depict the forms in which women participate in government environment programmes and in programmes of people's groups and organisations.

Table 7.1: Forms of Women's Participation in Government Programmes

S. No.	*Forms of Participants*	*Women Respondents (Percentage)*	*Men Respondents (Percentage)*
1.	Implementers	8.51	29.60
2.	Beneficiaries	57.44	40.78
3.	Implementers cum Beneficiaries	13.48	8.94
4.	Non-Participants	20.57	20.68
	Total	100.0	100.0

As mentioned earlier people's participation and thereby women's participation in government programmes was confined to three different forms i.e. as implementers, as beneficiaries and as implementers cum beneficiaries.

The table revealed that in the study locale:

1. One-fifth of the women did not participate in any form in any of the government environmental programmes. The maximum number of women (57.5%) participated as 'beneficiaries only' in government programmes and

13.5 per cent participated in 'benefit-sharing together with implementation'. Thus, on the whole almost 76 per cent women participated as 'beneficiaries' in government programmes. However, it needs to be mentioned that benefits could also be in the form of occasional/one time provision of saplings for plantation, or intermittent wage employment due to environment related work undertaken under the Employment Guarantee Schemes or a one time help to Mahila Mangal Dals in the form of a small revolving fund at the time of registration). Thus, benefits did not usually have an ongoing or regular nature (This is examined further in the next section).

2. A very small proportion of the total women (i.e. 8.5%) participated as 'implementers only'. The total number of women who participated as 'implementers' (either as 'implementers only' or as 'implementers cum beneficiaries') was 31 (or 22% of the total women participants). This category mainly comprised of the women panchayat members who were involved in the implementation of certain environmental programmes at the Gram Sabha level.

3. Comparing the participation of women with that of men, it was found that approximately 38.5 per cent men participated as 'implementers' as compared to 22 per cent women respondents and 50 per cent men were 'beneficiaries', as compared to almost 71 per cent women. Thus, more women participated as 'beneficiaries' in government programmes. This indicates a strange contrast and that is, while the role that women play in managing the environment was reiterated time and again by agencies of the government, and there did exist a strong opinion that women could be strong allies in environmental programmes, there was almost no effort on the part of the government to enhance their capabilities and opportunities to participate fully in these programmes.

Most state programmes related to the environment are usually of two types: high investment projects that marginalise women or women-specific projects that are themselves marginalised from the mainstream programmes. Strategies to assist women are usually peripheral, limited to income and employment generation only. Thus, it is obvious that the role of women in environmental management and conservation and their inherent knowledge of the natural resource base has been primarily limited to being a subject of seminars and conferences. It is not capitalized upon by the government and does not find an important place in governmental programmes of environmental conservation.

The above table shows the different forms in which women participated in the environmental programmes of people's groups, as also the comparative figures for men respondents. Data shows that:

1. Women participated in five combinations, as far as forms of participation were concerned. These were 'Implementers' (5.7%); 'Beneficiaries' (7.8%);

Table 7.2: Forms of Women's Participation in Environmental Programmes of People's Groups

S. No.	*Forms of Participants*	*Female (Percentage)*	*Male (Percentage)*
1.	Planners	—	15.08
2.	Implementers	5.67	14.53
3.	Beneficiaries	7.80	7.26
4.	Planners cum Implementers	4.26	27.37
5.	Beneficiaries cum Implementers	14.18	13.41
6.	Planners cum Implementers cum Beneficiaries	68.09	22.35
	Total	100.0	100.0

'Planners cum Implementers' (4.3%); 'Beneficiaries cum Implementers' (14.2%); and 'Planners cum Implementers cum Beneficiaries' (68.1%). While no woman participated as 'Planners only', the largest proportion of women fell in the last of the aforementioned categories viz. a combination of planning, implementing and benefit sharing roles (i.e. 68.1% representation). This indicated a very important result i.e. most women were comprehensively involved in the environmental programmes of the people's groups, that is, right from planning to implementation to benefit sharing. The proportion of men falling in this category was only 22.3 per cent.

2. As many as 102 women (or 72.3%) participated as 'planners', compared to 64.8 per cent men. As far as women's participation in implementation was concerned, as many as 130 women respondents or 92.2 per cent women participated in the implementation of programmes. In comparison 77.65 per cent of the males were 'implementers' of environmental programmes.

3. Almost 90 per cent of the women respondents also perceived themselves to be 'beneficiaries' of the environmental programmes of the people's groups, compared to 43 per cent of the men respondents who fell in this category.

4. Data clearly indicated that unlike government programmes, all women participated in the people's programmes. They participated as 'planners', as 'implementers' and as 'beneficiaries'. As compared to men, their participation in all three forms was higher. This showed that people's groups and organisations had provided opportunities for women to participate more optimally in environmental programmes. Even within their gender ascriptive roles, women had been able to traditionally organise around a number of environmental concerns related to their needs, livelihood and a reverence for nature, even though the groups and organisations were often not formalized. This was despite the unusually high workloads of women in the hill society of Garhwal; their relative isolation; and the cultural norms of the hill society. Women had been able to participate as active subjects in programmes of the voluntary organisations and in the community based organisations, but were confined to become passive objects in the case of governmental programmes.

In fact, it was interesting to note that even in the World-Bank funded JFM programme, the government did not envisage a role for women, who were the prime users of the forest produce and the main conservators too. In spite of the fact that in the hills, there are several examples of women-led conservation movements, beginning with the Chipko Movement, the state government continues to look westward for inspiration instead of trusting the rich experiences of its own people.

Nature of Participation

As for the combined group of respondents, the nature of women's participation was analysed in terms of the directness and regularity of participation.

Data on the nature of participation revealed that women's participation as 'implementers' and 'beneficiaries' in government programmes was predominantly 'direct'. Comparison with participation of male respondents showed similar trends as far as participation in 'implementation' was concerned. While 94 per cent males participated as 'implementers' directly, 83.9 per cent women followed suit. However, as 'beneficiaries', more female respondents participated directly (88%) as compared to males (61%). This was mainly because of a few women oriented programmes like Mahila Uthan Yojana, wherein funding for MMDs provided direct benefits to women participating in environmental programmes.

The nature of participation in programmes of people's groups is characterised by the following:

(i) Women's participation in programmes of people's groups was predominantly 'direct' in all three forms, viz. as 'planners' (94.1%), 'implementers' (94.6%) and as 'beneficiaries' (95.3%).

(ii) In comparison the nature of men's participation, in these programmes was completely 'direct' in all three forms.

Scope of Participation

As had been reported for the combined group, women participants too reported a limited scope of participation in government programmes, as compared to programmes of people's groups. One important observation related to the educational status of the women. One graduate woman member was working with a voluntary organisation and two were local activists. They reported a greater scope of work in terms of tasks/roles like chairing meetings, mobilizing womenfolk, preparation of reports/proposals etc. They also represented their groups/organizations at different fora like meetings, training programmes, workshops etc. Similarly, out of the fourteen women who were matriculates, four were working with voluntary organisations, six were panchayat members, one was a local activist and three belonged to MMDs. All these women respondents also reported a greater scope of work in their respective settings, due to their educational status. They were given more responsibilities by their chairpersons/chief workers in terms of coordination of work, handling resources, writing minutes/reports etc. However, at the level of the Mahila Mangal Dals, women did not report much variation in scope with regard to educational attainment.

Regularity of Participation

The following two tables depict the participation of women with regard to the regularity of their participation in both categories of programmes:

Table 7.3: Regularity of Women's Participation in Governmental Programmes

S. No.	*Forms of Participation*	*Nature of Participation*		
		Regular	*Intermittent*	*Total*
1.	Planners	82 (80.39)	20 (19.61)	102 (100.0)
2.	Implementers	111 (85.38)	19 (14.62)	130 (100.0)
3.	Beneficiaries	127 (100.0)	—	127 (100.0)

While Table 7.3 shows that (i) all women participants participated as 'implementers', on 'intermittent' basis, in the context of government programmes. Table 7.4 shows that a majority of women participants (85.4%) participated in the implementation of the people's programmes on a 'regular' basis; (ii) A majority of the women respondents participated as 'beneficiaries' in government programmes on an 'occasional' basis, (i.e. 63%). However, in people's programmes all beneficiaries derived benefits on a 'regular' basis; (iii) While no woman respondent participated as a 'planner' in governmental programmes, a majority of women not only participated as 'planners', they did so on a 'regular' basis in programmes of people's groups. This was mainly due to the ongoing nature of people's programmes, especially programmes of MMDs, Village Councils, and Voluntary organisations.

Table 7.4: Regularity of Women's Participation in Programmes of People's Groups

S. No.	*Forms of Participation*	*Nature of Participation*		
		Intermittent	*Occasional*	*Total*
1	Implementers	31 (100.0)	—	31 (100.0)
2.	Beneficiaries	37 (37.0)	63 (63.0)	100 (100.0)

Duration of Participation

As mentioned earlier, the duration of people's participation, in general, varied with the nature of programmes and the structure of the agencies seeking participation. Participation of people (including women) in governmental programmes depended on the time frame of the programme. But the situation was different for people's programmes, where continuity of efforts also determined the duration, and thereby participation.

Almost an equal proportion of women showed 'short-term' and 'medium-term' duration of participation in environmental programmes (i.e. 37%) and 35.5 per cent respectively). Approximately 28 per cent women showed a 'long-term' duration of participation. Participation of women in women's groups (MMDs) was mostly 'long term' oriented (43%) or 'medium-term' oriented (40%). Similarly, a majority of the women functionaries of voluntary organisations also showed 'medium term' participation. Women activists showed 'long-term' or 'medium-term' duration of participation, and village council members (other than panchayat members) also showed 'medium' or long term' participation.

However, since panchayats are elected on a periodic basis, and most members were relatively new entrants to these bodies, almost all women panchayat members (28 out of 30) and all van panchayat members showed a short-term duration of participation.

Level of Participation

The same scale, as had been used to determine levels of participation of the integrated group was employed here to assess the level of participation. On the basis of the same, the levels of women's participation in governmental and people's environmental programmes were determined. The same is contained in Table 7.5 and 7.6.

Table 7.5: Level of People's Participation in Government Programmes, as per Forms and Gender

S. No.	*Nature of Participation*	*Levels of Participation*					
		Average		*Passive*		*Total*	
		F	*M*	*F*	*M*	*F*	*M*
1.	Implementers	13 (41.94)	45 (65.22)	18 (58.06)	24 (34.78)	31 (100.0)	69 (100.0)
2.	Beneficiaries	9 (9.0)	25 (28.09)	91 (91.0)	64 (71.91)	100 (100.0)	89 (100.0)

Table 7.5 presents a comparative picture between women and men with regard to levels of participation in governmental programmes. Data showed

that: (i) The levels of women's participation, both as 'implementers' and 'beneficiaries' in these programmes varied between being 'average' to 'passive', with almost 58 per cent of them showing 'passive' participation as 'implementers' and a significant majority (91%) being 'passive' beneficiaries (ii) In comparison, a majority of the men respondents (65.2%) showed 'average' participation as 'implementers'. However, even for men, a majority (about 72%) of them were 'passive' beneficiaries of government programmes.

Table 7.6: Level of People's Participation in Programmes of People's Group as per Forms and Gender

S. No.	Form of Participation	Level of Participation							
		Active		Average		Passive		Total	
		F	M	F	M	F	M	F	M
1.	Planners	62 (60.78)	71 (61.21)	27 (26.47)	35 (30.17)	13 (12.75)	10 (8.62)	102 (100.0)	116 (100..0)
2.	Implementers	87 (66.92)	71 (51.08)	28 (21.54)	51 (36.69)	15 (11.54)	17 (12.23)	130 (100.0)	139 (100.0)
3.	Beneficiaries	83 (65.35)	52 (67.53)	39 (30.71)	20 (25.97)	5 (3.94)	5 (6.49)	127 (100.0)	77 (100.0)

On the other hand, the following results were reflected from Table 7.6, about women's participation in programmes of people's groups:

1. Women showed higher levels of participation in all three roles, viz. as 'planners', 'implementers' and 'beneficiaries', which is a very positive trend. While 60.8 per cent women were 'active' planners, almost two-thirds of them were 'active' implementers and beneficiaries. Moreover, a little more than one-fourth of the women were 'average' participants in their planning roles, and a little more than one-fifth of them were 'average' participants in the implementation of programmes. About 31 per cent were 'average' in their participation in benefit-sharing. Only a minority of the women was 'passive' in terms of their participation in all three forms.
2. A comparison with men's participation (reflected in the same table) revealed unusual results, as data showed that women indicated the same (and at times higher) levels of participation in comparison to men. Almost 61 per cent of women and men respondents showed 'active' participation in planning and decision-making. More women (67%) were 'active' implementers as compared to men (52%). Almost an equal proportion of women and men showed an 'active' participation in benefit-sharing (65% and 67.5%)

Comparison between Women's Participation in Government Programmes and Programmes of People's Groups

1. There were more opportunities offered by programmes organised by people's groups and organisations to enable women to participate as compared to government programmes. Consequently, a majority of women participated in all three forms viz. as 'planners' (72.3%); as 'implementors' (92.2%) and as 'beneficiaries' (90%) in programmes of people's groups. In contrast, while there was no participation of women in planning/decision-making in the government programmes, the same in implementation was low (only 22%). A majority of women (71 %) were however 'beneficiaries' in the government programmes. This reflected the 'beneficiary' oriented approach of the government agencies as compared to the 'participatory' approach of the people's groups.
2. Nature of women's participation (as implementers and beneficiaries) in government programmes, and in programmes of people's groups (as planners, implementers and beneficiaries) was mainly 'direct'.
3. Scope of participation was limited in government programmes, as these were pre-determined in terms of their goals, nature, benefits etc. However, the programmes of people's groups presented sufficient scope for participation of women in a variety of ways. Moreover, scope of participation was enhanced for higher levels of educational attainment.
4. In terms of regularity of participation, participation of women was 'intermittent' or 'occasional' in government programmes, as the same depended on the availability of such programmes. However, a predominant majority of women showed a 'regular' participation in the people's programmes, due to the ongoing nature of people's initiatives.
5. Women's participation in government programmes was mostly 'passive' or 'average', on account of lack of interest of women in these programmes, as also lack of suitable mechanisms to elicit their participation. On the other hand, a predominant majority of women showed 'active' participation in people's programmes, due to ample scope and opportunities, as also the women perceiving these programmes as their 'own' programmes.

8
People's Perception about their Participation

The chapter examines the perception of people in relation to: (1) the factors hindering/promoting participation; (2) the impact of participation on their own self, on their families and on the state of environment; (3) The nature of environmental programmes required to be undertaken in future, and the desirable role to be performed by different organisations/agencies with regard to the programmes; and (4) suggestions for promoting the participation of people in general, and women in particular.

Factors Promoting/Hindering Participation

There was no single factor. Rather, a combination of factors was identified by the people in terms of their role in hindering or promoting their participation in environmental programmes. Moreover, these factors were interrelated or linked, as is evident from Table 8.1, which presents a detailed account of these factors:

An analysis of the responses revealed very interesting results. It was seen that there were multiple factors, influencing participation and these could be classified in terms of five broad categories. It was also important to note that most of the factors identified by the respondents had a positive and negative connotation in terms of their role as a facilitator of participation, or as an obstacle to participation.

It was seen that a number of **Operational Factors**, played a role in influencing the participation of people. The 'lack of communication and contact with government officials' hindered the participation of almost 61 per cent respondents, while a 'regular contact with functionaries and members of people's organisations' promoted the participation of almost one-fourth respondents. About 53 per cent respondents perceived 'lack of information about programmes' as a factor hindering participation, (especially in context of government programmes), while approximately 38 per cent respondents were facilitated in their participation by their 'awareness about on going programmes'. Again, almost 31 per cent respondents felt that the 'high level of centralization of planning and implementation,' associated with

Table 8.1: Factors Promoting/Hindering Participation in Environmental Programmes

S. No.	Factors	Distribution of Respondents (Percentage)	
		Factor acting as a 'Promoter'	Factor acting as a 'Hindrance'
A. Structural/Institutional Factors			
1.	Presence/absence of participatory mechanisms/institutions	55.3	25.9
2.	Presence/absence of catalysts (Voluntary organisations, activist groups, etc)	42.2	12.8
3.	Quality/Role of leadership	16.9	5.6
B. Operational Factors (Related to planning and management)			
1.	Centralisation/decentralisation of planning and implementation	35.6	30.6
2.	Functioning of agencies/organisations	–	5.3
3.	Availability/lack of information about programmes	37.8	53.1
4.	Management of programme	–	13.4
5.	Presence/absence of contact with officials/ functionaries	25.6	61.3
6.	Availability/lack of funding, resources and other supportive infrastructure	–	63.1
7.	Topography	–	9.7
C. Economic Factors			
1.	Livelihood/Survival Concerns	34.7	20.6
2.	Availability/Lack of Benefits: of distribution of benefits	58.7	10.6
D. Personal Factors			
1.	Knowledge/Awareness about environment	29.1	–
2.	Literacy and Educational Status	22.8	18.7
3.	Training and Capacity Building	15.9	–
4.	Personal Interest/Inclination	22.8	–
5.	Availability/Lack of time	–	50.3
6.	Occupation with Family/Household responsibilities	–	46.9
7.	Absence/Presence of family cooperation	24.2	15.0
E. Socio-Cultural Factors			
1.	Social/Religious Customs and Traditions	22.8	10.3
2.	Heterogeneity/Homogeneity of caste, class, structure	–	12.8
3.	Gender-Specific Cultural Factors	–	17.2
4.	Presence/Lack of Community Solidarity	16.9	5.9

governmental programmes was an obstacle, while almost 36 per cent of them considered the 'decentralized functioning of people's organisations' as an enabling factor for participation. However, as far as 'funding/resources' were concerned, 63 per cent respondents perceived the 'lack of funds, resources other supportive infrastructure', as deterrent to their participation especially in programmes of people's organisations.

The **Personal Factors** were also seen to affect people's participation, both positively and negatively. Two important personal factors identified mainly by women as impeding factors were 'lack of time' and ' preoccupation with family/household responsibilities' (by 50 per cent and 47 per cent respondents respectively). Apart from the unequal gender based work distribution, substantial out migration of men was also instrumental in unusually high work burdens for women leading to a curtailment in their participation in developmental initiatives. The 30 per cent respondents who perceived 'environmental awareness' as a facilitating factor were mostly educated, (i.e. 65 out of 93 such respondents). It is important to note that only women respondents acknowledged 'family support' as an important factor influencing their participation. While the 'presence of family support' facilitated 78 female respondents, the absence of it curtailed the participation of 48 female respondents.

It is also important to note that a small proportion of people perceived literacy/education as a facilitating factor (23%) and an even smaller proportion (i.e. 18.7%) perceived it as a factor impeding participation. When probed, many people mentioned that they had been managing and protecting their resources traditionally, and their traditional wisdom and understanding of their environment equipped them sufficiently for this work. However, more woman respondents (42 out of 60) felt hindered by lack of literacy and education than men respondents. As per them, lack of education deprived them of benefits of government programmes like technology, credit and other inputs available to men.

Although **Structural/Institutional Factors and Economic Factors** also worked both ways, more respondents perceived them in terms of their facilitating role. Almost 55 per cent of them acknowledged the 'availability of participatory mechanisms and existing institutions' for eliciting people's participation as a main facilitator of their participation (especially in context of people's programmes). On the other hand, absence of such mechanisms (especially in government programmes) proved to be a hindrance to the participation of 26 per cent respondents.

Almost 17 per cent respondents felt that a 'committed village leadership' facilitated their participation, while 18 persons acknowledged the negative influence of a 'corrupt/partisan oriented leadership' in hindering participation.

The **Economic Factors** were seen to have an important influence on participation. More respondents perceived both the Economic Factors as facilitating factors. 'Availability of benefits' was a facilitating factor for almost 59 per cent respondents. On the other hand, only a small proportion (11%) felt that 'lack of benefits' or 'inequitable distribution of benefits' limited their participation. 'Livelihood and survival concerns' acted as facilitating factors for almost 35 per cent respondents, who reported that since they depended on their environment for their sustenance, they felt compelled to protect/conserve it. However, almost 20 per cent of the respondents felt curtailed in their participation in environmental programmes due to their preoccupation with earning their livelihood.

As far as **Socio-Cultural Factors** were concerned, it was primarily female respondents who perceived these factors as affecting their participation. Contrary to expectations socio-cultural traditions had a more facilitating influence on people's participation. It was interesting to see that almost 23 per cent people felt facilitated in their participation on account of the social/cultural/religious customs and traditions, and only about 10 per cent were obstructed by the same. An analysis of the former category of responses revealed that the practice of traditional community management of natural resources, which was culturally determined, and the socio-religious practices followed by the people to protect and promote their environment (like sacred groves, nature-worship etc.), acted as facilitators of participation. The people were inclined to continue with such commonly accepted and often revered practices and traditions. Moreover, 23 female respondents from this group felt that their important role in the subsistence economy of the region gave them the social sanction to participate in environmental programmes. About 17 per cent female respondents however felt gender-specific factors (like curtailment of freedom, unfavourable attitude of family elders/male members, inability to travel outside village/block, frequent child-bearing etc.) hindered their participation in environmental programmes to some extent. Another 10 per cent respondents, who were all female, reported other social customs and traditions impeding their participation. These included women belonging to higher castes, who were not expected to go to public gatherings, as also young daughters-in-law who were expected to remain confined to the households. Thus, socio-cultural factors impinged more on women's participation in environmental programmes.

Factors Promoting/Hindering Women's Participation

The responses of women respondents with regard to factors promoting and hindering participation were analysed separately in order to develop an in depth insight into, women's participation as distinct from people's participation in general. Table 8.2 presents the factors, which promoted or hindered women's participation:

Table 8.2 reveals the multiple factors promoting and hindering women's participation in environmental programmes and they pertained to a mix of structural, economic, operational, personal and socio-cultural factors. A comparison of the factors promoting and hindering people's participation

Table 8.2: Factors Promoting/Hindering Women's Participation

S. No.	*Factors*	*Distribution of Female Respondents (Percentage)*	
		Acting as a 'Promoter'	*Acting as a 'Hindrance'*
A.	*Structural/Institutional Factors*		
1.	Presence/absence of participatory mechanisms/ institutions	59.6	23.4
2.	Presence/absence of catalysts	57.5	9.2
3.	Leadership	9.9	1.4
B.	*Operational Factors (Related to planning and management)*		
1.	Centralisation/decentralisation of planning and implementation	26.9	22.7
2.	Functioning of agencies/organisations		4.3
3.	Availability/lack of information about programmes	38.3	58.2
4.	Management of programme		10.6
5.	Presence/absence of communication and contact	15.6	66.0
6.	Availability/lack of funding, resources		57.5
7.	Topography		20.6
C.	*Economic Factors*		
1.	Livelihood/Survival Concerns	48.23	22.7
2.	Availability/Lack of Benefits:	53.9	5.7
D.	*Personal Factors*		
1.	Knowledge/Awareness about environment	26.2	
2.	Literacy and Educational Status	17.0	29.8
3.	Training and Capacity Building	7.8	
4.	Personal Interest/Inclination	16.31	
5.	Availability/Lack of time		70.2
6.	Occupation with Family/Household responsibilities		83.7
7.	Absence/Presence of family cooperation	55.3	34.0
E.	*Socio-Cultural Factors*		
1.	Social/Religious Customs and Traditions	32.6	23.4
2.	Heterogeneity/Homogeneity of caste, class, structure		9.9
3.	Gender-Specific Cultural Factors		39.0
4.	Presence/Lack of Community Solidarity	6.4	2.1

(generally), and women's participation (particularly) revealed that while most factors were common to both categories, certain factors distinctly promoted or hindered women's participation. A brief description of these follows:

Important Factors Promoting Women's Participation

1. 'Presence of catalyst' in the form of voluntary organisations, local activists etc., was a very important factor promoting women's participation (reported by 57.5% women). Traditionally, women of the region had been mobilized, organised and supported by the local voluntary organisations, Chipko activists and Sarvodaya leaders.

Thus, they were perceived as playing a significant role in facilitating women's participation in environmental and even other developmental initiatives.

2. 'Presence of institutional/participatory networks' tended to play an important role in facilitating the participation of almost 60 per cent of the women respondents. In such institutions, women found a common forum to raise and work for issues related specifically to them, without these issues being undermined by the menfolk. Women acknowledged developing self-confidence, a sense of empowerment, and an opportunity for leadership, a chance that is difficult when men are also members. They felt that they could participate more effectively, as meetings were arranged around their work schedules, and usually held informally, allowing more participation of all members. Moreover, common struggles and common problems brought a sense of solidarity to the group, which increased their enthusiasm to become involved in activities to improve their status and living conditions.
3. 'Livelihood and survival concerns' were also perceived as important promoters of participation by almost half of the total women respondents. As per them, their basic dependence on their natural resource base to eke out a livelihood/sustenance for themselves, and their families provided a strong incentive for them to participate in environmental conservation initiatives. In fact, most of them reported that the protection of environment was a part of their basic strategy for survival and long-term security.
4. The 'presence of family support' was another important factor, which facilitated the participation of 55 per cent women. Since women of the region bear unusually heavy work burdens and responsibilities, and are also bound by cultural traditions, the presence of family consent, support and cooperation was seen as an essential pre-requisite to women's participation in outside activities. Many women acknowledged that the helpful attitude of their husbands, and their support enabled them to participate. Sharing of responsibilities by other female members, daughters and support of family elders was perceived as an extremely important facilitator for their participation.

Important Factors Hindering Women's Participation

1. 'Lack of time' was perceived as the most important factor impeding women's participation in environmental programmes. For almost 70 per cent women, time was the biggest constraint to undertaking any development activities. The heavy work burdens and the increasing

time spent in gathering biomass resources for household and livestock rendered their participation difficult, if not impossible.

2. A related factor hindering women's participation was their 'preoccupation with household and other family responsibilities'. Almost 84 per cent women respondents acknowledged this preoccupation (both physical and mental) as an obstacle to effective participation.
3. Certain 'gender specific cultural factors' were also perceived by 39 per cent of the women respondents as hindering their participation. These mainly related to: culture-imposed restrictions on women attending public gatherings and other male dominated fora; restrictions on women's mobility outside village community; women's lack of confidence in approaching officials with requests; their own inhibitions in articulating their views and opinion in male-dominated groups; frequent pregnancies, child births and the resultant ill-health, etc. A few women even reported a feeling of jealousy felt by male family members on account of women's election to Panchayats, Van panchayats and other formal bodies and their efforts to curb their participation, as a gender specific factor curtailing women's participation. However, looked at in a more positive perspective, only 39 per cent women reported gender specific constraints as hindering their participation. This could be due to their dominant role in the subsistence economy of the region, which gives the hill women a freedom of action that allows them a role outside the household, unlike their counter parts in the plains.
4. 'Lack of family support and cooperation' was a hindering factor only for women participants. No male respondent perceived this constraint.
5. 'Topographical constraints' also posed as a factor hindering women's participation in programmes organised at venues outside the village. Many programmes organised at block or district headquarters or at distant voluntary organisations could not be attended by women due to the distance factor, poor transport infrastructure and other topographical constraints.

Impact of Participation

The respondents acknowledged that their participation had led to an impact at three levels that is, on their own self; on their families and on the state of their environment.

It is important to note that most people took some time to think and articulate their perception about the impact of their participation, as they had never really given much thought to the same But with a little help from researcher, they were able to report their perceptions. The women were more forthcoming in sharing their perceptions.

A. Impact on 'Self'

A dominant majority of the respondents, i.e. 282 or 88.12 per cent perceived a 'positive' impact of their participation on themselves. The rest of the 38 respondents felt that the impact was both 'positive' and 'negative'. Table 7.3 depicts the perception of respondents with regard to the impact of their participation on their own self:

Table 8.3: Perception about Impact of People's Participation on 'Self'

S. No.	*Nature of Impact*	*Distribution of Respondents (Percentage)*		
		Males	*Females*	*Total*
Positive Impact				
I Economic Impact				
1.	Increase in income and standard of living	61.2	38.8	30.6
2.	Better availability of fuel, fodder, water, etc.(impacting expenditure)	58.3	41.7	15.0
II. Impact on 'Quality of life'				
1.	Decline in drudgery due to improvement	–	100	17.5
2.	Improvement in quality of life due to better environment	49.4	50.6	25.9
III. Impact on Personal self				
1.	Development of general and Environmental awareness	54.1	45.9	69.4
2.	Development of self-confidence, autonomy, expression and articulation of views/opinions	27.6	72.4	47.5
3.	Development of leadership quality/decision making ability	46.9	53.1	20.0
4.	Development of skills	60.5	39.5	26.9
5.	Enhancement of self-esteem/self fulfilment	25.6	74.4	13.4
IV. Impact on Social Image and Social Networking				
1.	Improvement of position in family	17.9	82.1	24.4
2.	Creation of positive image in society/social recognition	61.3	38.7	52.5
3.	Establishment of new contacts/opportunities	86.9	13.1	19.1
Negative Impacts				
I.	Additional burden on self/responsibilities	–	100	11.3
II.	Neglect of Self	–	100	3.7
III.	Increase in tension/stress due to family problems/ opposition	16.0	84.0	7.8
IV.	Tension due to adverse community/group dynamics	91.7	8.3	3.7
V.	Increase in expenditure/financial burden	76.2	23.8	6.6

Table 8.3 shows that the majority of the people perceived a 'positive' impact of their participation on themselves and this 'positive' impact could be categorised into five broad categories, (depending on the nature of the

impact.). Most people perceived 'Personal development' as an important positive impact of their participation. Within this category, almost 70 per cent respondents acknowledged 'developing awareness' (general and environmental), as a result of their participation. A little less than half the total respondents developed self confidence, autonomy and ability to articulate views, and one-fifth of them developed leadership and decision making abilities. More than one-fourth of the respondents developed diverse skills (mostly due to training in nursery development, water harvesting, plantation, environmental sanitation, income generation from NTFPs etc). Many respondents perceived enhancement of 'social image and social recognition' as a positive impact of significance. Under this category, 'creation of improved position in family situation' was perceived as a positive impact by one-fourth of the respondents and the 'creation of positive societal image and social recognition' was perceived as positive impacts of participation on self by more than half of the respondents

'Increase in income and standard of living' was an economic impact arising out of the participation of approximately 31 per cent respondents. Further, a gender-based analysis of responses showed very important results. It was seen that for women respondents the impact on 'quality of life' and on personal development' occupied primary importance. The former category included impacts like 'reduction in drudgery' (all 56 respondents who perceived this impact were women), while the latter category included 'development of confidence, autonomy, expression and articulation', (approximately 72% of all respondents reporting this impact were women): leadership and decision making ability (53%); and 'enhancement of self-esteem and self-fulfilment' (74%), Furthermore, a majority of the respondents who perceived an 'improvement in their position in family situation' as a result of their participation were also women (82%). This are important observations, as they support the point of view that women's participation in environmental initiatives positively contributes to an enhancement of their self image, position in the family and personal development, as also towards an improvement in their quality of life.

The 'negative' impacts of participation were also felt more by womenfolk. These included additional workload (for 11.3% respondents, who were all female): decline in leisure time; neglect of self; increase in tension due to family problems (arising out of travel, participation in meetings etc.).

B. Impact on 'Family'

The following table highlights the perception of the respondents about the impact of their participation on their families:

As far as the perception of respondents with regard to the impact of their participation on their families is concerned, a majority of them reported a 'positive' impact (that is, 244 respondents or 76.3%). While 48 respondents reported a mix of 'positive' and 'negative' impacts, 16 of them reported a 'negative' impact only. Another 12 respondents did not perceive any significant impact of their participation on their families.

Table 8.4: Perception of Respondents about the Impact of their Participation on their Families

S. No.	*Nature of Impact*	*Distribution of respondents (Percentage)*
Positive Impacts		
I. Economic Impact		
1.	Supplementation of income and improvement in standard of living	30.6
2.	Better availability of fodder, fuel, etc.	15.0
II. Impact on Quality of Life		
1.	Improvement in quality of life due to better availability of fuel, fodder, water, etc.	42.5
III. Socio-Psychological Impact		
1.	Increase in awareness among family members	38.7
2.	Development of progressive atmosphere in family	11.9
3.	Involvement of other family members in development work	20.6
4.	Enhancement of status and prestige of family	60.6
Negative Impacts		
I.	Neglect of Household/Family responsibilities	20.0
II.	Neglect of children and Elderly	16.3
III.	Additional Work Burden on family members	12.8
IV.	Family Tension/dissatisfaction on account of participation	7.8
V.	Differences with other families/community	2.5
VI.	Financial Burden on Family	6.6

As far as the 'positive' impact of participation was concerned, it was felt in four main ways: (1) Enhancement of status and prestige of families for 60.6 per cent respondents; (2) Increase in awareness among family members, for about 39 per cent respondents. [These two comprised the socio-psychological impact of participation] (3) Improvement in the quality of life of families (42.5%); and (4) Economic impact, in terms of supplementation of family income (30.6% of the respondents). It is important to note that 64 respondents, who comprised one-fifth of the total respondents, perceived certain ill effects of their participation on their families. Out of these 64 respondents, 52 of them were female respondents. 'Neglect of household work and family responsibilities' and 'neglect of children and elderly family members' were the two main negatives, acknowledged by 20 per cent and 16 per cent respondents respectively.

Thus, for these 52 respondents, who comprised more than one-third of the total female respondents, participation in tasks/activities outside their culturally assigned work roles entailed a neglect of their families and household work. It was observed that most of these women felt a sense of guilt and remorse that their families and households suffered on account of their participation. The study has already revealed that lack of time, and heavy domestic burdens posed as important hindrances to women's participation (in the preceding section). It automatically follows that a reduction in work burdens of women and provision of support systems for them will go a long way in facilitating women's participation in developmental initiatives.

C. Impact of Participation on the 'State of the Environment'

The perception of respondents about the impact of their participation on the general state of their environmental was also gathered. It was revealed that all respondents perceived their participation as having a 'positive' impact on the environment. Although 32 per cent of the respondents felt that this impact was not discernable in physical terms, the rest (that is, 218 respondents or 68% of them) felt that the 'positive' impact was discernable. Table 8.5 presents the positive impact of people's participation on the state of their environment.

Table 8.5: Impact of People's Participation on the State of the Environment

S. No.	*Nature of Impact*
Forest and Forestry Related	
1.	Regeneration of degraded community lands (58.8%)
2.	Improvement in forest cover in adjoining forests (62.5%)
3.	Improvement in quality of reserved forests (due to protection efforts) (37.8%)
4.	Availability of trees on private lands (16.3%)
5.	Promotion of mixed tree cover (47.5%)
Pasture development and development of grasslands	
6.	Replenishment of grasses, shrubs (44.4%)
Soil conservation	
7.	Improvement in soil fertility (23.4%)
8.	Decline in soil erosion (10%)
Water conservation	
9.	Improvement in water availability/recharging of water resources (25.6%)
10.	Decline in water pollution (15%)
Environmental Sanitation	
11.	Improvement in village sanitation (31.9%)
12.	Decline in use of non-biodegradable materials (10%)
Other impacts	
13.	Conservation/promotion of medicinal herbs (20.63%)
14.	Revival/use of local varieties of seeds/local species of vegetation (13.1%)

The data shows that a majority of the respondents perceived multiple benefits for the state of their environment, as a result of their participation in environmental programmes. Impact on 'forests' occupied primary focus, as most of the benefits were related to improvement in the state of the forests (both community and reserved forests). Regeneration of forests (59%) and improvement in forest cover (62.5%), as also promotion of mixed tree cover (47.5%), was the specific benefit derived by the forests of the area. Grassland development was also perceived as an important positive impact stemming from the participation of people (by 44.4% respondents). Since forests and grasslands played an important role in the life and living of the people, they were the focus of most environmental initiatives, and so quite naturally, they tended to be impacted more positively by people's participation in the same.

Suggestions for Future Environmental Initiatives

All the respondents perceived an urgent need for continuing with the environmental protection and promotion programmes in the future. As far as the primary responsibility for environmental initiatives was concerned, an overwhelming majority (296 respondents or 92.5%) opined that the government, and people's organisations should partake joint responsibility for future environmental conservation. While 8 respondents felt that the government should assume full responsibility, 16 respondents attributed the entire responsibility for environmental conservation on people and people's organisations. Thus, it was amply clear that almost all respondents (312 or 97.5%) perceived the importance of people's participation in future environmental initiatives for the area.

The suggestions of the respondents about the nature of programmes and the requisite role to be played by the different agencies/organisations has been discussed below:

A. *Nature of Environmental Programmes Required*

Table 8.6 presents the suggestions of the respondents regarding the nature of environmental programmes required to protect and promote the environment.

Table 8.6 shows that a dominant majority of respondents offered suggestions pertaining to forests. Almost 94 per cent respondents were in favour of forest protection. Most of them were critical of the massive, target-oriented afforestation programmes undertaken by the Forest Department, and opined that regeneration through protection was a more effective strategy to improve the quality of forest cover. Many respondents also stressed a need for vigilance against the forest mafia and outside contractors who clandestinely felled green trees, along with the dead trees. A few local activists even felt that the Forest Corporation, which was a party to such illegal felling should be disbanded and forest management handed to the Forest Department and the people.

Almost 89 per cent respondents suggested plantation of broad-leaved and people-friendly trees generating fuel and fodder for the local populace. Many of them felt that mixed forests should be revived even in the reserve forests, and monocultures should be discouraged.

Table 8.6: Suggestions Regarding Nature of Environmental Programmes Required

S. No.	*Suggestions about Nature of Environmental Programmes*	*Distribution of Respondents (Percentage)*
1.	Protection of forests from illegal felling, overgrazing, commercial exploitation (Regeneration through protection)	94.1
2.	Plantation of trees, with emphasis on broad-leaved, local varieties of trees (yielding fuel and fodder) in community and reserve forests	88.7
3.	Promotion of Non-conventional energy sources/alternate sources of energy	72.2
4.	Prevention and Control of forest fires	25.6
5.	Conservation and regeneration of medicinal plants/herbs	16.6
6.	Grasslands/Pasture Development	60.0
7.	Promotion of Water conservation/water harvesting/recharge of natural springs and traditional sources of water	52.8
8.	Promotion of soil conservation measures/measures for prevention of landslides	22.5
9.	Prevention and control of water	15.0
10.	Promotion of village sanitation/construction of toilets, compost pits/soak pits/proper garbage disposal	18.4
11.	Environmental awareness generation	22.8
12.	Promotion of use of fuel efficient and non-polluting devices like smokeless *chulhas*, pressure cookers, etc.	7.2
13.	Control of population growth	4.1
14.	Wildlife Protection	1.9
15.	Curbing local practices leading to environmental degradation	5.6
16.	Other programmes	3.4

It is important to note that almost 72 per cent respondents opined that unless they were provided with alternate sources of energy, they could not be expected to give up their dependence on fuel wood. People mostly suggested LPG and solar energy as options, as they were familiar with these. However, they also felt that the price of LPG was high and beyond the reach of most people. Moreover, the availability was restricted to roadside villages only. It is however ironical that presently the government is not making any significant efforts to promote non-conventional/alternate energy sources (as has been indicated by the discussion on environmental programmes).

Grasslands/Pasture Development, and regeneration of grasses were also important environmental initiatives suggested by 60 per cent respondents.

Almost one-fourth of this group recommended stall-feeding instead of grazing in order to prevent overgrazing.

Concern with shortage of water and drying up of perennial sources of water prompted almost 53 per cent respondents to suggest promotion of water conservation measures. Many people suggested growing oak trees in the catchment areas of the sources of water, as they play an important role in the regeneration of ground water. Besides the other environmental programmes suggested by people (indicated in Table 7.6), an interesting set of suggestions pertained to the curbing of certain local practices detrimental to environmental. One such practice related to the cutting down of four young chir pine trees for every wedding ceremony taking place in the region. Discouraging such practices and finding suitable alternatives (like using branches instead of trees) was the suggestion offered by 18 respondents. A few respondents also suggested curbing tourist related pollution and environmental degradation.

B. Role of Organisations/Agencies in Environmental Conservation

The respondents were also asked to articulate the specific role and functions of different agencies and organisations partnering environmental conservation initiatives, viz. government agencies, and people's groups including voluntary organisations. The following categorisation of roles emerged:

1. Role of Government

Forest Related

- (a) Plantation/afforestation in Reserved forests and community forests;
- (b) Nursery development and distribution of saplings/seeds, etc. for plantation;
- (c) Prevention and control of forest fires;
- (d) Prevention of illegal tree felling, regulation of commercial exploitation of forests;
- (e) Promotion and Provision of alternate sources of energy.

Water Related

- (f) Provision of technical inputs and funding for water conservation/ water harvesting;
- (g) Afforestation in catchment areas of water sources.

Land/Soil Related

- (h) Soil conservation measures;
- (i) Measures for prevention of landslides.

General Role

- (j) Support to people's groups (both formal and informal) like panchayats, van Panchayats, women's groups, youth groups, co-operatives and voluntary organisations;

(k) Provision of training and technical inputs to people's groups and voluntary organsations;
(l) Formulation of relevant policies and legislation pertaining to environmental conservation.

2. Role of Voluntary Organisations

(a) Mobilisation of people for participation in environmental programmes;
(b) Awareness generation on environmental issues and programmes;
(c) Support to People's groups;
(d) Provision of training/capacity building of people for environmental conservation;
(e) Experimental action for demonstration impact;
(f) Action as an intermediary between the government and people.

3. Role of People's Groups

(a) Forest protection through fencing, appointment of chowkidars, control of grazing;
(b) Plantation on community lands and private lands;
(c) Curbing social practices leading to environmental degradation;
(d) Proper Garbage disposal, cleanliness/sanitation of villages, water resources, etc.;
(e) Promotion of medicinal herbs, local varieties of trees, seeds etc.;
(f) Action as watchdogs for the prevention of illegal tree felling.

An analysis of the above categorisation shows that people expected the government to primarily take up regeneration/promotional work pertaining to the environment, as also provide support to people's organisations, including Van Panchayats, voluntary organisations and people's groups. Voluntary organisations were mainly expected to provide training, support and environmental awareness to people, as also intermediate with government agencies on people's behalf. People's groups were primarily expected to perform the role of protection of the natural resource base, both by curbing their own wasteful use and over-exploitation, as also by acting as a watchdog for the prevention of illegal tree felling by vested interests. They were also to be entrusted the task of preserving the local, indigenous varieties of plants, medicinal herbs; seeds etc.

Suggestions for Enhancement of People's Participation

A. Enhancement of people's Participation in Governmental Environmental Programmes

Multiple suggestions were offered by the people towards the adoption of different strategies/approaches for enhancing people's participation in government programmes. It is important to note that suggestions from respondents mainly pertained to government programmes, as by and large people were dissatisfied with their present level of participation in these programmes. The main suggestions offered include:

1. Making existing people's institutions like Mahila Mangal Dals, Nav Yuvak Mangal Dals, Village level committees, voluntary organisations strong and effective, by providing funds, material support, training, technical inputs etc. (81.9%).
2. Encouraging the constitution of Van Panchayats in the region, and investing them with due authority, resources and control (45.3%).
3. Providing for adequate mechanisms/institutional framework within government programmes for enabling people to participate (62.2%).
4. Enlisting the support of local voluntary organisations and using their experience and understanding of local needs, problems and resources (35%).
5. Ensuring frequent communication and contact between government officials and people through regular visits, meetings, workshops etc. (79.4%).
6. Evolving environmental programmes based on local issues and concerns and after consultation with people to understand their needs, problems and perspectives (and not thrust them on people) (32.5%).
7. Decentralizing planning and implementation; involving people right from the conception of the programme; delegating responsibilities to people's groups/committees etc; using ideas, inputs and traditional knowledge of the people in programme formulation and implementation (55.3%).
8. Ensuring widespread information dissemination about government programmes to people on a timely basis; apprising people about the progress of programmes; ensuring transparency about the programme targets, funding and other details (41.6%).
9. Informing people about the benefits of the programmes (17.5%).
10. Recognising the rights of the local people/user groups in their natural resources, particularly forests and enabling them to fulfill their genuine needs of fuel, fodder, timber, non-timber forest produce etc. (72.8%).
11. Fulfilling people's economic aspirations and other needs in a sustainable manner, as a first step (8.4%).
12. Providing alternate and cheap sources of energy to people to minimise their dependence on forests (10.9%).

13. Providing incentives for successful people's initiatives (25%).
14. Constituting joint committees of government officials and people/ people's representatives to monitor programmes (13.1%).
15. Holding frequent awareness generation camps on environmental issues and programmes (31.6%).
16. Providing training to people for enhancing their capabilities for environmental protection and management (23.1%).
17. Giving representation to women in different bodies/organisations (27.2%).
18. Providing support to women for participation; promoting women's literacy, education, skill development, economic sustenance and awareness levels; giving greater benefits to women; constituting and strengthening women's groups (15.9%).

B. Enhancement of People's Participation in Programmes of Voluntary Organisations

The people, by and large, expressed their satisfaction with the efforts of the voluntary organisations to elicit people's participation. However, some suggestions were provided. These included the following important ones:

1. Generating a wider awareness among people about the environmental issues and problems confronting the area through discussions, meetings, Eco development camps, indigenous communication media, etc. (69.7%).
2. Educating people about their role and responsibilities in the protection and promotion of the environment; and on ways to use their resources judiciously (23.4%).
3. Providing training and technical inputs to people for working towards environmental conservation (40.3%).
4. Evolving suitable low cost rural technologies, based on the preferences of people, revival of traditional systems/indigenous approaches of environmental conservation (25%).
5. Providing information to people about ongoing programmes, (both governmental and non-governmental); new policies, laws, etc. (57.8%).
6. Mobilizing people and helping them to organise themselves into suitable groups for participation in environmental initiatives (62.5%).
7. Helping people to manage their own programmes; assisting people in resource mobilization from government agencies and through self contribution (shramdan, voluntary contributions etc.) (16.3%).
8. Initiating demonstration projects for motivating people's involvement in similar projects (10%).

9. Initiating suitable income-generation programmes for people, so that they could have time/inclination for participating in larger social issues and concerns (24.1%).
10. Training people for forest-based cottage industries, promotion of forest-based cottage industries (8.7%).
11. Strengthening women's participation by involving women in all programmes; capacity building for women through literacy, education, training, health and awareness (44.4%).
12. Reducing women's work burden/drudgery by developing suitable technology, fuel efficient, non-polluting devices, women's toilets etc. (48.1%).
13. Evolving support systems for women to elicit women's participation, like day care centres, balwadis, creches, etc. (10%).
14. Developing and providing alternate energy sources like wind mills, micro hydels, solar cookers, biogas etc. (13.4%).
15. Organizing mass programmes like Van Sammelans, Van Suraksha Abhiyans, Padyatras, Rakshasutra Andolans etc. for collective mobilization of people for common issues and concerns (38.1%).

C. Suggestions for Promoting Women's Participation

1. Mobilizing and organising women of all villages into women's groups (Mahila Mangal Dals); strengthening and supporting the Dals to sustain and take up need-based programmes (83.1%).
2. Ensuring greater involvement of women in all programmes of governmental and non-governmental organisations by introducing special women-centred components in programmes (38.1%).
3. Capacity-building of women through literacy, education, training/ skill-development (86.6%).
4. Ensuring better communication facilities, i.e. an information delivery system to generate awareness about ongoing programmes, benefits, women's initiatives in other regions (51.9%).
5. Giving greater say to women in management and protection of their natural resource-base by ensuring their representation and active participation in committees and organisations like Van Panchayats, JFM committees etc. (72.2%).
6. Training women members of committees/Panchayats/Van Panchayats in environmental conservation and management strategies. (34.4%).
7. Facilitating women's access to resources, including credit, agricultural inputs and technology (24.7%).
8. Providing employment/self-employment/income generation opportunities for women to make them economically secure (25%).

9. Undertaking programmes/initiatives for reduction of women's workload/drudgery, by developing suitable technology like fuel efficient chulhas, pressure cookers, solar cookers, village based Mahila complexes (toilets) etc. (72.2%).
10. Promoting the use of alternate energy sources like provision of subsidised cooking gas (LPG) connections, kerosene, coal, solar and thermal devices, biogas etc. to reduce women's dependence on forests and the resultant drudgery (30%).
11. Ensuring certainty of fodder, fuel, NTFPs etc. to free women for participation in developmental initiatives (13.7%).
12. Evolving support systems for women to reduce women's responsibilities pertaining to household and family, like balwadis/ day care centres, creches, community networks etc. (40.6%).
13. Educating men about the role of women in development; influencing them to share in the responsibilities of women (20.3%).
14. Influencing community leaders to create public opinion in favour of women's participation (11.3%).
15. Changing the customs and traditions, which are discriminatory in nature (10%).
16. Providing special incentives for women's participation (13.7%). An analysis of the suggestions forwarded by the respondents for enhancing people's participation in governmental programmes showed that the four main suggestions offered by a majority of the respondents to the government were: (1) strengthening the existing people's institutions by provision of funding, training, technical inputs, and support (81.9% respondents); (2) Ensuring frequent contact/communication between government officials and people (79.4%); (3) Recognising the rights of the local people/users to their natural resource base (72.8%); and (4) Providing for mechanisms/ institutional framework within government programmes for securing participation (62.2%).

The four main suggestions forwarded by the respondents to voluntary organisations for improving people's participation in environmental programmes included: (1) Generating widespread awareness about environmental problems and issues (69.7%); (2) Mobilizing people for organisation into groups for participation (62.5%); (3) Providing information about on going programmes, legislations and policies (57.8%); and (4) Reducing women's work burden and drudgery and evolving support systems for them to enhance women's participation (48.1%).

As far as women's participation was concerned, respondents had again offered multiple suggestions to enhance the participation of women in environmental programmes, both governmental and non-governmental. The main suggestions offered by a majority of the respondents were: (1) enhancing the capacity of women through the provision of literacy, education, training/ skill development (86.6% respondents); (2) Mobilizing and organising women of all villages into women's organisations (Mahila Mangal Dals) and strengthening of these organisations (83.1%); (3) Ensuring greater representation and participation of women in village committees, groups and organisations to provide them a greater say in the protection and management of the natural resources (72.2%); and (4) Reducing women's workload/ drudgery by developing suitable technology, to enable them the time and opportunities for participation (72.2%).

9
The Way Forward

In the foregoing parts of this book, an attempt has been made to understand the participation of people in the protection and promotion of the environment in the Bhilangana block, located in the Garhwal region of Uttarakhand with special focus to the participation of women in environmental conservation programmes, keeping in view the important role traditionally played by the hill women as users, protectors and promoters and managers of their natural resource base.

This final chapter delineates the suggestions and recommendations for the enhancement of people's participation in government programmes and programmes of voluntary organisations. Suggestions for improvement of women's participation in environmental action programmes have been listed separately. The scope of social work intervention stemming from the problems delineated by the study and the suggestions offered by the respondents follows as the final section of this chapter.

Suggestions and Recommendations

The suggestions for the improvement of people's participation in the protection and promotion of the environment that emerged from an engagement with the stakeholders are presented in the ensuing section. As has been seen, people's participation holds the key to a better protection and promotion of the environment. Suggestions to improve such participation have been developed separately for the government and the voluntary organisations, and have been based on the suggestions offered by different categories of respondents. Additionally, suggestions for enhancement of women's participation (to be considered both by the government and the voluntary agencies) have been listed separately.

I. Suggestions for Government's Role in the Improvement of People's Participation in the Protection and Promotion of the Environment

1. Strengthening the existing people's institutions, like Mahila Mangal Dals, Nav Yuvak Mangal Dals, Village Forest Protection Committees, and such others; and developing suitable institutional framework,

where the same is required, taking into consideration the needs and requirements of the area, its environment, and the people is an imperative for a state which is committed to people's participation. The first priority needs to be given to the existing institutions, as they are the most viable and sustainable options. Having the acceptance of the people, they offer the best option for participatory action. These institutions can be strengthened or revived through the provision of resources, training, technical inputs and other requisite support. The development of new institutional framework is the alternative option which would require an in depth understanding of the context, followed by the identification of existing groups and their representatives willing to devote time and efforts; creating within them the desirable competencies and skills; and bringing them together to form an organisation.

In this regard, the constitution of Van Panchayats at the village settlement level, and based on the model of successful Van Panchayats in the Kumaun region, but invested with due functional responsibilities, authority, control, resources and flexibility can be a viable option.

2. Promoting a better communication between the government officials and the people through meetings, discussions, workshops, shivirs (camps) etc. was necessitated, in order to generate mutual respect and confidence as also mutual cooperation in each other's programmes and initiatives was needed. This could take the form of joint coordination committees comprising of representatives of both. The huge gap between the people, the government agencies and government programmers needs to be urgently bridged.
3. Bringing about a bureaucratic reorientation to transform a predominantly 'beneficiary-oriented' approach of the officials to a 'participatory' approach is mandated. This bureaucratic reorganisation would involve: (a) changes in modes of operation and programme administration; (b) evolution of more open and transparent working practices; (c) changes in the perceptions and attitudes of officials by sensitising them to the needs of the local people and enabling them to develop respect for people's indigenous knowledge and capability to protect and manage their own natural resource base.
4. Ensuring widespread information dissemination about government programmes, programme benefits and progress on a timely basis; maintaining transparency about programme targets, funding and other details should be interwoven.

5. Enlisting the support of local voluntary organisations, and using their localised experience, understanding of local problems, needs and resources, and grassroots contacts to elicit support and participation of the people emerged as a highly desirable option.
6. Recognising the rights of the local people/user groups in their natural resources, particularly forests, and enabling them to fulfill their genuine needs of fuel, fodder, timber and non-timber forest produce would help.
7. Combining poverty alleviation and food security with environmental management, as income generation activities enhance the availability and motivation of the local people in participatory management of natural resources.
8. Ensuring the 'visibility of benefits' in the environment programmes. Benefits should be 'visibly perceived' as a concrete reality by people, especially those who live at the subsistence level. For them any change to a new system of management and protection (like land management or livestock management) can threaten livelihood and thus, only when such people see the benefits accruing to them do they provide cooperation in 'social fencing' and other environmental initiatives.
9. Fulfilling people's economic aspirations and other critical needs in a sustainable manner, should be seen as the first step. This could be done by providing employment/self employment/income generation opportunities to the local people and ensuring certainty of fuel, fodder and NTFPs, prior to seeking their involvement in environmental programmes.
10. Validating and integrating the rich diversity of indigenous knowledge of the local people and their traditional resource use and management systems into environmental initiatives, should be focussed on, as and when possible, instead of thrusting technical and 'expert' knowledge on people on a routine basis.
11. Organising frequent training for people and people's groups for enhancing their skills and capabilities for undertaking environmental conservation programmes like nursery development, soil conservation, non-conventional energy, etc. and also sustainable livestock management, agriculture etc.
12. Providing and promoting use of alternate and cheap sources of energy to people to minimise their dependence on forests.
13. Providing incentives and recognition for successful people's initiatives needs to be amalgamated within the government's perspective and pedagogy for strengthening people's participation in environmental conservation and management.

14. Strengthening women's participation through the promotion of literacy, education and skill development; giving special incentives; strengthening women's groups and providing for women's participation in formal groups and organisations.

II. Suggestions for the Enhancement of Peoples's Participation in the Protection and Promotion of the Environment in Voluntary Organisations

1. Generating a wider awareness about the environmental issues and problems confronting the area through the organisation of meetings, discussions, and other media. The 'Paryavaran Shivirs' or 'Eco-Development camps' organised by a few organisations have proved to be very effective fora to enhance people's understanding about the environment and environmental problems, as also to create sensitivity for, and knowledge of possible cost-effective solutions. This could also include provision of information about ongoing programmes, environmental policies, legislations etc.
2. Educating people about their role and responsibilities in the protection and promotion of the environment; and on ways to use their resources judiciously and sustainable needs to be further emphasised.
3. Providing training to people on strategies/techniques for environmental protection and promotion emerged as an area of improvement and expansion.
4. Strengthening existing people's groups, both formal and informal, through the provision of appropriate support; as also mobilizing people to organise themselves into suitable groups/user organisations, where required. This could also take the form of revival/resurgence of the traditional forms and systems of community management of common property resources, where these existed and are functional. Traditional resource management systems need to be integrated with current information and knowledge.
5. Establishing linkages/networking with government agencies, funding organisations, technical/specialised agencies and other voluntary organisations to enable people an access to funds, materials, technical inputs, acquisition of skills and other support was deemed necessary.
6. Helping people to revive the traditional and indigenous practices and approaches to sustainable resource use and environmental conservation was something that derived full support and whole hearted consensus of people.
7. Initiating demonstration projects for motivating people's involvement in similar programmes of environmental conservation, like nursery development, non-conventional energy, environmental sanitation, herb cultivation etc could be an excellent way to engage people.

8. Identifying and promoting suitable employment/income generation programmes for people so that they could have the time and inclination for participating in larger social issues and concerns.
9. Developing and promoting alternate and low-cost energy sources like solar cookers, solar lights, wind mills, biogas. etc. to diminish people's dependence on forests. Options for harnessing non conventional sources of energy needed to be context specific and should be determined by the larger centralised options, pursued at the behest of planners, who were not familiar with the local conditions, culture and practices.
10. Strengthening women's participation, through access to literacy, education, training, health services, credit, technology and incentives was imperative.
11. Introducing a system of positively rewarding the people/groups who sustainably use, restore and maintain biodiversity could go a long way in enhancing people's connect with initiatives.
12. Undertaking documentation highlighting the need and impact of people's participation was also a much desired outcome, as that could contribute towards an extension of the 'best practices' and thereby to people's participation in environmental action.
13. Using people's power in social action for environmental protection and promotion. People's collective action, based on the traditional/indigenous approaches (like Rakshasutra Andolan, Chipko or hugging of trees) could be initiated and sustained by local organisations desirous of working against illegal tree felling, commercial exploitation of natural resources, and other such issues.

Thus, it was advocated that although voluntary organisations cannot replace governmental organisations and people's institutions at large, they can play a very important role as communicators, facilitators, catalysts and stimulators, to supplement, develop and provide the impulse for eco-friendly development, based on people's full participation, at less cost and with much greater acceptance.

III. Suggestions for Promotion of Women's Participation in Environmental Protection and Promotion

1. Mobilising and organising women of all villages into women's groups (Mahila Mangal Dals); strengthening and supporting the Dals to sustain and take up need-based programmes had worked, with excellent results in the locale under study.
2. Ensuring greater involvement of women in programmes of governmental and non-governmental organisations by introducing

special women-centred components is an option that needs to be further strengthened.

3. Giving greater say to women in the management and protection of their natural resource-base by ensuring their representation and participation in formal groups and other bodies like Van Panchayats, JFM committees, FDA, etc is urgently needed to be keyed in.
4. Training and capacity building for elected women members of Panchayats, Van Panchayats, and Village Forest Committees in environmental conservation and management, micro-planning, monitoring, is required to enhance women's ability to seek their rightful place and share in development/governance.
5. Integrating women's knowledge and experience of conservation and management of natural resources in environmental programmes; building programmes based on women's perception and indigenous knowledge of the environment; promoting provision of environmentally sound technologies designed and developed in consultation with women is an integral component that may go a long way in harnessing women's 'real' participation in environmental conservation and management.
6. Capacity building of women through literacy, education, training and skill development and facilitating women's access to resources including credit, agricultural inputs, and technology, and to property rights is the necessary pre requisite to strengthened women's participation.
8. Providing employment/self employment/income generation opportunities for women to make them economically secure. Also, ensuring for them, a certainty of fodder, fuel and NTFPs, in order to free women for participation in developmental initiatives.
10. Undertaking initiatives for the reduction of women's workload/ drudgery, by developing suitable technology like suitable agricultural implements (for use by women), fuel-efficient chulhas, pressure cookers, Mahila Complexes (toilets), water harvesting structures, etc. Also, promoting the use of non-conventional/ alternate energy sources like provision of subsidised cooking gas (LPG) connections, solar devices, biogas, and hydro power are necessary to reduce women's dependence on forests, and the resultant drudgery.
11. Evolving support systems for women to reduce their responsibilities pertaining to the household and family like balwadis, day-care centres, creches, community support networks, etc needs a thrust to free women from the household responsibilities, and to enable them to participate in community matters and processes.

12. Providing gender awareness and sensitisation to menfolk, government officials, community leaders and village elders, to create attitudes conducive to women's participation, and educating them about the role of women in development; sensitising men to shoulder women's work burden to enable women to have time to participate: influencing community leaders to create public opinion in favour of women's participation needs urgent consideration.
13. Increasing recruitment of women officers at grassroots level and in the extension machinery; providing orientation and training to extension workers to mobilise women's participation.
14. Improving women's access to health and family welfare services with special focus on family planning.
15. Providing women with access to information and educating them about their rights. Also a focus on changing customs, traditions and practices which are discriminatory in nature, through the enactment of social legislation is a necessary step to step up women's participation.
16. Organising separate meetings and interactive sessions for women, if needed, as women often feel inhibited in expressing themselves freely in the presence of community elders.

Scope for Social Work Intervention

There is inbuilt scope for social workers' intervention in the protection and promotion of the environment, considering the problems delineated by the study and the suggestions emanating from the same. The following areas of social work intervention emerge as important:

I. Research and Documentation

1. Developing, documenting and publicizing research on the state of the environment, environmental issues and problems at the local, regional and national levels, as also the linkages between the quality of environmental conditions and the socio, economic and health conditions of the people.
2. Documenting and publicizing successful environmental initiatives of the government, voluntary organisations and people's groups, and highlighting the need and impact of people's participation on environmental conservation.

II. Awareness Generation

1. Initiating a process of discussion, reflection, questioning and analysis of environment and environmental issues with different groups of people, in order to create awareness and sensitivity towards the

problems, as also alternative solutions based on people's own understanding and perceptions.

2. Enabling people to develop awareness about the environmental policies, legislation and ongoing environmental programmes.
3. Facilitating people to develop a better understanding of their rights and responsibilities towards the environment.
4. Creating awareness about the need and importance of people's participation and participatory development; highlighting the changing roles of women and educating men and community leaders about the importance of women's participation in development activities.
5. Generating widespread awareness about the sustainable use of biomass/natural resources; ways and means of reducing consumption of energy and adoption of eco-friendly practices by people and organisations.

III. Orientation and Training

1. Facilitating the organisation of suitable training for people and people's groups in the maintenance, management and regeneration of their resource base, including revival of traditional patterns of environmental conservation.
2. Organising training programmes for women representatives of informal groups, as also formal groups like Panchayats, Van Panchayats, JFM committees etc. in microplanning, programme administration, monitoring/evaluation and other need-based areas.
3. Organising training and gender sensitization programmes for government officials, community leaders, and for other menfolk.

IV. Mobilisation and Organisation

Facilitating the process of community mobilisation around local environmental issues and problems, and organisation of people into suitable groups like user groups, women's groups, youth groups, etc is imperative. In case such groups already exist, strengthening of such groups can be facilitated through provision of appropriate support.

V. Initiation of Action

1. Facilitating the revival/resurgence of traditional community management systems, which are acceptable to the people.
2. Enabling community groups to initiate action on accepted solutions; promoting developmental action independently and in relation to people's groups, (both formal and informal); facilitating mechanisms for equitable distribution of benefits and local conflict resolution.

VI. Networking and linkages

1. Facilitating linkages between people and government agencies, funding organisations, and voluntary organisations to procure access to funds, material and technical support, as also acquisition of skills.

VII. Campaign and Advocacy

1. Seeking to influence public opinion about use of sustainable ways of resource consumption, and adoption of energy efficient and non-conventional sources of energy, as also promotion of eco-friendly, personal lifestyle changes.
2. Creating public opinion for gender equality; women's participation in development; and changing customs and traditions discriminatory to women.
3. Influencing environmental policy and legislation to acknowledge and incorporate the rights of local and impoverished communities to their natural resource base and pressing for the incorporation of people's participation as an essential component of policy framework.

Appendix I

Interview Schedule

I. Background Information

1. Name
2. Address
3. Sex
4. Age
5. Marital Status:
   (a) Married
   (b) Unmarried
   (c) Widowed/Separated
6. Religion
7. Caste
8. Educational Background
9. Training (if any)
10. Family structure:
    (a) Joint
    (b) Nuclear
11. Family Composition
12. Family Size
13. Occupation:
    (a) Own Occupation
    (b) Family Occupation
14. Income (Annual):
    (a) Own Income
    (b) Family Income
15. Ownership Status
    (a) Land: Yes/No Extent of Land
    (b) House: Yes/No Nature of House
    (c) Livestock Yes/No Number of Animals
    (d) Other Household goods (with details)

II. Organisation/Group Affiliation

1. Name of organization/Group
2. Address
3. Designation/Membership details
4. Duration of Affiliation/Membership
5. Source of Inspiration for Affiliation
6. Year of Establishment of organization/Group
7. Founder of Organisation/Group
8. Objectives of Organisation/Group
9. Programmes
10. Target Area

11. Target Groups
12. Environmental Programmes of Organisation/Group

Name of Programme	*Year*	*Activities*	*Target Group*	*Impact*

13. *Source* of Information

III. Environmental Awareness

1. Importance of Environment in life and Living: Yes/No.
2. Nature of Importance (Specify)
3. Environmental Changes in the Last 10 years
4. Environmental Problems (Specify)
5. Awareness about Environmental Programmes:

A. Government Programmes

Name of Programme	*Year of Establishment*	*Activities*	*Target Group*	*Impact*

B. Programmes of Voluntary Organisations

Name of Programme	*Year of Establishment*	*Activities*	*Target Group*	*Impact*

C. Programmes of People's Groups

Name of Programme	*Year of Establishment*	*Activities*	*Target Group*	*Impact*

6. *Source* of Information

Government Programmes	*Programmes of Voluntary Organisations*	*Programmes of People's Groups*

7. Scope of People's Participation in Programmes:

Government Programmes	*Programmes of Voluntary Organisations*	*Programmes of People's Groups*
Yes/no If Yes (Nature)	Yes/No If Yes (Nature)	Yes/No If Yes (Nature)

IV. Participation in Environmental Programmes

1. Participation in Government Programmes:
   (a) Forms of Participation
      (i) As Planner
      (ii) As Implementer
      (iii) As Beneficiary
      (iv) As Evaluator
   Give Details
   (b) Nature of Participation
      (i) Direct/Indirect (Give Details)
      (ii) Regularity of Participation Occasional/Intermittent/
   Give Details
   (c) Duration of Participation
   Long Term/Medium Term/Short Term Give Details
   (d) Level of Participation (Use Scale)
   (e) Scope of Participation Yes/No
   Give Details
2. Participation in Programmes of People's Groups:
   (a) Forms of Participation
      (i) As Planner
      (ii) As Implementer
      (iii) As Beneficiary
      (iv) As Evaluator
   Give Details
   (b) Nature of Participation
      (i) Direct/Indirect
   Give Details
      (ii) Regularity of Participation Occasional/Intermittent/
   Give Details
   (c) Duration of Participation
   Long term/Medium term/Short term
   Give Details.
   (d) Level of Participation (Use Scale)
   (e) Scope of Participation Yes/No
   Give Details.

(f) Methodologies Used to Secure Participation

By Government	*By Voluntary Organisations*	*By People's Groups*

V. Factors Hindering/Facilitating Participation

1. Factors Hindering Participation
   - (i) Organisation/Group Related Factors
   - (ii) Personal Factors
   - (iii) Social/Cultural Factors
   - (iv) Any Other Factors
2. Factors Facilitating Participation
   - (i) Organisation/Group Related Factors
   - (ii) Personal Factors
   - (iii) Social/Cultural Factors
   - (iv) Any Other Factors

VI. Impact of Participation

(i) On Self: Positive/Negative
Specify

(ii) On Family: Positive/Negative
Specify

(iii) On the State of the Environment: Positive/Negative
Specify

VII. Future Environmental Initiatives

(i) Need for Future Environmental Action: Yes/No

(ii) Responsibility for Environmental Action:

		Reasons
a. Government	Yes/No	
b. Voluntary Organisations	Yes/No	
c. People's Groups	Yes/No	

(iii) Environmental Programmes which should be Taken Up:

- By Government
- By People's Groups/Organisations

VIII. Suggestions for Improvement of People's Participation

(i) In Government Programmes

(ii) In Programmes of Voluntary Organisations/People's Groups

(iii) Suggestions for Improvement of Women's Participation

Appendix II

Scale for Measurement of Level of Participation

I. Planners

S. No.	*Indicators*	*Level of Participation*		
		Active (Score 3)	*Average (Score 2)*	*Passive (Score 1)*
1.	Regularity in attending meetings	Attend more than 75% meetings	Attend between 50% to 75% meetings	Attend less than 50% meetings
2.	Raising relevant issues in meeting	In more than 50% meetings	In 25% to 50% meeting	In less than 25% meeting
3.	Participation in discussion	In more than 75% meetings	Between 50% 75% meetings	Less than 50% meetings
4.	Role played in arriving at decisions	Yes	Sometimes	No

II. Implementers

S. No.	*Indicators*	*Level of Participation*		
		Active (Score 3)	*Average (Score 2)*	*Passive (Score 1)*
1.	Regularity in attending meetings	Attend more than 75% meetings	Attend between 50% to 75% meetings	Attend less than 50% meetings
2.	Expression of views/ opinion on implementation of programmes	In more than 75% meetings	In 50% to 75% 75% meetings	In less than 50% 50% meetings
3.	Extending new ideas/strategies	Yes	Sometimes	No
4.	Carrying out assigned tasks satisfactorily	Yes	Sometimes	No
5.	Participation in training/orientation	Yes	Sometimes	No

III. Beneficiaries

S. No.	Indicators	Level of Participation		
		Active (Score 3)	*Average (Score 2)*	*Passive (Score 1)*
1.	Selection as beneficiaries	Full role	Partial role	No role
2.	Decision on nature of benefits	Full choice	Partial choice	No Choice
3.	Redressing grievances through meetings and discussions with officials/members	Yes	Sometimes	No
4.	Confrontation, in case grievances are not met	Yes	Sometimes	No

For arriving at the levels of participation of planners, implementers and beneficiaries, the scores of 3, 2 and1 were marked for each indicator pertaining to the particular form of participation. Therefore, Summated Scores were worked out for each respondent after adding the individual indicator scores. Respondents were categorized on the basis of their Summated Scores as 'active', 'average' or 'passive' in terms of their levels of participation as 'planners', 'implementers' and 'beneficiaries' in the following manner:

I.	**Planners**	**Summated Scores**
	Active Participation-	Between 12 and 10
	Average Participation-	Between 9 and 7
	Passive Participation-	Between 6 and 4
II.	**Implementers**	**Summated Scores**
	Active Participation	Between 15 and 13
	Average Participation-	Between 12 and 9
	Passive Participation-	Between 8 and 5
III.	**Benefit-sharing**	**Summated Scores**
	Active Participation-	Between 12 and 10
	Average Participation-	Between 9 and 7
	Passive Participation-	Between 6 and 4

Select Bibliography

Abbott, A. (1995). Defining the Boundaries of Social Inquiry. *Social Research: A International Quarterly. 63*(1), 857-882.

Adas, M. (1981). From Avoidance to Confrontation: Peasant Protest in Pre-colonial and Colonial South East Asia. *Comparative Studies in Society and History, 23*(2).

Agarwal, A. and Narain, S. (1985). *Strategies for the Involvement of the Landless and Woman in Afforestation*. New Delhi: Centre for Science and Environment

______ and Narain, S. (1989). *Towards Green Villages: A Strategy for Environmentally Sound and Participatory Rural Development*. New Delhi: Centre for Science and Environment.

______, and Narain, S. (1992). *Towards Green Villages*. New Delhi: Centre for Science and Environment.

______ (ed.). (1992). *The Price of Forests*. New Delhi: Centre for Science and Environment.

______ (1994). *An Indian Environmentalist's Credo*. In R. Guha (Ed.), Social Ecology. New Delhi: Oxford University Press.

Agarwal, B. (1986). *Cold Hearths and Barren Slopes: The Wood Fuel Crisis in the Third World*. London: Zed Press.

______ (1991). *Engendering the Environment Debate: Lesson from the Indian Subcontinent*. East Lansing: CASID.

______ (1992). The Gender and Environment Debate: Lessons from India, *Feminist Studies, 18*(1), 119-158.

Agarwal, C.M. (1993). *Dimensions of Indian Womanhood*. Almora: Shri Almora Book Depot.

Agarwal, J.C., and Agarwal, S.P. (1995). *Uttarakhand: Past, Present and Future*. Concept Publishing Co. New Delhi.

Amar, F. (1997). *Colonial Forest Policy in Uttarakhand 1890-1928*. New Delhi: Kitab Publishing House.

Anderson, R., and Walter, H. (1988). *The Hour of the Fox: Tropical Forests, the World Bank and Indigenous People in Central India*. New Delhi: Vistar Publications.

Armitage, A. (1988). *Social Welfare in Canada: Ideals, Reality and Future Paths*. (Second edition). Toronto: McClelland and Stewart.

Arne, K., and Persoon, G. (ed.). (1998). *Environmental Movement in Asia*. Great Britain: Curzon Press.

Arnold, D. and Guha, R. (eds). (1995). *Nature, Culture, Imperialism: Essays on the Environment History South Asia*. New Delhi: Oxford University Press.

Arnold, J.E.M., and Stewart, W.C. (1991). *Common Property Resource Management in India*. London: Oxford Forestry Institute.

Arnstein, S.R. (1969). A Ladder of Citizen Participation. *Journal of the American Institute of Planners*, *35*(4).

Arora, H., and Khare, A. (1993). People's Participation. *Wastelands News*, *8*(4), 5.

Atkinson, E.T. (1981). *The Himalayas Gazetteer*, Reprint. Vol. I, Part II and Vol. III Part I. New Delhi: Cosmo Publications.

Azad, R.N. (1978). *Integrated Rural Development in Dynamics of Development: An International Perspective*. Vol II. Delhi: Concept Publishing House.

Bahuguna, S. (1974). *Uttarakhand mein Ek Sau Bis Din*. Dehradun.

______ (1979). The Himalaya: Towards a Programme of Reconstruction. In K.M. Gupta and Desh Bandhu (eds.), *Man and Forest*. Delhi.

______ (1980). *Chipko*. Silyara.

______ (1983). *Paryavaran aur Chipko Yatra*. Silyara.

______ (1983). *Walking with the Chipko Message*. Silyara.

Bailabh, V., and Singh, K. (1988). Managing Forest through Peoples Institutions: A Case Study of Van Panchayat in Uttar Pradesh Hills. *Indian Journal of Agriculture Economics*, July-September.

Bajaj, M. (1991). Natural Regeneration versus Afforestation: An Examination of the Potential for Investment in Natural Regeneration of Degraded Forests with Community Participation. In A. Agarwal (ed.), *The Price of Forests*. New Delhi: CSE.

Bamberger, M. (ed). (1986a). *Readings in community participation*. (2 volumes).

______ (1986b). *The Role of Community Participation in Development Planning and Project Management*. Washington D.C.: Economic Development Institute.

Bapat, A.R. (1992). *People's Participation for Ecological Restoration of Aravallis Region*. National seminar on Ecological Restoration of Aravalli Hill Ecosystem of Rajasthan, March 25-24.

Barker, R.L. (1991). *The Social Work Dictionary*. (Second Edition). Silver Spring: National Association of Social Workers.

Bartelmus, P. (1986). *Environment and Development*. Boston: Ailen and Unwin.

Becker, H. (1997). *Social Impact Assessment*. London: UCL Press.

Barthwal, C.P., Rawat, K.S. and Semwal, M.M. (1992). Environmental Management through People's Participation: The Chipko Way in Garhwal Himalayas. In H. Singh (ed.) *Environmental Policy and Administration*. Jaipur: Print well.

Baviskar, A. (1999). The Case of the Great Himalayan National Park. In R. Jeffery, and N. Sunder (eds.) *A New Moral Economy for India's Forests? Discourses of Community and Participation*. New Delhi: Sage Publications.

Beadon, B.F. (1896). *Working Plan of Garhwal Forests Division*. Central Circle: North West Provinces and Oudh.

Bergdall, T.D. (1993). *Methods for Active Participation: Experiences in Rural Development from East and Central Africa*. Nairobi: Oxford University Press.

Berreman, G.D. (1983). The UP Himalaya: Culture, Cultures and Regionalism. In O.P. Singh (ed.) *The Himalaya: Nature, Man and Culture*. Delhi.

Bhatt, Chandi Prasad and Kunwar, S.S. (eds.). 1982. Hill Women and Their Involvement in Forestry. In S.S. Kunwar (ed.). *Hugging the Himalaya: The Chipko experience*. Gopeshwar.

Bhatt, H.P. (1993). *Environmental Dimensions of Rural Settlements in Hill Areas*. New Delhi: Ashish Publication House.

Bhatt, Sanjai. (1991). Eco-Regeneration Through People's Participation: A CECOEDECON Experience in Rural Rajasthan. Paper presented at the 11th Asia Pacific Regional Seminar on Social Work. Hong Kong. 21-24 August, 1991.

Bourai, Himanshu. (2001). Hill Women: Strengths, Opportunities and Problems, In O.P. Kandhari, and O.P. Gusain (eds.), *Garhwal Himalaya: Nature, Culture and Society*. Srinagar (Garhwal): Transmedia.

Brager, G., Spetch, H., and Torczyner, J. (1987). *Community Organising (Third Edition)*. New York: Columbia University Press.

Burkey, S. (1996). *People First A Guide to Self-Reliant Participatory Rural Development*. London: Zed Books Ltd.

Burns, D., and Taylor, M. (2000). *Auditing Community Participation: An Assessment Handbook*. Bristol: Policy Press.

Campbell, J.Y., (1992). Joint Forest Management in India. *Social Change*, *22*(1), 37-54.

Capila, A. (2002). *Images of Women in the Folk Songs of Garhwal Himalayas A Participatory Research*. New Delhi: Concept Publishing Company.

Carson, R. (1962). *Silent Spring*. Boston: Houghton Mifflin Co.

Centre for Science and Environment. (1982). *The State of India's Environment 1982: A Citizen's Report*. Delhi.

_______. (1985). *The State of India's Environment 1984-85: A Citizen's Report*. Delhi.

Champion, H.C., and Seth, S.K. (1968). *Revised Forest Types of India, Govt. of India, Delhi*.

Chani, S. (1990). *Contribution of Voluntary Organisations in the Field of Rural Development*. M. Phil Thesis Submitted to the Department of social work, University of Delhi.

Chatterjee, M., and Ramble. *Himalayan Culture and Environment*. Shimla: Indian Institute of Advanced Studies.

Chatterjee, M., and Roy, S.B. (1995). *Reflections on Gender Issues in Joint Forest Management*. New Delhi: Inter India Publications.

Chaturvedi, A.N. 1992. Environmental Value of a Forest in Almora. In A. Agarwal (ed.), *The Price of Forests*. New Delhi: CSE.

Chaubey, A.C., and Pandey, D.N. (1993). Community Participation for Joint Forest Management and use of generated funds of World Food programme. UNWFP Workshop on Joint Forest management, 13-15 January, New Delhi.

Chen, M.A. (1993). Women and Wasteland Development in India: An Issue Paper. In M. Singh, Andrea and N. Burra, (eds), *Women and Development in India*. New Delhi; Sage Publications.

Chopra, K., Kadekodi, G.K., and Murty, M.N. (1990). *Participatory Development: People and Common Property Resources*. New Delhi: Sage Publications.

Chopra, K. (1998). "Watershed Management Programmes: An Evaluation of Alternative Institutional and Technical Options" (Paper presented in National workshop for Watershed Approaches to Wastelands Development). New Delhi. April, 1998.

Choudhary, M., Hasan, Z., and Majumdar, V. (1983). *Women's Participation in Political Life in India (mimeo)*. New Delhi: Centre for Women's Development Studies.

Choudhuri, A.B. (1992). *Himalayan Ecology and Environment*. New Delhi: Ashish Publication House.

Chowdhury, A.N. (1996). *Let grassroots speak: People's participation, Self-Helpgroups and NGO's in Bangladesh*. Dhaka: The University Press Ltd.

Cohen, J.M. and Uphoff, N. (1977). *Rural Development Participation: Concepts and Measure for Project Design, Implementation and Evaluation*. Center for International Studies, Rural Development Committee, Monograph no. 2, Ithaca: Cornell University.

Cohen, J.M. and Uphoff, N. (1980). Participation's Place in Rural Development: Seeking Clarity through Specificity. *World Development*, 8, 213-235.

Cole, D.W., and Rapp, M. (1981). *Dynamic Principles of Forest Ecosystems*. London: Cambridge University Press.

Curtis, D. *et al.* (1978). *Popular Participation in Decision-Making and the Basic Needs Approach to Development: Methods, Issues and Experiences*. Geneva: ILO.

Curtis, D. *et al.* (1982). *Popular participation in decision-making and the basic needs approach to development*. WEP Working Paper. Geneva: ILO.

Dangwal, D. (1998). Forests and Social Change in Tehri Garhwal, 1850-1950. Unpublished PhD thesis, Jawaharlal Nehru University, New Delhi.

Das, A.N. (1991). Organising Rural Poor. In P. Wignaraja, A. Hussain, H. Sethi, and G. Wignaraja. (eds.), *Participatory Development: Learning from South Asia*. UNU/ Oxford.

Das, J.C., and Negi, R.S. (1983). Chipko Movement. In K.S. Singh (ed.), *Tribal Movements in India*, Volume II. Delhi.

Das, R.D., Barul, J.K., Sahu, N.C., and Mishra, M.K. (1998). *The Environmental Divide: The Dilemma of Developing Countries*. New Delhi: A.P.H Publishing Corp.

Dasgupta, S. (1986). *Forest, Ecology and the Oppressed*. New Delhi: People's Institute for Development and Training (PIDT).

Dayal, G. (1993). Role of Women in Environmental Protection. In C.M. Agarwal (ed.) *Dimensions of Indian Womanhood*. Nainital: Sri Almora Book Depot.

Desai, A.R. (ed.). (1987). *Agrarian Struggle in India since Independence*. Delhi.

Dev, M.S. (2001). Village Institutions and Common Property Resources: Socio-Economic Impact and Lessons for Tree Growers Cooperatives. In Mishra and Bajpai (eds.), *Community Participation in Natural Resources Management*. Jaipur and New Delhi: Rawat Publications.

Devasia, L. (1997). *Safe Drinking Water and Basic Health Facilities: Rural Women's Participation in Development*. New Delhi: PRIA.

Devasia, V.V. (1996). *Tribal Women's Participation in Sustainable Tribal Development*. New Delhi: PRIA.

Dewan, M.L. (1990). *People's Participation in the Himalayan Eco-System Management. (A Plan for Action)*. New Delhi: Concept Publishing Company.

Dhar, T.N. (1994). *Environmental Friendly Hill Development: An Approach for District Chamoli*. Himavikas Occasional Publication, No. 4. G.B Pant Institute of Himalayan Environment and Development, Almora.

_______ (1999). The Tragedy of Commons Must be Averted. *Wastelands News, XIV* (4).

Ecology and Statistical Division. (1992). *U.P Statistical Diary*. Lucknow: State Planning Division.

Ecology and Statistical Division. *Sankhkiya Patrika: Janpad Tehri Garhwal*. Lucknow: State Planning Division.

Economic Commission for Latin America. (1973). Popular participation in Development. *Community Development Journal. 6*(1).

Economic and Social Commission for Asia and the Pacific. (1977). *Methods and Techniques of Promoting People's Participation in Local Development*. Bangkok.

Envis Bulletin. (2001). *Himalayan Ecology and Development*, Vol. 9, No. 1. Almora, U.P: G.B. Pant Institute of Himalayan Ecology and Development.

Evens, P. (1974). *Community Work: Theory and Practice*. Oxford: Alistain Shownach Ltd.

F.R.I. Dehradun. (1961). *100 Years of Indian Forestry*, Volumes I and II. Dehradun, U.P.

FAO. (1985). *The Ecological Effects of Eucalyptus*. FAO Forestry Paper 59. Geneva: FAO.

FAO. (1982). *Research Guidelines and Participation of the Poor in Rural Organisations*. Rural Organisation Action Programme (ROAP). Rome.

Farooquee and Rawat. (1997). Development Dilemma. In *Development Dilemma: Indian Scenario and Rural Himalayas (A Himalayan Perspective)*. Nainital: Gyanodaya Prakashan.

Farrington, J. *et al.* (eds.). (1999). *Strengthening Participatory: Processes with Emphasis on Increasing the State of the Poor*. London: Oxford University Press.

Fernandes, W., and Menon, G. (1988). *Deforestation, Forest Dweller Economy and Women*. New Delhi: Indian Social Institute.

Ferrer, M.E. (1988). People's Participation in Coastal Area Management. Paper presented at the Regional Policy Workshop on Coastal Area Management. Johor Bahru.

Fisher, R.J., Singh, H.B., Pandey, D.R., and Lang. H. (1991). *The Management of Forest Resources in Rural Development: A Case Study of Sindhu Palchok and Kabhre Palanchok district of Nepal*. Nepal Australia Forestry Project, ICIMOD Joint case study.

Freire, P. (1985). *The Politics of Education: Culture, Power and Liberation*. Boston: Bergin and Garvey.

Forum 85. (1985). Women and the Environmental Crisis (A Report of the Proceedings of the workshop on Women, Environment and Development). Nairobi, July 10-20, 1985.

Gadgil, M. (1982). Towards an Indian Conservation strategy, paper presented at the workshop on a New Forest Policy. Indian Social Institute, New Delhi, 12-14 April.

_______ (1983). Forestry with Social Purpose. In W. Fernandes and S. Kulkarni, (eds.), *Towards a New Forest Policy*. Delhi.

Gadgil, M. (1995). Ecology and Equity: The Use and Abuse of Nature in Contemporary India. London and New Delhi.

______, Prasad, S.N., and Ali, R. (1983). Forest Management and Forest Policy in India: A Critical Review. *Social Action. 33*(2).

______ and Berkes, F. (1991). Traditional Resource Management Systems, Resource Management and Optimization. *8*(3-4), 127-141.

______ and G.R. (1992). *This Fissured Land: An Ecological History of India*. New. Delhi: Oxford University Press.

______ (1991). Deforestation: Problems and Prospects. In A.S. Rawat (ed.) *Forestry in India*. New Delh: Indus Publishing Company.

______ (1992). Perverse Incentives for Industrialization and its Impact on Forest Resources. In A. Agarwal (ed.). *The Price of Forests*. New Delhi: Centre for Science and Environment.

Gamble, D.N., and Weil, M.O. (1995). Citizen Participation. In R.L. Edwards, (Ed.). *Encyclopaedia of Social Work*, Vol. 1, 19th Edition (pp. 483-494). Washington D.C: National Association of Social Workers Press.

Ghai, D., and Vivian, M.J. (eds). (1992). *Grassroots Environmental Action: People's Participation in Social Development*. London and New York: Routledge.

Gandhi Peace Foundation. (1998). Ripples in Society. FAO.

Gawande, S.P. (2001). Community Participation in Integrated watershed Management for Sustainable Productivity. In G.P. Mishra and B.K. Bajpai (eds.), *Community Participation in Natural Resources Management*. Jaipur and New Delhi: Rawat Publications.

Gispert, P.S.J. (1973). *Fundamentals of Sociology*. Bombay: Orient Longman.

Gradwohl, J., and Greenberg, R. (1988). *Saving Tropical Forests*. London: Earthscan Publications Ltd.

GoI. (1983). *Eliciting Public Support for Conservation*. New Delhi: Department of Environment.

Guha, R. (1983). Forestry in British and Post-British India: A Historical Analysis. *Economic and Political Weekly*, 29 October and 5-12 November.

______ (1999). *The Unquiet Woods, Ecological Change and Peasant Resistance in the Himalaya*, New Expanded Edition. New Delhi: Oxford University Press.

______ (ed.) (1994). *Social Ecology*. Delhi: Oxford University Press.

Guha, R., and Gadgil, M. (1989). State Forestry and Social Conflict in British India: A Study in the Ecological Bases of Agrarian Protest. *Past and Present*. No. 123.

Guhathakurta, P., and Sharma, B. (1995). Case study: Gender and Forest Resources: Three Villages of West Bengal, India. In V.L. Wilde and A.V. Mattila. (eds.), *Gender Analysis and Forestry*, pp. 37-65.

Guhathakurta, P. and Sarin, R. (1995). Case Study: Gender and Forest Resources: Three Villages of West Bengal, India. In V.L. Wilde and A.V. Mattila. (eds.), *Gender Analysis and Forestry* (pp. 67-85).

Gunanidhi, P. (2000). *Ecology and Development in Conflict: A Gandhian Approach*. New Delhi: APH Publication Corp.

Gupta, R.K. (1983). *The Living Himalaya*, Volume I: Aspects of Environment and Resource Ecology of Garhwal. Delhi.

Gurung, J.D. (1999). *Searching for Women's Voices in the Hindu Kush-Himalayas*. Kathmandu, Nepal: International Centre for Integrated Mountain Development.

Hamison, W.D. (1995). Community Development. Encyclopaedia of Social Work, Vol. 1, 19th Edition. Washington DC: National Association of Social Workers Press.

Haug, E. (1997). A global analysis for Social Work education in Canada: A twenty-first century imperative (A research proposal). Faculty of Social Work, The University of Calgary.

G.B. Pant Institute of Himalayan Environment and Development. (1992). *Himalayan Environment and Development: Problems and Perspectives* (Himvikas Occasional Publication No. 1). Nainital: Gyanodaya Prakashan.

Himalayas Sewa Sangh. (1977). *People and the Forests*. Rishikesh.

Hoff, M.D. and McNutt, J.G. (1992). *The Global Environmental Crisis: Implications for Social Welfare and Social Work*. Avebury, Aldershot, Brookfield and Hong Kong.

Huby, M. (1988). *Social Policy and the Environment*. Buckingham: Open University Press.

Human, J., and Pattanaik, M. (2000). *Community Forest Management: A case Book from India*. Great Britain: OXFAM.

Involve. (2004/05). *People and Participation: How to put citizens at the heart of decision-making*. UK: Togetherwecan.

Jacob, K.K. (1989). *Social Policy in India*. Udaipur/Delhi: Himanshu Publications.

_______ (1992). Social Development Perspectives. Himanshu Publications, Udaipur/ Delhi: Himanshu Publications.

Jayal and Bandopadhyaya, J. (1984). *Indian Environment Crises and Responses*. New Delhi.

Jena, N.R. (1994). An Inquiry into "Popular Participation". *Participation and Governance, 1*(1); 8-17.

Jodha, N.S. (1986). Common Property Resources and Rural Poor in Dry Regions of India. *Economic and Political Weekly*, 21.

Joseph, M. (1997). *Women Participation and Development Strategies*. New Delhi: Kanishka Publishers.

Joshi, A., Garia. and Hasnan, I. (1999). *Uttarakhand Update: A State's Profile for Development Planning*. New Delhi: Kanishka Publishers.

Joshi, B.K. (1983). 'Underdevelopment of Hill Areas of UP', (mimeo). GIDS, Lucknow.

Joshi, Gopa. (1982). 'Men propose Women Dispose'. Indian Express, 14 January.

Joshi, M. (2000). "People's Participation in Management of Natural Resources. *Indian Journal of Forestry*, September.

Joshi, S.C. (ed.). 1984. *Rural Development in the Himalaya: Problems and Prospects*. Gyanodaya Prakashan, Nainital.

______ (1998). *Rural Development in the Himalayas: Problems and Prospects*. Gyanodoya Prakashan, Nainital.

Kadekodi, G.K., Murthy, K.S.R., and Kumar, Kireet. (eds.). *Water in Kumaon: Ecology, Value and Rights*. Nainital: Gyanodaya Prakashan.

Kant, S., Singh, N.M., and Singh, K.K. (1998). Community Based Forest Management

Systems (Case studies from Orissa). Bhopal and New Delhi: Indian Institute of Forest Management and SIDA.

Kapoor, A. (2000). Hill Women Succeed Where Government Fails. *Humanscape*, February, 2000.

Kaufĩnan, M. and Alfonso, H.D. (1997). *Community power and grassroots democracy: The transformation of social life.* Ottawa: International Development Research Centre (IDRC).

Khan, W. and Tripathy, R.N. (1976). *Plan for Integrated Rural Development in Pauri Garhwal*. Hyderabad.

Khoshoo, T.N. (1987). Environment: Concept. In R.P. Anand (ed.) *Law, Science and Environment*. New Delhi: Kalinga Publishers.

Kindleberger, C.P. and Herrick, B. (1977). *Economic Development*. Tokyo: McGraw Hill Kogukusha Ltd..

Korten, D.C. (1990). Getting to the 21st Century: Voluntary action and global agenda. Connecticut: Kumarian Press.

Kothari, A., Suri, Saloni. and Singh, N. (1995). Conservation in India: A New Direction. *Economic and Political Weekly*, October 28, 1995.

Kothari, P., and Vania. (2000). Where Communities Care (Report of the South Asian Regional Review of Community Involvement in Wildlife Management in Asia).

Kulkarni, S. (1987). Forest Legislation and Tribals: Comments on Forest Policy Resolution. *Economic and Political Weekly*, December 12, 1987.

Kumar, P. (1997). Uttarakhand Movement: Areas of Peripheral Support. *Mainstream*, 9 August, 1997.

Kumar, S. (1999). *Protecting Environment: A Quest for NGOs*. Delhi: Kalinga.

Sharma. K. (1984). Women in Struggle: A Case study of the Chipko Movement. *Samya Shakti*, Vol. I, No. 2.

Kunwar, S.S. (ed.). 1982. *Hugging the Himalaya: The Chipko Experience*. Gopeshwar.

Kurup, V.S.P. (1996) (ed.). *New Voices in Indian Forestry*. New Delhi: SPWD.

Lall, J.S. (1981). The Himalayan Aspects of Change. Oxford University Press, New Delhi.

Leach, M. (1991). Women's Use of forest Resources for Food Security and Income Generation. In *Women and the Environmen*t. London: Zed Books Ltd.

Lisk, F.A. (1981). Popular participation in basic-needs orientated development planning. *Labour and* Society, *6*(1).

Malhotra, K.C. and Poffenberger, M. (eds.). (1989). Forest Regeneration through Community Protection: The West Bengal Experience. Calcutta: West Bengal Forest Department.

Mathbor, G.M. (1990). *People's Participation in Upazila Rural Development Activities: Problems and Prospects*. Ministry of Planning, Government of Bangladesh.

Mehta, G.S. (2001). Participation in Forest Management A case study of Uttarakhand. In Mishra and Bajpai (eds.), *Community Participation in Natural Resourxes Management*. Jaipur and New Delhi: Rawat Publications.

Mehta, M. (1993). *Cash crops and the Changing Context of Women's Work and Status: A Case study from Tehri Garhwal* (ICIMOD Discussion paper series January). Kathmandu, Nepal.

Mishra, A. and Tripathi, S. (1978). *Chipko Movement, Peoples Action for Development and Justice*. New Delhi: Gandhi Peace Foundation.

Mitra, A. (1993). 'Chipko: An Unfinished Mission'. *Down To Earth,* 30 April.

Mukherjee, K.K., Pant, B. and Sharma, Y.K. (1982) Development: Concept, Programmes and Strategies (Changing Villages: Rural News and Views. Vol. 22). New Delhi.

Mukherjee, N. (1997). *Participatory Appraisal of Natural Resources*. New Delhi: Concept Publishing Company.

Mukherjee, S. (1992). Women's Participation in Rural Development Programmes: A Case Study of Rezapur Block. Unpublished Ph.D. Thesis, Jamia Millia Islamia University, New Delhi.

Mukhopadhyay, M. (1990). Women's Struggle to Save the Forest in India. In Women and Sustainable Development (A Report from Women's Forum). Centre for Information on Women and Development, Bergen, Norway, May.

Mukul. (1993). Villages of Chipko Movement'. *Economic and Political Weekly*, 10 April.

Nanda, N. (1982). *Tawang: The Land of Mon*. New Delhi: Vikas Publishers.

______(1992). Local Management of Community Property Resources. In A. Agarwal (ed.), *The Price of Forests*. New Delhi: CSE.

______ (1999). *Forests for Whom? Destruction and Restoration in the U.P. Himalayas*. New Delhi: Har-Anand Publications Pvt. Ltd.

Negi, S.S. (1983). *Forest Protection*. Delhi: BSMPS Publication.

______ (1986). *Managing the Himalayan Environment*. Delhi: PEBA Publication.

______ (1990). *A Handbook of the Himalaya*. New Delhi: Indus Publishing Co.

______ (1991). *Environmental Degradation and Crisis in India*. New Delhi: Indus Publishing Co.

______ (1994). *India's Forest, Forestry and Wildlife*. New Delhi: Indus Publishing Co.

______ (1997). *Forestry in India* (Vols. I and II). Delhi: M.D Publication.

______ (2000). *Himalayan Forests and Forestry*. New Delhi: Indus Publishing Company.

______ (2000). People's Participation in Management of Natural Resources. *Indian Journal of Forestry, 23*(3).

Nehal, A., Farooque, and Rawat, D.S. (1997). *Development Dilemma, Indian Scenario and Rural Himalaya (A Central Himalayan Perspective)*. Nainital: Gyanodaya Prakashan.

Oakley, P., and Maraden, D. (1984). *Approaches to Participation in Rural Development*. Geneva: International labour Organization.

______ (1989). *Community Involvement in Health Development: An Examination of the Critical Issue*. Geneva: WHO.

______ *et al.*, (1991). *Projects with People: The Practice of Participation in Rural Development*. Geneva: ILO.

Odum, E.P. (1978). Ecology (Second Edition). New Delhi: Oxford and IBH Publishing Co.

Osmaston, A.E. (1921). *Working Plan for the Garhwal Forest Division, United Provinces, 1921-22 to 1930-31*. Government Press Allahabad.

Pande, D.C. (1998) Forest Management. In S. C. Joshi, (ed.), *Rural Development in the Himalayas*. Nainital: Shri Almora Book Depot.

Pande, P.N. (1996). *Drudgery of the Hill Women*. New Delhi: Indus Publishing Company.

Pandey, D.N. (1991). Participatory Management and Sustainable Use of Biodiversity. *Yojana*, *35*(23), 11-14.

______ (1996). *Beyond Vanishing Woods: Participatory Survival Options for Wildlife, Forests and People*. (Centre for Sustainable Development, Lal Bahadur Shastri National Academy of Administration, Mussoorie). New Delhi: Himanshu Publications.

Pant, B.R., and Pant, M.C. (1995). *Glimpses of Central Himalaya: A Socio-Economic and Ecological Perspective*, Part I and II. New Delhi: Radha Publications.

Pant, G.B. (1922). *The Forest Problem in Kumaun*. Allahabad.

Pant, S.D. (1935). *The Social Ecology of the Himalayas*. Delhi: Mittal Publications.

Panwar, S.S. (1971). Garhwalis: The Warrior Race of the North. *The Commentator*, Dehradun, 16 August.

Parsons, R.J. (1991). Empowerment: Purpose and Practice Principle in Social Work. *Social Work with the Group*, *14*(2), 7-21.

Participatory Research in Asia. (1988). *Role of Women in Water and Environmental Sanitation Services: A Social Feasibility Study in Two States of India*. New Delhi: PRIA.

Parvitya, Prabhag, Rajya Niyujan Sanathan. (1988). *U.P Sankhikya Diary*. Lucknow, U.P: Parvitya Kshetra.

Pathak, N., and Kothari, A. (2000). Empowering Communities, Conserving Nature. *Humanscape*, February.

Pathak, S. (1985). Anti-Alcohol Movement in Uttarakhand. *Economic and Political Weekly*, 28 July.

Paul, S. (1987). *Community Participation in Development Projects*. World Bank Discussion Paper 6. Washington DC: World Bank.

Pawar, J.P. (1994). *Chipko ki Parampara mein ab Van Panchayatain Janta ko Andolit kar Rahi Hain*. Naini Tal Samachar, 1 September.

Pearse, A., and Mathias, S. (1979). Inquiry into Participation: A Research Approach. Geneva: UNRISD.

Poffenberger, M., and McGean, B. (eds.), (1996). *Village Voices, Forest Choices: Joint Forest Management in India*. Oxford University Press, New Delhi.

Poffenberger, M., and Chandra, S. (1989). Community Forest Management in West Bengal: FPC Case Studies. In *Forest Regeneration Through Community Participation: The W. Bengal Experience*. Calcutta: W. Bengal Forest Dept.

Pretty, J.N. (1996). Participation, Learning and Sustainability: Emerging Challenges for Agricultural Development. *Social Change*, *26*(1), March.

Putnam, R.D. (1993a). The Prosperous Community: Social Capital and Public Life. *The American Prospect,* 13 (Spring, 1993).

______ (1993b). *Making Democracy Work: Civic Tradition in Modern Italy*. Princeton: Princeton University Press

Raju, M.S. (1997). *Seeking Niches in Forest Canopy* (An Enquiry Into Women's Participation). New Delhi: Ford Foundation.

Rahman, M.A. (1990). The Case of Third World: People's Self-Development. *Community Development Journal*, 25(4).

_______ (1993). *People's Self-Development: Perspectives on Action Research (A Journey through Experience)*. London: Zed Books.

_______ (1995). *People's Self-Development: Perspectives on Participatory Action Research*. London: Zed Books.

_______ (1997). *Participation Development Dictionary-A Guide to Knowedge as Power*. New Delhi: Orient Longman.

Rajwar, G.C. (1993). *Garhawl Himalaya: Ecology and Environment*. New Delhi: Ashish Publication House.

Rangan, H. (1993). Romancing the Environment: Popular Environmental Action in the Garhwal Himalayas'. In J. Freedman and H. Rangan (eds.), *In Defence of Livelihood: Comparative Studies on Brutal action*. West Hartfort, C.T: Kumarion Press.

Rangarajan, M. (1996). *Fencing the Forest: Conservation and Ecological Change in India's Central Provinces, 1860-1914*. New Delhi.

Rawat, A.S. (1977). Political Movement in Tehri Garhwal State. *Uttarakhand Bharati*, 2(2).

_______ (1999). *Forest Management in Kumaon Himalaya: Struggle of the Marginalized People*. New Delhi: Indus Publishing Company.

_______ and Joshi, D.P. Forest Policy for the Regeneration of the Himalayan Environment'. In J.S. Singh (ed.) *Environmental Regeneration in the Himalaya. Concepts and Strategies*. New Delhi: Indus Publishing Company.

Rawat, D.S., Farooque, N.A., and Joshi, R. (1996). Towards Sustainable Land Use in the Hills of Central Himalaya, India. *The International Journal of Sustainablc Development and World Ecology*, (3), 57-65.

Rehman, K., and Rehman, M.M. (1998). *Participation for Development: A Resource Book of Strategy, Programmes and Procedures*. New Delhi: Manak Publications.

Reiger, H.S. (1981). Man versus Mountain. In J. Lall and Modie (eds.), *The Himalayas: Aspects of Change*. New Delhi: Oxford University Press.

Revathi, E. (1996). Development, Ecology and Women. *Mainstream*, February, 10, 22-24.

Robinson, M. *et al.* (1993). Participatory Action Research in Native Communities: Cultural Opportunities and Legal Implications. *The Canadian Journal of Native Studies*, XIII.

Rodda, A. (1991). *Women and the Environment*. London and New Jersey: Zed Books Ltd.

Rogers, Adams. (eds). (1995). Taking Action An Environmental Guide for You and Your Community. United Nations Environmental Programme. In association with the UN Non-Government Liaison Service, Nairobi, Kenya.

Roy, S.B. (1995). *Experiences From Participatory Forest Management*. Inter India Publications, New Delhi.

Rude, G. (1980). *Ideology and Popular Protest*. London: Zed Books.

Sah, N.K. (ed.), (1990). *Himalaya: Environment, Resources and Development*. Almora: Shree Almora Book Depot.

Samal, P.K. (1993). The Status of Women in Central Himalaya: A Cultural Interpretation. *Man In India*, *73*(1).
Saxena. N.C. (1995). The People are Covered. *Down To Earth*, January 31.
______ (1995). *Towards Sustainable Forestry in the U.P Hills*. Centre for Sustainable Development, LBS National Academy of Administration, Mussorrie, U.P.
______ (1987). Social Forestry in the Hill Districts of Uttar Pradesh (mimeo). Kathmandu, Nepal: ICIMOD.
______ (1990). *Farm Forestry in North West India*. New Delhi: Ford Foundation.
______ and Sarin, M. (1999). The Western Ghats Forestry and Environment Project. In R. Jeffery and N. Sunder (eds.), *A new Moral Economy for India's Forests? Discourses of Community and Participation*. New Delhi: Sage Publications.
Selvam, S. (1997). *Participatory Structures: Concept and Forms (A Study on People's Participation in Burari Village)*. New Delhi: PRIA.
Shah, S.A. (1993). Important Imperatives of Joint Forest Management. *Wasteland News*, *8*(4), 38-39.
Shankar, R. and Srivastava. D. (1991). Snow, Ice and Glaciers: A Himalayan Perspective. (Invited Papers. Symposium on Snow, Ice and Glaciers: A Himalayan Perspective). G.S. I, Lucknow.
Shankar, U. (1993). Digging their own Grave. *Down To Earth*, *2*(7), 25-32.
Sharma, Kumud. (1984). Women in Struggle: A Case Study of the Chipko Movement. *Samya Shakti*, Vol. I (2).
Sharma, K., Nautiyal, K., and Pandey, Balaji. (1987). Women in Struggle: Role and Participation of Women in the Chipko Movement in Uttarakhand Region of Uttar Pradesh. New Delhi: *Centre for Women's Development Studies*.
Sharma, P.N., and Shastri, L. (1993). *Social Planning: Concept and Technologies*. Lucknow: Print House.
Shashikant. (1992). Privatization of Common Property Resources: Case of Tree Patta Scheme in U.P. In A. Agarwal (ed.), *The Price of Forests*. New Delhi: Centre for Science and Environment.
Shepherd, G. (1986). *Forest policies: Forest politics*. ODI Social Forestry Network Paper 3a, London.
Sheth, P. (1997). *Environmentalism: Politics, Ecology and Development*. Delhi: Rawat Publications.
Shiva, V. (1988). *Staying Alive: Women, Ecology and Survival in India*. New Delhi: Kali for Women.
______ (1991). *Ecology and the Politics of Survival: Conflicts over Natural Resources in India*. New Delhi: Sage Publications.
______ and Bandhopadhyay, J. (1986). *Chipko: India's Civilisational Response to the Forest Crisis*. New Delhi: The Indian National Trust for Art and Cultural Heritage.
Shreshta, K.B. (1996). Community Forestry in Nepal, An Overview of Conflicts. (Discussion paper series). International Centre for Integrated Mountain Development, Kathmandu, Nepal.
Singh, A.K., and Rawat, D.S. (1993). A Note on Woman and Work in Kumaun Himalaya. In C.M. Agrawal (ed.), *Dimensions of Indian Womanhood*. Almora: Shri Almora Book Depot.

Singh, C. (1998). *Natural Premises: Ecology and Peasant Life in the Western Himalaya. 1800-1950*, New Delhi.

Singh, J.S., *et al.* (1985). *Environmental Regeneration in the Himalayas Concepts and Strategies*. Nainital: Gyanodoya Prakashan.

——— Pandey, U., and Tiwari, A.K. (1984). Man and Forests: A Central Himalayan Case Study. *AMBIO*, 13, 80-87.

Singh, K. (1992). *People's Participation in Natural Resource Management*. Anand, Gujarat: Indian Rural Management Institute.

Singh, S. (1999). Collective Dilemmas and Collective Pursuits: Community Management of Van Panchayats in the U.P Hills. *Wastelands News*, XIV(4).

Sinha, A. (1995). Towards Evolution of a Concrete Agenda for Sustainable Development in India. *The Administrator*, (Special Issue on Sustainable Development) XL (2).

Smith, B.C. (1998). Participation without Power: Subterfuge or Development. *Community Development Journal*, *33*(3), UK: Oxford University Press.

Society for Himalayan Environmental Rehabilitation and Peoples' Action. (1986). Seminar on Environmental Security and Watershed Management Relevance of Peoples' Participation, Pantnagar, June 1986.

Somanathan, E. (1991). Deforestation, Incentives and Property Rights in Central Himalaya. *Economic and Political Weekly*, 26 January.

Staples, L.H. (1990). Powerful Ideas about Empowerment. *Administration in Social Work*, 14 (2), 29-42.

State Planning Institute. (1995). *Sankykiya Patrika*, Lucknow, U.P.

Stebbing, E.P. (1922-27). *The Forest of India*, (3 Volumes). London.

Stiefel, M., and Wolfe, M. (1994). *A Voice for the Excluded. Popular Participation in Development: Utopia or Necessity?* Geneva: UNRISD; London: Zed Books.

Sunder, N., Jefferey, R., and Thin, N. (2001). *Branching Out-J.F.M in India*. New Delhi.

Suresh, B., and Manoj B. (1995). Van Kataan ke Virudh "Raksha Sutra" Andolan. *Man and Nature*, 18 (6).

Swami, P. (1995). Blundering Progress: The Tehri Project and growing Fears. *Frontline*, 30 June.

Swaminathan, M.S. (ed.), (1998). *Gender Dimensions in Biodiversity Management*. New Delhi: Konark Publisher Pvt. Ltd.

Swayam Shikshan Prayog. (1998). *Women's Eye View Grassroots Women's Approach to Settlement*. Bombay.

Pasha, S. A. (1992). CPRs and Rural Poor: A Micro Level Analysis. *Economic and Political Weekly*, 14 November.

TERI. (2000). Green Beginnings-Joint Forest Management in Jhabua. SIDA.

Tewari, G.C. (1982). An Economic Profile of the hill Region of Uttar Pradesh, Occasional paper no. 10. Allahabad: G.B. Pant Social Science Institute.

Weber, T. (1989). *Hugging the Trees*, New Delhi: Penguin.

Thurani, K. (1985). *Women, Participation and Development: A Case Study from Rural Punjab*. New Delhi: Centre for Women's Development Studies.

Ullah, M.I. (1996). Community Participation in Social Forestry. In V.S.P. Kurup (ed.), *New Voices in Indian Forestry*. Delhi: Society for Promotion of Wastelands Development.

UNDP. (1988). *Role of Women in Water and Environmental Sanitation Services*.

_______ (1993). *Human Development Report-1993*. New Delhi: OUP.

_______ (1993). *Human Development Report 1993: People's Participation*. New York: UNDP.

_______ (1994). *People Helping People: A Participatory Development Programme for the UN Volunteers*. New Delhi: OUP.

_______ (1998). Ecö-regional Co-operation for Biodiversity Conservation in the Himalaya (Report on the International Meeting on Himalaya Eco-Regional Co-op).

_______ (1988). Role of Women in Water and Environmental Sanitation Services: A Social Feasibility Study in two States of India-Orissa and Rajasthan (PROWESS), New Delhi: PRIA.

United Nations Environmental Programme (UNEP). (1996). Environmental Impact Assessment Training Manual. Nairobi, Kenya: Environment and Economic Unit (EEU).

Uphoff, N. (1997). Learning about participation and for participation: From theoretical and empirical studies to practical experience, and back to theory. A keynote paper presented at the Annual Meeting of the Canadian Association for the Study of International Development. St. John's, Newfoundland, Canada.

Uttarakhand Prabhag Rajya Niyojan Sansthan. 1995. U.P., Sankhikya Diary Parvatya Kshetra, U.P., Lucknow.

Uttranchal Prabhag, Rajya Niyojan Sansthan. 1993. U.P. Statistical Diary, Uttranchal, U.P., Lucknow.

Valdiya, K.S. 1995 (ed.). *Uttarakhand Today*. Shree Almora Book Depot, Almora.

Venkateswaran, Sandhya. 1995. *Environment, Development and Gender Gap*. Sage Publications, New Delhi.

Vettivel, Surendra. K. 1993. Participation and Sustainable Development: *Theory and Practice in Government and Non-Governmental Organisations*. Vetri Publications, New Delhi.

Vohra, C.P. (1981). *Himalayan Glaciers: Aspects of Change*. Delhi: Oxford University Press.

Westergaard, K. (1986). *People's participation, local government, and Rural Development: The Case of West Bengal, India*. CDR Research Report 8. Copenhagen: Centre for Development Research.

White, A. (1989). Coastal Management Two Community Based Marine Resources Projects: Lessons for Coastal Development. ICARARM Conference Proceedings.

Whittaker, W. (1984). Migration and Agrarian Change in Garhwal District, Uttar Pradesh'. In Bayliss-Smith and Wanmali (eds.), *Understanding Green Revolutions: Agrarian Change and Development Planning in South Asia*. Cambridge.

Wignaraja, P. (1991a). The Knowledge System. In P. Wignaraja *et al.* (eds.), *Participatory Development: Learning from South Asia*. Tokyo and Karachi: UN University Press and Oxford University Press.

_______ Hussain, A., Sethi, H., and Wignaraja, G. (1991b). In P. Wignaraja *et al.* (eds.), *Participatory Development: Learning from South Asia*. Tokyo and Karachi: UN University Press and Oxford University Press.

Wignaraja, P. (1991c). Towards Praxis and Participatory Development. In P. Wignaraja *et al.* (eds.), *Participatory Development: Learning from South Asia*. Tokyo and Karachi: UN University Press and Oxford University Press.

Wilson, M. and Whitmore, E. (1994). Gender and International Development Praxis. Social Development Issues, 16(1). USA: Inter-University Consortium for International Social Development (KJCISD).

Women's Development Council. (2000). Women and Environment: Impact of Environmental degradation on Rural Women (Case Studies from Selected Villages of Orissa). New Delhi: Council of Professional Social Workers, Kalp Vriksh and International Institute of Environment and Development.

Workshop on Women, Environment and Development. (1985). Women and One Environment: A Call for Action (Report of Proceedings). New Delhi: Centre for Women's Development Studies.

World Bank. (1992). *The World Bank Development Report-1992*: Development and Environment. Oxford University Press, New York. 264.

______ (1993). The World Bank in Forestry Sector: Policies and Issues in India. *Wastelands News*, 9(1), 5-39.

______ (1995). *Environment Department Papers: Toward Environmentally and Socially Sustainable Development*. World Bank Participation *Source*book. Washington D.C: The World Bank.

______ (2000/01). *World Development Report*. Washington DC: World Bank.

World Commission on Environment and Development. (1987). *Our Common Future*. London: Oxford University Press.

Yadama, G.N. (1995). Participation in non-governmental and governmental development programmes: An empirical study of community forestry programs. *Social Development Issues*, 17(l).

Zachariah, M., and Sooryamoorthy, R. (1994). *Science in Participatory Development: The Achievements and Dilemmas of a Development Movement—The Case of Kerala*. London: Zed Press.

Zimmerman, M.A., and Rappaport, J. (1988). Citizen Participation, Perceived Control, and Psychological Empowerment. *American Journal of Community Psychology*, 16(5), 725.

Index